Understanding Economic Statistics

AN OECD PERSPECTIVE

Enrico Giovannini

ORGANISATION FOR ECONOMIC CO-OPERATION AND DEVELOPMENT

The OECD is a unique forum where the governments of 30 democracies work together to address the economic, social and environmental challenges of globalisation. The OECD is also at the forefront of efforts to understand and to help governments respond to new developments and concerns, such as corporate governance, the information economy and the challenges of an ageing population. The Organisation provides a setting where governments can compare policy experiences, seek answers to common problems, identify good practice and work to co-ordinate domestic and international policies.

The OECD member countries are: Australia, Austria, Belgium, Canada, the Czech Republic, Denmark, Finland, France, Germany, Greece, Hungary, Iceland, Ireland, Italy, Japan, Korea, Luxembourg, Mexico, the Netherlands, New Zealand, Norway, Poland, Portugal, the Slovak Republic, Spain, Sweden, Switzerland, Turkey, the United Kingdom and the United States. The Commission of the European Communities takes part in the work of the OECD.

OECD Publishing disseminates widely the results of the Organisation's statistics gathering and research on economic, social and environmental issues, as well as the conventions, guidelines and standards agreed by its members.

> This work is published on the responsibility of the Secretary-General of the OECD. The opinions expressed and arguments employed herein do not necessarily reflect the official views of the Organisation or of the governments of its member countries.

Chapters 1, 2, 3 and 5 of this book are translated and adapted from *Le statistiche economiche* by Enrico Giovannini, Bologna, Società editrice il Mulino, 2006. Copyright © 2006 by Società editrice il Mulino, Bologna.

Corrigenda to OECD publications may be found on line at: *www.oecd.org/publishing/corrigenda*.
© OECD 2008

You can copy, download or print OECD content for your own use, and you can include excerpts from OECD publications, databases and multimedia products in your own documents, presentations, blogs, websites and teaching materials, provided that suitable acknowledgment of OECD as source and copyright owner is given. All requests for public or commercial use and translation rights should be submitted to *rights@oecd.org*. Requests for permission to photocopy portions of this material for public or commercial use shall be addressed directly to the Copyright Clearance Center (CCC) at *info@copyright.com* or the Centre français d'exploitation du droit de copie (CFC) *contact@cfcopies.com*.

Cycles of the Century

Shelagh Kendal

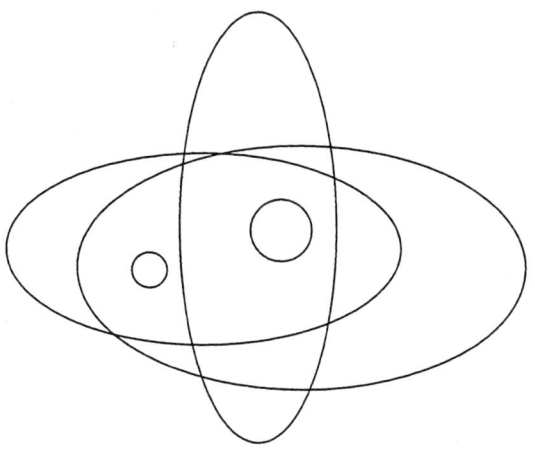

Copyright © Shelagh Kendal, 1999

All rights reserved. The use of any part of this publication reproduced, transmitted in any form by any means, electronic, mechanical, photocopying, recording, or otherwise, or stored in a retrieval system, or on the Internet, without the prior written consent of the publisher, or, in the case of photocopying or other reprographic copying, a licence from Canadian Reprography Collective, is an infringement of the copyright law.

Canadian Cataloguing in Publication Data

Kendal, Shelagh
    Cycles of the century

ISBN 0-9686309-0-1

    1. Astrology   I. Title

BF1708.1.K45 1999   133.5'4   C99-901516-8

First printing, 1999

Printed and bound in Canada

Ptolemy Press
c/o S. Kendal
200 Rideau Terrace
Ottawa, Ontario K1M 0Z3 Canada
E-mail: skendal@travel-net.com

Cover design by Maurice Gagnon.

Foreword

The aim of this book is to help the reader to better understand how to use economic statistics in general and OECD statistics in particular. It introduces the main concepts used by statisticians and economists to measure economic phenomena and provides tables and charts with relevant data. Moreover, the book describes how the production of international statistics is organised, who are the main data producers, what are the main databases available over the Internet and how can the quality of statistics be assessed. Thanks to this book, the users will better understand where to find and how to use OECD statistics on gross domestic product, government's public deficit and debt, short-term economic indicators, different sectors of economic activity, globalisation, innovation, labour market, etc. Special attention is paid to indicators used to assess both macroeconomic and structural policies. In each section, references to sources and suggestions for further reading are provided.

Why this book? As Jean-Claude Trichet, President of the European Central Bank, said at the 2004 OECD Forum on "Statistics, Knowledge and Policy", nowadays we are bombarded by statistics, the volume of which often creates confusion, rather than information. The challenge to find the most appropriate figures for a particular phenomenon becomes even harder when international comparisons are needed. The number of sources increased dramatically over the last decade and the use of search engines on Internet sometimes help in finding the best source, but often they list websites that contain conflicting data or do not provide appropriate metadata to assess their quality.

The OECD is recognised worldwide as a formidable source of statistical information on economic, social and environmental topics and this book aims to help students and researchers better understand the world in which they live and find appropriate evidence to carry out their work. It also aims to help journalists and analysts evaluate economic trends and assess the effectiveness of policies. Finally, it is designed to help policy advisors compile meaningful statistical reports to compare economic performances and provide evidence-based advice to decision makers.

Some chapters in the book (chapters 1, 2, 3 and 5) are adapted from my earlier work "Le statistiche economiche", published by Il Mulino in 2006. The chapter focusing on OECD statistics, (chapter 4), is the result of a collective effort by several OECD statisticians and I would like to collectively thank them for their contribution, not only to the book, but especially for their invaluable effort in continuously providing innovative and high-quality statistics to the whole world, with professionalism and ethical integrity. In doing so, we provide our contribution to better decisions, better policies and finally to a better world. I would also like to thank the colleagues working in the Publishing and Communications Directorate who contributed to the publication of this book.

Enrico Giovannini,
OECD Chief Statistician

This book has...

StatLinks
A service that delivers Excel® files from the printed page!

Look for the *StatLinks* at the bottom right-hand corner of the tables or graphs in this book. To download the matching Excel® spreadsheet, just type the link into your Internet browser, starting with the *http://dx.doi.org* prefix.
If you're reading the PDF e-book edition, and your PC is connected to the Internet, simply click on the link. You'll find *StatLinks* appearing in more OECD books.

Table of contents

Chapter 1 The Demand for Economic Statistics 11

1.1. From the period after the Second World War to the first oil crisis 14
1.2. From the early 1980s to globalisation 15
1.3. A look to the future 18

Chapter 2 Basic Concepts, Definitions and Classifications 23

2.1. The economic system 24
2.2. Economic agents 26
    2.2.1. Households 26
        Table 2.1 – Resident households and breakdown by size of household and geographical distribution 28
        Table 2.2 – Average monthly household expenditure by occupational status of reference person 28
    2.2.2. Enterprises 29
        Table 2.3 – ISIC Rev. 3.1 industrial classification of economic activities – Categories and divisions 31
        Table 2.4 – Enterprises and employees by size class in the total industry (excluding construction) 33
        Table 2.5 (a) – Groups, enterprises and employees belonging to groups, by number of employees 34
        Table 2.5 (b) – Groups, enterprises and employees belonging to groups, by number of enterprises involved in the group 35
        Table 2.6 – Exporting enterprises, employees and exports by number of employees 35
        Table 2.7 (a) – Enterprises and employees by legal form 36
        Table 2.7 (b) – Enterprises and employees by legal form 36
        Table 2.8 – Farms (including publicly owned holdings) and total area by total area class and type of occupancy (area in hectares) 38
    2.2.3. General government 38
        Figure 2.1 – Procedure for classifying units in the general government sector 40
        Table 2.9 – Institutions, local units and employees by geographical distribution 41
2.3. Economic aggregates 42
    2.3.1. Production, intermediate costs and value added 43
        Table 2.10 – Production account 45
    2.3.2. Consumption, capital formation and net foreign demand 45
        Table 2.11 – National final consumption and domestic final consumption 46

TABLE OF CONTENTS

	2.3.3. From gross domestic product to national income	48
2.4.	Values at current prices and constant prices	49
2.5.	Index numbers	50
2.6.	Time series	54
	Figure 2.2 – Components of a time series: trend-cycle, seasonal variation, irregular variation	55
	Figure 2.3 – General industrial production index – Raw data	56
	Figure 2.4 – Consumer price index – All items	56
	Figure 2.5 – General industrial production index – Seasonally adjusted data	56
	2.6.1. Measuring the movements of a time series	56
	2.6.2. Seasonal adjustment procedures	59

Chapter 3 **The Main Producers of Economic Statistics** 65

3.1.	The international statistical system	66
3.2.	The OECD statistical system	72
3.3.	The European Statistical System and the European System of Central Banks	73

Chapter 4 **An Overview of OECD Economic Statistics** 77

4.1	Agriculture and fishery statistics	78
	Figure 4.1.1 – Outlook for world crop prices to 2017	79
	Figure 4.1.2 – Total Support Estimates for OECD countries	80
	Further information	81
4.2	Energy statistics	82
	Figure 4.2.1 – Total primary energy supply per unit of GDP	84
	Figure 4.2.2 – Crude oil spot prices	84
	Further information	85
4.3	Industry and services statistics	86
	Business demography	86
	▶ Key definitions	87
	Figure 4.3.1 – Birth and death rates	87
	Enterprises by size classes	87
	Figure 4.3.2 – Enterprises with less than 20 persons engaged	88
	Insurance	89
	▶ Key definitions	89
	Figure 4.3.3 – Penetration of insurance industry	90
	Funded pensions	90
	▶ Key definitions	91
	Figure 4.3.4 – Importance of pension funds relative to the size of the economy in OECD countries	92
	Bank profitability	92
	▶ Key definitions	93
	The OECD Product Market Regulation Database	93

TABLE OF CONTENTS

	Figure 4.3.5 – Product market regulation...	94
	Further information	95
4.4	General government	96
	General government accounts	96
	▶ Key definitions...	96
	Figure 4.4.1 – Government net borrowing/net lending	97
	Social expenditure	97
	Figure 4.4.2 – Public social spending	99
	Revenue statistics...	99
	▶ Key definitions...	100
	Figure 4.4.3 – Total tax ratio	100
	Taxing wages	101
	▶ Key definitions...	101
	Table 4.4.1 – Tax burden..	102
	Central government debt...	102
	▶ Key definitions...	103
	Table 4.4.2 – Central government debt..	104
	Further information	105
4.5	Science, technology and innovation	106
	Research and development...	106
	▶ Key definitions	108
	Figure 4.5.1 – R&D intensity	109
	Innovation..	109
	Figure 4.5.2 – Firms collaborating in innovation activities, by size	111
	▶ Key definitions	112
	Table 4.5.1 – Percentage of enterprises' total turnover from e-commerce...	113
	Biotechnology	114
	▶ Key definitions...	115
	Figure 4.5.3 – Total expenditures on biotechnology R&D by biotechnology-active firms	116
	Patents	117
	▶ Key definitions...	117
	Figure 4.5.4 – Share of countries in nanotechnology patents filed under PCT...	118
	Further information	119
4.6	Globalisation	120
	International trade...	121
	▶ Key definitions...	122
	Figure 4.6.1 – Relative growth of exports of goods	123
	Figure 4.6.2 – Relative annual growth in exports of services	123
	Foreign direct investment	124
	▶ Key definitions	124

TABLE OF CONTENTS

	Figure 4.6.3 – FDI Flows to and from OECD	125
	Activity of multinationals	126
	▶ Key definitions	127
	Figure 4.6.4 – Employment in manufacturing and services in affiliates under foreign control	128
	Migration statistics	128
	Figure 4.6.5 – Foreign-born persons with tertiary attainment	129
	Development aid statistics	131
	Figure 4.6.6 – Net ODA in 2006	132
	Further information	133
4.7	Short-term economic indicators	134
	Economic activity indicators	134
	▶ Key definitions	134
	Figure 4.7.1 – Industrial production	136
	Figure 4.7.2 – Mean absolute revision to first published estimates of quarter-on-previous-quarter growth rates for GDP at different intervals	137
	Cost of labour	138
	Figure 4.7.3 – Unit labour cost (industry)	139
	Consumer prices and other inflation measures	139
	Figure 4.7.4 – Different measures of inflation, United States	141
	Figure 4.7.5 – Producer price indices: manufacturing	142
	Business tendency surveys and consumer opinion surveys	144
	▶ Key definitions	145
	Figure 4.7.6 – Business confidence indicator	146
	Composite leading indicators	146
	Figure 4.7.8 – OECD leading indicator	147
	Further information	148
4.8	Labour statistics	149
	▶ Key definitions	149
	Figure 4.8.1 – Unemployment rates	151
	Further information	151
4.9	Income distribution and households' conditions	152
	Figure 4.9.1 – Distribution of household disposable income among individual	152
	Further information	154
4.10	Monetary and financial statistics	155
	Monetary aggregates	155
	▶ Key definitions	155
	Figure 4.10.1 – Broad Money	156
	Balance of payments statistics	156
	Figure 4.10.2 – Current account balance of payments	157
	Interest rates	157

TABLE OF CONTENTS

	▶ Key definitions..	158
	Table 4.10.1 – Interest rates February 2008	159
	Further information..	160
4.11	National accounts	161
	Economic accounts	161
	Figure 4.11.1 – Real GDP growth	162
	Figure 4.11.2 – GDP per capita	163
	Productivity..	164
	Figure 4.11.3 – Growth in GDP per hour worked	165
	Input-output tables	166
	Financial accounts and balance sheets	167
	▶ Key definitions...	168
	Quarterly national accounts	168
	Figure 4.11.4 – OECD total, GDP volume	169
	Figure 4.11.5 – Quarterly GDP volume growth...	170
	Purchasing power parities	170
	▶ Key definitions...	171
	Figure 4.11.6 – Comparative price levels and indices of real GDP per head.	172
	Further information	173
4.12	OECD Economic forecasts...	174
	Table 4.12.1 – Economic Outlook N.82, Summary of projections	175
	Further information	176
4.13	Territorial statistics..	177
	▶ Key definitions	178
	Figure 4.13.1 – Index of geographic concentration of GDP	179
	Figure 4.13.2 – Gini index of inequality of GDP per worker	179
	Further information	180
4.14	Economic history: long-term statistics of the world economy.........................	181
	Table 4.14.1 – Comparative Levels of Economic Performance, China and Other Major Parts of the World Economy	182
	Table 4.14.2 – Shares of World GDP	182
	Further information	183
Chapter 5	**Assessing the Quality of Economic Statistics**	185
5.1.	The dimensions of quality	186
5.2.	International initiatives for the evaluation of quality	188
	Figure 5.1 – Trust in official statistics and belief that policy decisions are based on statistics...	195

Chapter 1
The Demand for Economic Statistics

The media publish economic data on a daily basis. But who decides which statistics are useful and which are not? Why is housework not included in the national income, and why are financial data available in real time, while to know the number of people in employment analysts have to wait for weeks? Contrary to popular belief, both the availability and the nature of economic statistics are closely linked to developments in economic theory, the requirements of political decision-makers, and each country's way of looking at itself. In practice, statistics are based on theoretical and interpretative reference models, and if these change, so does the picture the statistics paint of the economic system. Thus, the data we have today represent the supply and demand sides of statistical information constantly attempting to catch up with each other, with both sides being strongly influenced by the changes taking place in society and political life. This chapter offers a descriptive summary of how the demand for economic statistics has evolved from the end of the Second World War to the present, characterised by the new challenges brought about by globalisation and the rise of the services sector.

1 THE DEMAND FOR ECONOMIC STATISTICS

One of the major functions of economic statistics is to develop concepts, definitions, classifications and methods that can be used to produce statistical information that describes the state of and movements in economic phenomena, both in time and space. This information is then used to analyse the behaviour of economic operators, forecast likely movements of the economy as a whole, make economic policy and business decisions, weigh the pros and cons of alternative investments, etc.

Before embarking on an analysis of the economic statistics available for international comparisons, it is important to clarify some of the concepts that shape the type of information in existence, and hence the results it is possible to derive from these data. In the first place, it should be noted that the measures used to define any economic system depend on a particular conceptual framework. All types of measurement, in practice, require defined goals, and these goals, in turn, are derived from a particular "view" of reality, in other words a particular theory. In the case of economic statistics, there is no one single view of reality, but a number of theories, each of which tends to generate demand for specific instruments of measurement. Because of this, the development of economic statistics throughout the years can be closely linked to developments in economic theory. For example, the definition of the economic cycle (and the instruments for measuring its main features, such as amplitude and duration) can vary according to which theoretical framework is adopted (post-Keynesian, real business cycle, etc.), as can the definitions of well-being and employment/unemployment.

Despite the existence of a variety of theories about the way economic systems work, a substantial portion of the economic statistics produced today is based on concepts and definitions broadly shared at the international level. The conceptual framework most widely used is the one codified in the System of National Accounts (SNA), published in 1993 by the major international/supranational organisations (United Nations, UN; the Organisation for Economic Cooperation and Development, OECD; the International Monetary Fund, IMF; the World Bank, WB; and the Statistical Office of the European Communities, Eurostat). The SNA, like its European version, which is called the "European System of National and Regional Accounting" (ESA) and received official approval in 1996 in a European Council regulation, contains a huge body of mutually consistent concepts, definitions and classifications for measuring economic activity and several economic phenomena. In practice, it is also used as a base of reference for the production of sectoral and territorial economic statistics. The SNA could, therefore, be said to be the reference text for many recent developments in statistics aiming to measure the results of economic activity.

The conceptual framework used to develop the SNA is based on the neoclassical synthesis of the Keynesian economic theory. Thus, the focus of the SNA is on economic activities that translate into market transactions, rather than on all activities, or on social and environmental phenomena. It must be noted, however, that the SNA offers interesting ideas for extending the measurement of strictly economic facts to social and environmental phenomena. Lastly, it should also be noted that the SNA is subject to periodic reviews of its basic concepts, definitions of individual phenomena and classifications. A significant revision of the 1993 SNA has been agreed in 2008 by the

THE DEMAND FOR ECONOMIC STATISTICS

international statistical community, to address 44 measurement issues considered relevant to make the SNA able to deal with changes in the economic systems coming from globalisation, the development of the so-called "new economy", etc. This evolutionary approach shows that the SNA itself, the instrument that for many represents the most complete collection of concepts used to produce economic statistics, is by its nature purely a matter of agreement.

Economic statistics are produced to satisfy user demand, which is extremely varied and can be classified according to a number of different dimensions. The first and most fundamental distinction is based on whether the user is interested in analysing the *level* of economic variables or the way they *change* over time. In the first instance, the demand is normally for an absolute value of a certain variable (for example, the value of goods and services produced by an economic system); in the second, users are interested in how a particular variable changes over time (for example, the variation in production between the latest year and the one before). Despite the importance of the first type of question, in a variety of discussions of an analytical or political nature, a large part of the demand for statistical information is for temporal comparisons. This preference derives not only from user requirements, but also from the fact that statistical methods are more capable of assessing variations in economic magnitude over time, rather than their absolute value.

In this context, the question economic statistics are mainly required to answer pertains to the "health" of a particular economic system. The attention of the media, economic policy makers and economic operators is primarily focused on the level of, and movements in, the gross domestic product (GDP), which represents the flow of goods and services produced by the units of production residing in a given country (in other words by the national economy) over a certain period of time (a year or a quarter). While the level of GDP per head of population is the most commonly used shorthand measurement of the economic well-being of a given country (most of all in international comparisons), its variation over time in real terms (in other words at constant prices) measures economic growth, the maximisation of which is usually considered to be the main goal of economic policy.

Beyond comparing levels or variations in GDP, spatial and temporal analyses of economic data on specific sectors of activity, geographic areas, etc., as well as their structural features, are also extremely important. There is also strong growth in demand for information on the behaviour of individual economic operators, such as households and businesses. For instance, the study of the success factors for businesses, which is fundamental in defining industrial policy, requires the analysis of longitudinal data concerning individual businesses. Similar data of a longitudinal nature on the educational and employment history of individuals can allow the identification of groups "at risk" for poverty or unemployment, thus providing useful information for devising policies on employment or supporting income levels.

While measurement of GDP has for decades been the main pillar of economic information, since the end of the Second World War the demand for economic statistics has shown a constant tendency to increase and diversify. The reasons for this development are numerous, and closely related to developments in economic systems and policies. This is why, in order to better understand the current state

1 THE DEMAND FOR ECONOMIC STATISTICS

of economic statistics in OECD countries, it can be helpful to look briefly at the historical development of the demand for economic statistical information, in order to identify both ongoing trends and mid-term perspectives.

1.1. From the period after the Second World War to the first oil crisis

During the 1950s, development of economic theories based on the "neoclassical model", establishment of the major international organisations, growth in international trade, changes in the economic structure due to new technologies, and the growing role of the State in economic and societal matters led to an extraordinary flowering of new concepts and statistical methods for measuring economic phenomena. In particular, studies by J. Meade (1907-1995), R. Stone (1913-1991) and S. Kuznets (1901-1985) laid the foundations for what was later to become the first *System of National Accounts* (published in 1952) and strongly influenced how statistical information was gathered, compiled and distributed. Of course, the work of the national statistical institutes depended not only on their own traditions, but also on the impact of war (in some European countries, for example, there was no population census in 1941). Nor should the role played by academic research centres and scholars in the development of economic statistics be forgotten, since they not only drew up the theoretical models but were unafraid to "get their hands dirty" gathering statistical data in the field and integrating them into the relatively scant information available from official statistics sources.

The 1960s saw a steep rise in demand for statistical information, mostly to guide and support economic policy development. The duty of the State expanded to include intervening in the economy to stabilise cyclical fluctuations, creating new infrastructures, maintaining the standard of living, as well as managing major enterprises considered of strategic interest. These new functions resulted in growing pressure on the statistical institutes to significantly broaden their fields of activity. In parallel, there was also a remarkable acceleration in demand for statistical information from both public and private research institutions. In this context, the development of econometric modelling played a significant role: large-scale models required data disaggregated by economic sector – production, consumption, employment, foreign trade, etc. – as well as monetary and financial variables. In addition, the growing role of the international currency markets greatly increased demand for internationally comparable statistical data. This resulted in a major commitment to develop internationally comparable statistics, not only by the Bretton Woods institutions themselves (the UN, IMF and WB), but also by relatively new organisations such as the European Economic Community and the OECD.

The 1970s, characterised by the end to the post-war system of international payments, major instability in the international financial system and economic upheavals following the 1973 oil crisis, represented a period of growth in the demand for economic statistics. International financial instability and conversion to a regime of freely floating currencies stimulated demand for monetary and financial statistics, both at the national and international levels. Strong and persistent increases in the general level of prices (inflation and hyperinflation), coupled with marked fluctuations

THE DEMAND FOR ECONOMIC STATISTICS 1

in economic activity and levels of employment in many countries, industrialised or not, placed exceptional pressures on national statistical systems, central banks and international institutions, which were required either to produce new statistical information, or to publish their data more frequently.

Consistent with an "interventionist" view of economic policy, governments and central banks were expected to make frequent decisions on the level of interest rates, the management of public spending, the control of capital movements, etc., in response to movements in the main economic variables, and the timing of decisions came to be viewed as critical in determining whether a policy would be effective. At the same time, businesses had to reformulate their mid-term production strategies in line with the dramatic changes in the relative prices of oil and other products, which led in turn to corporate restructurings and related movements in the flow of labour. Lastly, the problem of economic and social growth in the poorer countries acquired a prominent place on the international political agenda, in the strategies of the national banking systems and also in public opinion.

At the European level, given the development of Community institutions, the demand for internationally comparable statistical information grew significantly. In the past, it was mainly the fields of agriculture and foreign trade that were affected by this process, since these were the areas in which most European policy was concentrated. But by the 1970s, the definition of standards for the production of European statistics extended to national economic accounting, statistics concerning trends in various economic sectors, as well as to the classification of economic activity and products.

During this period, there was a marked increase in interest shown by the media and the economic operators themselves in economic statistical information. Coupled with this, the growing role played by trade unions and business organisations in economic policy discussions in many western countries resulted in broadening the user base for economic statistics. The difficulty of predicting future movements in critical variables, such as international exchange rates, income, inflation (hence wages), and interest rates led to a greater emphasis on economic statistics. Research centres were asked to provide ever-more-frequent economic policy forecasts or advice came up with new models, either for analysing the economic cycle or for evaluating future changes in the structures of various economies. As a result, demand for international statistics grew further still, whether to assess the economic and financial position of countries (especially developing countries) in the throes of financial and monetary crises, compare the relative performance of various economic policy measures, or even to formulate production and marketing strategies of multinational corporations.

1.2. From the early 1980s to globalisation

Throughout the 1980s, both economic theory and the direction of economic policy underwent important changes, given a second oil crisis, an increase in the trend towards the internationalisation of systems of production, and the expansion of the international financial system. With acceptance of the new classical macroeconomics,

1. THE DEMAND FOR ECONOMIC STATISTICS

based on the real business cycle and supply side economics, demand for economic statistics focused mainly on the behaviour of companies and markets (including the job market). There was also demand for in-depth exploration of the interaction among businesses of different sizes and ownership structures (such as the issue of vertical integration and the development of corporate groups) and between sectors of production (outsourcing of services functions, the growth in sub-contracting, etc.). In addition, the development of modern time-series analysis increased demand for sub-annual (typically monthly and quarterly) economic indicators on real, as well as financial, phenomena. Increasing numbers of research centres were basing their econometric models on data observed quarterly, prompting the statistical institutes either to produce sub-annual and ever-more-frequent assessments of the main products or activity sectors statistics within the scope of the national accounting systems, or to develop new indicators.

The 1980s also saw a boom in monetary and financial transactions, as well as in the stock and bond markets, in which households were showing ever greater interest. In addition to the attention devoted to the measurement of income and overall demand (consumption, investment, etc.) there was also a greater amount of data being produced on the dynamics of supply and on productivity, with particular emphasis on measuring the so-called "non-observed economy" (or "underground economy").

Changes in economic systems and in industrial relations, as well as the greater degree of interest shown by households in the financial markets, meant that the demand for economic information spread throughout the different parts of the society. Mass media devoted more attention to economic information, which became part of the daily flow of information to economic agents, households included. Economic terms once considered useful only to "those in the know" became part of everyday language. Finally, new techniques of time-series analysis were developed and applied to the study of economic phenomena, significantly altering approaches to forecasting economic aggregates and increasing the numbers of research centres and individual scholars capable of carrying out quantitative analysis and forecasting, and therefore needing detailed and timely statistics.

In Europe, demand for comparable economic data was strong, above all on the part of policy makers. The gradual transfer of competence to the Community institutions begun in the late the 1950s and the use of statistical indicators to calculate either the amount of national contributions to the budget of the Community institutions, or the flows of "structural funds" directed at economically disadvantaged areas, made it indispensable to have an assessment of the relative position of each country/region, requiring more timely and detailed data by sector and territory. Towards the end of the 1980s, because of the process of setting up the European Union (EU), the demand of the Community institutions for statistics was becoming broader still. Regulations were approved by the European Council to encourage member States to produce economic statistics more compliant with international standards. In many countries, those demands came on top of the existing requirements of national users, greatly increasing the operating costs of the national statistical institutes. At the international level, work towards the development and updating of methodological standards intensified to keep pace with new economic realities.

1. THE DEMAND FOR ECONOMIC STATISTICS

The 1990s saw the birth of the "information society", on the wave of change brought about in economic and social systems by the "technological revolution" and globalisation.

"The concept of the "Information Age" suggests a number of propositions. It implies that there is more information now than ever before, which is indisputable. The concept also implies that more people spend more time producing and using more information than ever before, which is also indisputable. Beyond that, the concept of a new "Information Age" also suggests that the role of information is more important in the economy than ever before, and that information is replacing some earlier "fuel" of the American economy. These two propositions are forcefully debated and disputed".

The above was written in 1993 by J.W Duncan and A.C. Gross in their book *Statistics for the 21st Century*. However, as the last decade of the 20th century progressed, the concept of the "information society" gradually came to be accepted, not only by academics but by political decision-makers and society as a whole, so that significant research programmes and political action were directed towards it. The following factors have wrought a profound transformation in society and economic systems, and as a result have influenced the development of economic statistics: the concepts of the knowledge economy and the digital economy; the extraordinary transformation in many production processes thanks to new information and communication technologies (ICT); the globalisation of economic and social systems; the creation of the Internet giving millions of users access to enormous amounts of information; the fall of many barriers to the free circulation of goods, people and production factors.

These phenomena, together with the growing role of service businesses and other forms of intangible activity (research and development, electronic commerce, new financial services, etc.), the expanding operations of multinational corporations, and the rethinking of the role of the State in the regulation of economic systems, have severely affected the national statistical apparatus. They have produced radical changes (which are still ongoing) in the techniques used for gathering and disseminating information (for example, increased use of administrative data, or relying on the Internet for collecting and disseminating data). Even the "strategic positioning" of the national statistical institutes has been questioned. Thanks to the availability of new information technology, new producers of statistical information have gradually appeared on the market, while corporations begun using data produced in real time by their own information systems instead of (or in addition to) "official" statistical data. Policy makers required ever more detailed and timely economic statistics, not only on short-term trends, but also on the characteristics of, and changes in, the production structures within their own countries or abroad.

The media and the financial market operators begun turning their attention to each new piece of information supplied not only by official sources, but also by every single business or association in the field. The growing awareness of the interaction between economic development and social and environmental balance has required the development of more integrated statistical frameworks to provide comprehensive

1 THE DEMAND FOR ECONOMIC STATISTICS

evaluations of the state of a given country. Lastly, the intensifying international mobility of goods, units of production and persons has forced a rethinking of the concepts, definitions and classifications of economic statistics, which have been reinforced but are still demonstrably ill-adapted to the task of accurately reflecting some economic realities (for example, the activity of multinationals).

In Europe, the processes of preparing, introducing and managing the European Monetary Union resulted in an unprecedented increase in the demand for economic statistics. Both the European Commission (through the Statistical Office of the European Communities - Eurostat), and the European Central Bank (ECB) have added to the pressure on national statistical systems to produce economic data that are extremely timely and detailed. On the other hand, also because of the role played by the EU in the maintenance of regional policies, an equally strong demand for information has emerged at the sub-national level (regional, provincial and local), sustained by the trend towards federalism in a number of European countries.

Finally, the availability of large databases relating to single economic agents (businesses, persons, households, etc.) has spurred the development of new statistical and econometric techniques of analysis designed to summarise and comprehend the behaviour of individuals (or particular subject typologies), used in applied research, or for deciding on economic or social policy interventions. At the same time, the abundance of data coming from various sources has forced the statistical authorities, as well as end users, to devise statistical methods for integrating this data, and also for "selecting" which information is relevant for different needs and uses. This is a significant reversal in the trend seen for decades, when statistics were mainly supposed to "extract" the greatest possible amount of information from the collection of limited and partial data.

1.3. A look to the future

The previous brief account of demand trends for economic statistical information in the last 50 years should help the reader realize that producers of statistics have a significant and growing demand to satisfy. It should also show how wide is the range of users who needs economic statistics and why a full-fledged taxonomy of users is very difficult. For example, within the category of policy makers, it is possible to distinguish between those who are mostly interested in the supranational dimension from those whose main aim is to ascertain the position at national or subnational level. As a result, the former are very interested in the comparability of macroeconomic statistics, while the latter are mainly focused on sectoral or territorial detailed data, as well as the data's ability to depict the behaviour of particular groups of operators (successful businesses, individuals at risk of poverty, etc.). Within the media, it is possible to distinguish the press agencies, radio and television (especially interested in the speed at which data can be acquired, but much less so in thematic or sectoral detail), from the daily newspapers and the more in-depth periodicals, whose main concern is to tell a "story" based on the statistics.

In the world of business, medium-to-large companies are interested in receiving timely information not only about national and international macroeconomic

THE DEMAND FOR ECONOMIC STATISTICS

developments, but also on various aspects concerning the sectors in which they operate, at a meaningful level of territorial detail. By contrast, small businesses want information more limited in scope, possibly relating to the local market in which they work, or to their own sector of economic activity. Then there are research centres, either public or private, whose needs for information go in all directions, depending on the subject matter. Lastly, households mainly want information that is quite general (or "curious"), expressed in a form they can understand, almost exclusively "consumed" via the different media (television, the press, Internet, etc.).

Looking to the future, it is possible to identify certain trends in the demand for economic statistics that will presumably strengthen in the years to come. In the first place, demand will focus more and more on the services sector (which already accounts for over 70% of GDP in many developed countries), with new forms of production playing a more important part. The measurement of "intangible" activities will take on increased importance and this should bring about greater integration of economic statistics with social statistics: concepts such as those of human and social capital are already generating interest and becoming the subject of quantification, albeit still in embryonic form.

While the international dimension of various phenomena is set to increase with the integration of production activities dispersed over several countries, this will make it more and more difficult to measure the results of individual national economies. This will require a rethinking of the way in which economic statistics are currently compiled, especially with regard to the exchange of data between national statistical institutes in order to make national statistics more representative and consistent.

Thanks to the development of microeconometric models for the design and evaluation of public policy, there will presumably also be an increase in the demand for access to databases containing statistical information on single units (microdata). Such a trend, which is already apparent at the national and international levels, will inevitably present national statistical institutes as well as international organisations with new regulatory and organisational challenges (especially in terms of the protection of privacy). Finally, it is to be assumed that demand for greater integration of economic, social and environmental statistics will lead to new integrated accounting frameworks capable of bringing together these three main themes, mainly to enable policies that make economic growth socially and environmentally sustainable.

Demand for better integration of economic, social and environmental dimensions is also fostering the development of composite indicators, *i.e.* indicators that aggregate data covering specific phenomena into a single aggregated index, to be used to rank countries (regions, cities, etc.). These indices, very much appreciated by the media, are often used to advocate particular policies or to call public attention to issues not well covered by official statistics (corruption, human rights, etc.). Although the development of composite indicators is criticised by some statisticians and should require the use of an extensive set of statistical methodologies, it is putting pressure on the more traditional statistical sources to move towards new areas of work, including subjective well-being and happiness (or life satisfaction).

1. THE DEMAND FOR ECONOMIC STATISTICS

Additionally, the increasing role of large emerging countries, such as China, Russia, Brazil, is putting pressure on international organisations to produce more comparable statistics. The limited availability of national statistics adhering to international standards, as well as the high speed with which these countries' economies and societies evolve, make the measurement of key statistics – including population, GDP, employment and international trade – difficult. Therefore, uncertainties still exist on the dimensions of some global phenomena, such as unbalances in the international financial system or migration flows.

A large degree of uncertainty also exists about the condition of several developing countries, especially the poorest, where the availability and quality of key statistics is low. Notwithstanding the efforts made by the international community to support statistical capacity in these countries, several of them do not have basic figures, or they are produced under the control of political authorities, and thus considered unreliable.

Of course, even if statistical data and metadata are available, the capacity to transform this statistical *information* into *knowledge* to be used in decision-making by individuals, households, businesses and political institutions largely depends on the users' degree of statistical education, and this in turn depends on the country's level of economic development and also on purely cultural factors. Taking as an example the countries in the OECD, major differences can be observed: in the countries with an English-speaking culture (the United States, Canada, the United Kingdom, Australia, etc.) and in the countries of Northern Europe (Sweden, Finland, Norway, etc.) statistics play a fundamental role in political and cultural life, while in other countries the situation is much more nuanced. In the former, the greater degree of commitment to a culture of statistics is reflected not only in the greater levels of public funds devoted to the production of "official statistics", but also in greater levels of investment in applied economic research by academic institutions, foundations and major private sector companies, as well as training that is more geared to scientific disciplines and to quantitative aspects (including statistics) right down to the primary school level. By contrast, in some other countries there is less public investment in official statistics, a lower level of ability to distinguish between reliable statistical information and opinion polls, and political debate is mostly abstract and less likely to be based on statistically measured "facts".

A greater investment in statistical culture not only tends to improve the capacity to benefit from statistical data, but also creates the means by which information is communicated more accurately, a factor that is all the more important in an era of information oversupply. Naturally, this does not altogether prevent statistics being used for partisan purposes, or errors being made in interpretation. However, in countries with higher levels of statistical culture, there is a clear perception of official statistical information as a "public good", the production of which must be freed from any political influences. This consideration has led some countries to recognise the public function of statistics either in their constitutions or in laws that protect the independence of institutions producing official statistics. The inevitable effect of such recognition is to enhance the credibility of official statistics, and thus increase the demand for them.

THE DEMAND FOR ECONOMIC STATISTICS

That said, field studies have shown that even in the more statistically advanced countries, the proportion of people who know little or nothing about the country in which they are living and working is still high. As an example, a survey carried out in 2003 on a sample of citizens in the United States showed that the ability to correctly indicate the dimensions of key variables such as the public deficit or the tax burden, the level of the minimum wage or benefits under the social welfare system is quite limited, especially among people with the lowest levels of income or education, whose main source of information is television (or speeches by political and religious leaders), and who have no particular political leanings and no wish to be better informed about what is happening in their country.

The main conclusions of the authors are threefold: 1) in forming opinion about the direction of economic policy, ideology seems to play a greater role than accurate information; 2) the key hypothesis underlying economic models (*i.e.* that economic operators are fully informed, rational and basically selfish) seems to be a long way from reality, because it appears instead that individuals' actions are confused and basically generous; 3) there is still room for hope that increased knowledge might result in a better approach to decision-making, even though results obtained to date from the information society would seem somewhat limited.

In conclusion, the role played by statistics in orientating public policies and private decisions seems destined to grow in the near future, as will the difficulty users have in distinguishing reliable statistics from those of a lesser quality. Thus, the main challenge in the years to come for the producers of economic statistics will be based not on their capacity to provide quality statistics, but to offer a product whose quality will be clearly evident to the user. Fundamental to this challenge will be the growth in the statistical culture at every user level, with special attention to the world of the media. Following the principles of national accounting, the value of a service should be measured in terms of the change in the status of the consumer. In the case of statistics (a non-market service), we expect the consumer to experience an increase in his/her knowledge of the real world, enabling better choices for the individual and collective well-being. Until now, little attention has been paid to measuring the actual impact of official statistics. Instead, the focus has been limited to measuring the quantity of data published or the annual gathering of data, in other words the processes of production and not the outcome of the statistical function. One of the future challenges will be how to measure the impact of official statistics on the decision-making processes, both of individuals and of those responsible for political decisions.

Chapter 2

Basic Concepts, Definitions and Classifications

How is an economic system defined? Who are the economic agents, and how is a household distinguished from an enterprise? How is the growth of an economy measured? How is a time series defined, and what is the difference between a trend, a cycle and a seasonal variation? This chapter provides an overview of the main concepts and methodological tools necessary to read and analyse the main economic statistics described in Chapter 4. After introducing the main definitions concerning the economic system, we shall analyse the characteristics of the principal economic agents (households, enterprises and public and private institutions) using examples drawn from OECD countries, and then we shall review the main economic aggregates as defined in national accounts, from gross domestic product to national income. The second part of the chapter will be devoted to a brief presentation of index numbers and time series analysis, which are indispensable tools for "reading" economic statistics.

2. BASIC CONCEPTS, DEFINITIONS AND CLASSIFICATIONS

2.1. The economic system

The term *economic process* refers to to those activities through which goods and services aimed at satisfying human needs are produced, distributed and used. For example: daily consumption of food and other goods and services by individuals; an enterprise's production of machinery used to produce other goods; or even the writing of a book on economic statistics intended to be bought by university students.

One of the fundamental characteristics of activities defined as economic processes is that they involve relations between various agents. The definition of economic agent is therefore absolutely fundamental in determining the nature of the economic processes: *economic agent* refers to a person or legal entity that plays an active role in an economic process. An economic agent can therefore be an individual consumer who purchases goods and services, an enterprise that organises factors of production to generate income, a worker who provides his or her labour in a production process, etc. These individual agents (to which economic theory habitually attributes preferences, objectives, behaviour, etc.) are then normally grouped into *institutional sectors* that represent groupings of institutional units (corporations, households, general government, etc.), each of which:

- is entitled to own goods or assets in its own right; it is therefore able to exchange the ownership of goods or assets in transactions with other institutional units;
- is able to take economic decisions and engage in economic activities for which it is held to be directly responsible and accountable by law;
- is able to incur liabilities on its own behalf, to take on other obligations or future commitments and to enter into contracts;
- has either a complete set of accounts (including a balance sheet of assets and liabilities) or it would be possible and meaningful, from both an economic and legal viewpoint, to compile a complete set of accounts for the unit, if required.

These institutional units are the categories of economic agents normally referred to in the System of National Accounts (SNA).

All the agents within a given territory (a region, country, etc.) and the ways they interact with each other and with other agents outside that territory are defined as an *economic system*. An economic system is not only characterised by the physical or technological factors that determine how its production is oriented (*i.e.* mainly towards agriculture, industry, etc.), but also by cultural and institutional factors that regulate how it functions (laws, regulations, etc.). Thus, there are systems in which the economic relations between individual agents are heavily regulated and systems that freely allow agents to undertake new activities or terminate existing activities. There are economic systems completely open to trade with other systems as well as highly regulated systems; systems in which a few large enterprises produce most of the goods and services and others with a vast number of small enterprises and only a few large ones.

2 BASIC CONCEPTS, DEFINITIONS AND CLASSIFICATIONS

The characteristics of an economic system are also important because they can influence the quality of the statistics describing how the system functions. For example, when economic systems are characterised by the presence of a few large enterprises, it is relatively simple to collect statistics to measure the functioning of the system, but when the economic system is composed of a myriad of small enterprises, it can become extremely difficult and/or time consuming to do so. Similarly, in a system that has a particularly large "underground" (or "non-observed") economy, *i.e.* the economy that is not visible to the tax and administrative authorities, production of accurate economic statistics can be a challenge.

An economic system is generally defined in terms of territorial boundaries. The *economic territory* is the area in which the units reside, operate and pursue their interests. Traditionally, the following types of areas are identified:

- *supranational* economic systems: systems composed of groups of sovereign States that have come together through international treaties that set common standards for the functioning of national economic systems (for example, the group of countries that belong to the European Union);
- *national* economic systems: systems having an economic territory that coincides with the administrative boundaries of a sovereign State (France, Canada, etc.);
- *regional* economic systems: systems defined using the administrative boundaries of sub-national areas (regions, provinces, etc.);
- *local* economic systems: systems not defined on the basis of administrative boundaries, but in terms of specific economic, social or environmental characteristics (for example, "local labour systems" or "industrial districts").

The concept of territory is extremely important in statistics because it allows us to distinguish between *agents residing* in a specific territory and *non-resident agents*, thereby making it possible to measure the contribution of each type of agent to economic variables, such as consumption, production, etc. If an agent has its "centre of economic interest" within the national territory, *i.e.* if that is where it conducts its most important economic transactions for a prolonged period (at least one year), it is defined as "resident". If it does not, it is defined as "non-resident".

In reality, with the development of international trade and the processes of "globalisation", it has become extremely difficult to know the relations existing between resident and non-resident agents and to assess the contribution each makes to the overall economic system. Given the expanding operations of multinationals and the introduction of electronic commerce, it is becoming increasingly difficult to describe in statistical terms the amounts and characteristics of the flow of goods, services and activities among agents residing in different countries and their interrelations.

2 BASIC CONCEPTS, DEFINITIONS AND CLASSIFICATIONS

2.2. Economic agents

As we have just seen, in order to be defined as such under the SNA, institutional units (*i.e.* the basic economic decision-making centres) must have autonomy of decision-making in carrying out their principle function and keep (at least potentially) complete accounting records. Institutional units are then aggregated according to the principle function they perform. In this regard, a distinction is made between three "institutional sectors":

- *households*, which perform three principle functions: 1) consume the goods and services produced by other institutional sectors; 2) produce goods and services that can be sold; and 3) acquire real and financial assets. The household sector also includes *non-profit institutions serving households*, which provide non-market (*i.e.* not intended for sale) services consumed by households;

- *enterprises*, which produce goods and services intended for sale to generate profits and which acquire real and financial assets. This sector also includes *non-profit institutions serving enterprises*, which produce services intended for sale to be consumed by companies;

- *general government*, which, in addition to fulfilling its political responsibilities and role of economic regulation, produces principally non-market services (possibly goods) for individual or collective consumption and redistributes income and wealth.

Transactions between resident and non-resident units are normally measured by aggregating all of the latter into a single institutional sector, defined as *rest of the world*. Let us now examine in detail the characteristics of the main economic agents.

2.2.1. Households

From a statistical standpoint, a *household* consists of a small group of people sharing the same living accommodation, who pool some, or all, their income and wealth and who consume certain types of goods and services collectively, mainly housing and food. This group of people can be bound by ties of marriage, family relationship, affinity, adoption, guardianship or ties of affection, and they habitually reside in the same municipality (even if they are not yet registered by the municipality as residents). A household may consist of a single person. Someone who is temporarily absent remains a member of the household even if he or she is living in a different accommodation, be it in the same municipality or in another municipality within the same country or abroad.

As can be seen, the statistical concept of household is not directly related to that used in legislation, and this is a necessary condition given the need to compare statistics on households over time and space. It should also be pointed out that, as we shall see later, many existing statistical surveys refer to individuals rather than to households. However, some surveys are designed also to provide information

BASIC CONCEPTS, DEFINITIONS AND CLASSIFICATIONS 2

by household, as do the so-called "multi-purpose" surveys or those on household consumption and wealth.

It is important to classify households on the basis of the number of families that constitute them. The *family* within the household is defined as those members of the household who are related, to a specific degree, through blood, adoption or marriage. Consequently, the concept of family is normally more restrictive than that of household; in fact, a household may include one or more families or even no families at all (as in the case of single-person households), or may include several families and isolated family members (for example, a child living at the parental home after being legally separated from his/her spouse) or isolated family members (for example, two siblings whose parents are dead).

For example, according to Italian census data (Table 2.1), in 2001, for nearly 57 million persons residing within the national territory, there were 21.8 million resident households, a sharp increase over 1991 (up by nearly 2 million). Of these, nearly 5.5 million consisted of a single person (mostly widows and widowers) and nearly 6 million of two persons (of which nearly 500,000 were unmarried couples). There were slightly fewer than 6 million households with four or more persons. Some 4.5 million households consisted of couples without children and there were some 9 million couples with children. Lastly, in roughly 2 million cases only one of the two parents was present in a household with children. The average number of members per household was 2.6 (2.8 in 1991), with values ranging from 2.4 in the North-West to 2.9 in the South. The regions with the lowest average were Liguria and Valle d'Aosta (2.2), while Campania had the highest (3.1).

In the case of households with more than one member, a problem of classification arises. Given the individual members' different demographic and social characteristics (employed, unemployed, students, young, elderly, etc.), how can the entity "household" be classified unambiguously on the basis of accurate demographic and socio-economic characteristics? The response normally adopted for household surveys is to refer to the characteristics of the *reference person*. The reference person is the "the person registered in the public records in relation to whom family relationships are defined". Thus, if there is a father in a household, he will usually be the reference person, while the wife will be indicated as the spouse, their offspring as children, etc. If there is no father, then the mother will usually act as the reference person and so on. This means that households can now be classified not only by the *number of members*, but by the *labour market status* of the reference person (economically active or inactive), his or her *employment status* (employed, unemployed, job-seeker, etc.), *age*, *income*, *housing tenure* (owner, renter, etc.) and so on.

2 BASIC CONCEPTS, DEFINITIONS AND CLASSIFICATIONS

Table 2.1 – **Resident households and breakdown by size of household and geographical distribution**
Italy, 2001

Geographical distribution	Households by number of members						Total		
	One person	Two persons	Three persons	Four persons	Five persons	Six or more persons	Households	Members	Average number of members per household
North-West	1 767 208	1 840 037	1 390 009	966 118	207 367	46 461	6 217 200	14 813 530	2.4
North-East	1 116 042	1 208 212	962 636	701 273	184 009	59 838	4 232 010	10 530 285	2.5
Centre	1 061 905	1 188 248	941 315	780 561	208 574	61 596	4 242 199	10 820 324	2.6
South	940 888	1 100 449	935 550	1 150 759	474 806	145 822	4 748 274	13 860 137	2.9
Islands	541 578	568 465	476 696	537 495	191 070	55 689	2 370 993	6 569 745	2.8
Italy	5 427 621	5 905 411	4 706 206	4 136 206	1 265 826	369 406	21 810 676	56 594 021	2.6

StatLink http://dx.doi.org/10.1787/336610548652

Source: Italian Statistical Office.

These classifications are used in many statistical surveys. For example, in the household consumption survey for France, consumer spending can be compared based on the number of household members, the occupational status of the reference person (Table 2.2) or the type of household.

Table 2.2 – **Average monthly household expenditure by occupational status of reference person**
France, 2001

Occupational status of reference person	Food		Non-food		Total
	Value (in euros)	Percentage	Value (in euros)	Percentage	Value (in euros)
Farmer	6 092	19.3	25 553	80.7	31 645
Self-employed	7 165	16.3	36 696	83.7	43 861
Managers and professional workers	8 327	15.5	45 508	84.5	53 835
Employees	4 789	18.6	20 926	81.4	25 715
Manual workers and similar	5 551	19.6	22 782	80.4	28 333
Retired	4 576	20.7	17 529	79.3	22 105
Others not employed	3 201	20.2	12 675	79.8	15 876
Total	5 513	18.4	24 450	81.6	29 963

StatLink http://dx.doi.org/10.1787/336618155337

a) Including expenses for restaurants, bars, cafés and canteens.

Source: INSEE, *Le Budget des Familles en 2001*.

To consume the goods and services produced by companies, general government and the rest of the world, households spend the income they receive from participating in productive activities. They may also engage in productive activities themselves, such as running family businesses (a shop, a restaurant, etc.) or renting accommodation (apartments or houses). In this case, they are defined as *unincorporated enterprises*. More precisely, an unincorporated enterprise is a producer unit not incorporated

BASIC CONCEPTS, DEFINITIONS AND CLASSIFICATIONS 2

as a legal entity separate from its owner (in this case the household, but it could also be the government or a foreign resident); the fixed and other assets used by unincorporated enterprises do not belong to the enterprises but to their owners; the enterprises as such cannot engage in transactions with other economic units nor can they enter into contractual relationships with other units nor incur liabilities on their own behalf; in addition, their owners are personally liable, without limit, for any debts or obligations incurred in the course of production.

Finally, NPISHs (Non-Profit Institutions Serving Households) provide goods and services (usually for free, being financed by regular membership subscriptions or dues) that benefit households, such as assistance to disabled persons, recreational activities for children, etc. NPISHs are created by associations of persons to provide goods or services primarily for the benefit of the members themselves (such as professional or learned societies, political parties, trade unions, consumers' associations, churches or religious societies, and social, cultural, recreational or sports clubs).

The distinction between consuming and producing households is typical of national accounts, while other statistical sources tend to view households above all as entities primarily aimed at consumption (when the survey is of an economic nature) or as the place where interpersonal ties are established and where key functions for society as a whole take place (when the survey is focused on studying demographic or social aspects). In these cases, households are classified by criteria that differ from those adopted in the national accounts, although it is still possible, at least at the conceptual level, to conduct cross-classifications, for example by distinguishing consuming households on the basis of social-demographic characteristics.

2.2.2. Enterprises

The enterprise sector includes various types of entities. The term *enterprise* in the strictest sense refers to the organisation of an economic activity on a professional basis for the purposes of producing goods or providing services intended for sale. An enterprise has a certain autonomy regarding its choices in the field of production, sales and distribution of profits. The entity responsible for the enterprise consists of one or more persons acting individually or in partnership or of one or more legal entities.

Enterprises can operate in all sectors of economic activity (agriculture, industry or services). In the agricultural sector, however, there is a specific type of economic entity, defined as an *agricultural holding*. For agricultural census purposes, an agricultural holding is a techno-economic unit of agricultural production comprising all livestock and all land used wholly, or partly, for agricultural purposes and managed by one person or more, without regard to title, legal form, size or location. In terms of national accounts, it is defined as an economic unit under a single management engaged in agricultural production. The unit may also be engaged in non-agricultural activities, so this concept should not be interpreted too strictly; the aim is rather to value the final production of all agricultural products. Also, establishments or specialised units that provide agricultural services on a fee or contract basis should, in general, be included. The fundamental difference between an enterprise and an agricultural holding is that

2. BASIC CONCEPTS, DEFINITIONS AND CLASSIFICATIONS

the basic requirement for the former is its business-oriented organisation (independent of the sector of activity), while for an agricultural holding, it is the specific activity of agriculture, forestry or animal production that is fundamental.

Enterprises may be classified on the basis of many characteristics. In the SNA, enterprises are aggregated in the institutional sector of "corporations", which comprises corporations and unincorporated enterprises. Moreover, quasi-corporations are unincorporated enterprises that function as if they were corporations, and which have complete sets of accounts, including balance sheets.

Within the institutional sector of corporations two typologies are distinguished:

- *non-financial corporations*: corporations whose principal activity is the production of market goods or non-financial services;
- *financial corporations*: institutional units principally engaged in financial intermediation or in auxiliary financial activities.

Among the various ways of classifying enterprises, classification based on *economic activity* is certainly of key importance. This type of classification is based on the characteristics of the the activity of production units, *i.e.* the characteristics of the goods and services produced, the uses for which these are intended, the factors of production and the production process and technology used. The importance given to these criteria varies from one category to the next. For example, for goods characterised by a particularly complex production process, the final use, the technology and the organisation of production are given priority over the type of goods produced.

The reference classification for economic activities is the *International Statistical Industrial Classification* (ISIC Rev. 3.1) published in 2002. At the European level, the corresponding classification is known as NACE Rev. 1.1, which is totally aligned with ISIC Rev. 3.1. NACE Rev. 1.1 has the following levels:

- Level 1: Categories (one-letter alpha code – A to Q);
- Level 2: Divisions (2-digit codes);
- Level 3: Groups (3-digit codes);
- Level 4: Classes (4-digit codes).

In several countries, the statistical office prepares a national version of the international classifications. These classifications, although roughly consistent with the international ones, take into account the specificity of national production structures and may contain an additional level of detail useful for identifying activities particularly important to that country.

BASIC CONCEPTS, DEFINITIONS AND CLASSIFICATIONS   2

Table 2.3 – **ISIC Rev. 3.1 industrial classification of economic activities – Categories and divisions**

A		Agriculture, hunting and forestry
B		Fishing
C		Mining and quarrying
D		Manufacturing
	15	Manufacture of food products and beverages
	16	Manufacture of tobacco products
	17	Manufacture of textiles
	18	Manufacture of wearing apparel; dressing and dyeing of fur
	19	Tanning and dressing of leather; manufacture of luggage, handbags, saddlery, harness and footwear
	20	Manufacture of wood and of products of wood and cork, except furniture; manufacture of articles of straw and plaiting materials
	21	Manufacture of paper and paper products
	22	Publishing, printing and reproduction of recorded media
	23	Manufacture of coke, refined petroleum products and nuclear fuel
	24	Manufacture of chemicals and chemical products
	25	Manufacture of rubber and plastics products
	26	Manufacture of other non-metallic mineral products
	27	Manufacture of basic metals
	28	Manufacture of fabricated metal products, except machinery and equipment
	29	Manufacture of machinery and equipment n.e.c.
	30	Manufacture of office, accounting and computing machinery
	31	Manufacture of electrical machinery and apparatus n.e.c.
	32	Manufacture of radio, television and communication equipment and apparatus
	33	Manufacture of medical, precision and optical instruments, watches and clocks
	34	Manufacture of motor vehicles, trailers and semi-trailers
	35	Manufacture of other transport equipment
	36	Manufacture of furniture; manufacturing n.e.c.
	37	Recycling
E		Electricity, gas and water supply
F		Construction
G		Wholesale and retail trade; repair of motor vehicles, motorcycles and personal and household goods
H		Hotels and restaurants
I		Transport, storage and communications
J		Financial intermediation
K		Real estate, renting and business activities
L		Public administration and defence; compulsory social security
M		Education
N		Health and social work
O		Other community, social and personal service activities
P		Activities of private households as employers and undifferentiated production activities of private households
Q		Extraterritorial organizations and bodies

2. BASIC CONCEPTS, DEFINITIONS AND CLASSIFICATIONS

Enterprises may be classified on the basis of other criteria, such as size, organisation, legal form, purpose of products, technological description, etc. The classification by *size of enterprise* is based on the number of employees, with the term *employee* referring to a person who enters an agreement (either formal or informal) to work for an enterprise in return for remuneration in cash or in kind. Employees can have different types of contracts: for example, stable employees are those who have had, and continue to have, an explicit (written or oral) or implicit contract of employment, or a succession of such contracts, with the same employer on a continuous basis. On a continuous basis implies a period of employment longer than a specified minimum determined according to national circumstances. Regular employees are those with stable contracts for whom the employing organisation is responsible for paying taxes and social security contributions and/or where the contractual relationship is subject to national labour legislation.

The size classes can be defined on the basis of various criteria and purposes. For example, the definition adopted at the European level classifies enterprises with fewer than 250 employees as "small and medium-sized enterprises"; this classification is used both for statistical purposes and to identify enterprises that may qualify for special financing granted by the EU. In countries such as Italy, where a myriad of small and very small enterprises exist, the European size classification does not appear to be very useful; therefore, other thresholds are used to analyse these economic systems. Over time, the size distribution of enterprises can change significantly, partly because of legal acts that favour certain groups of enterprises. For example, Table 2.4 shows the evolution of the industrial sector in the United States, based on enterprise size.

Generally, an enterprise produces a variety of products. Furthermore, other activities, known as secondary activities, are often carried out in addition to the principal activity. The term *principal activity* refers to activity whose value added exceeds that of any other activity carried out within the same unit (the output of the principal activity must consist of goods or services capable of being delivered to other units, even though they may be used for its own consumption or own capital formation). An *ancillary activity* is a supporting activity undertaken within an enterprise to create the conditions within which the principal or secondary activities can be carried out; ancillary activities generally produce services commonly found as inputs into almost any kind of productive activity, and the value of an individual ancillary activity's output is likely to be small compared with the other activities of the enterprise (*e.g.* cleaning and maintenance of buildings). Finally, a *unit of homogeneous production* is a producer unit in which only a single (non-ancillary) productive activity is carried out (this unit is not normally observable and is more an abstract or conceptual unit underlying the symmetric input-output tables).

BASIC CONCEPTS, DEFINITIONS AND CLASSIFICATIONS 2

Table 2.4 – **Enterprises and employees by size class in the total industry (excluding construction)**
USA, 1992 and 2002

Size classes (number of employees)	1992 Enterprises	1992 Employees	2002 Enterprises	2002 Employees	Growth rates (percentages) Enterprises	Growth rates (percentages) Employees
1-9	214 626	707 793	210 322	693 444	-2.0	-2.0
10-19	55 629	758 189	52 299	711 304	-6.0	-6.2
20-99	68 632	2 809 125	64 467	2 588 453	-6.1	-7.9
100-499	17 203	3 070 757	17 732	2 703 843	3.1	-11.9
500 or more	5 431	12 420 510	10 635	9 600 428	95.8	-22.7
Total	361 521	19 766 374	355 455	16 297 472	-1.7	-17.5

StatLink http://dx.doi.org/10.1787/336664670860
Source: OECD 2006, *Structural and Demographic Business Statistics*, OECD publishing.

Another extremely important distinction is between enterprises situated *in a single location*, *i.e.* enterprises that carry out their activity in a single local unit (establishment), and enterprises with *a number of locations*. Naturally, many small enterprises have a single location, but this is also true of many medium-sized and large enterprises. In addition, enterprises with a number of locations often have local units scattered in many different regions and sometimes in other countries.

The trend towards the globalisation of production, the development of computer networks, the growing international mobility of capital, products and labour and the growing role of groups of enterprises have caused major changes in production units in recent years. Trends towards "relocation" of production have been particularly important, *i.e.* the transfer abroad of entire enterprises or of specific local units. These changes pose difficult problems of classification with regard to the location of enterprises, their ownership structure and the relations between local units operating in different countries. The distinction between individual enterprises and groups of enterprises is important in this regard.

According to the European Council Regulation EEC No. 696/93, an *enterprise group* is an "association of enterprises bound together by legal and/or financial links. A group of enterprises can have more than one decision-making centre (production, sales, etc.) and it may centralise centrain aspects of financial management and taxation". The concept of control is naturally crucial for the definition of a group: control of an enterprise implies the ability to appoint a majority of the board of directors, to run the enterprise, guide its activities and determine its strategy. This ability is exercised by a single direct investor or a group of associated shareholders acting in concert and controlling the majority (+50%) of ordinary shares or voting power. The control of an enterprise may be direct or indirect, immediate or ultimate. However, "effective control" may be exercised when the investor(s) holds a large block of voting stock, even when it is less than 50%, and the remaining shares are widely held by many smaller investors. Control of enterprises may also be exercised through interlocking directorates and inter-corporate ownership links between firms, as in the case of conglomerates.

2 BASIC CONCEPTS, DEFINITIONS AND CLASSIFICATIONS

The notion of *ownership* is different from that of control, since the former corresponds to financial ownership of an enterprise, be it majority or minority ownership. Majority direct ownership (+50%) of ordinary shares, or voting power, by a single investor could imply control of this enterprise by the investor, but minority ownership could also imply indirect control of this enterprise (through another enterprise). In other words, the notion of ownership is not sufficient to indicate if an enterprise is under influence or control.

Within groups, the following main types of enterprises can be identified:

- *holding corporation*: corporation that controls a group of subsidiary corporations and whose principal activity is owning and directing the group. When the holding corporation is resident in a different country from the enterprise controlled, the holding enterprise is considered to be "foreign";

- *the parent (controlled) enterprise*: an enterprise controlled by another institutional unit that controlled directly or indirectly more than 50% of the shares or voting rights of the first enterprise at 31 December of the reference year. When the controlled enterprise is resident within the national territory but is controlled by a non-resident institutional unit, the controlled enterprise is considered to be "foreign".

Using the statistical register ASIA (Table 2.5), the Italian Statistical Institute has estimated that in 2003 there were more than 59 000 groups, which comprised some 138 000 enterprises and employed more than 5.1 million people. Groups involved 3.2% of economically active enterprises and one-third of employed persons. However, this number rose to 20% (and 57% of employment) if it was calculated with reference to the number of corporations only. Some 63.4% of groups are concentrated in enterprises with 1-9 employees (accounting for 4.7% of employment), but those with 500 employees or more, even though they only represent 2% of the total, account for over 3 million employees. There are 649 groups under the direct or indirect control of general government, which account for 12% of the employment of enterprises belonging to groups, while 9.2% of groups are foreign controlled.

Table 2.5 (a) – **Groups, enterprises and employees belonging to groups, by number of employees**
Italy, 2003

Number of employees	Groups		Enterprises		Employees	
	Number	%	Number	%	Number	%
1-19	38 045	63.4	65 155	46.9	239 225	4.7
20-99	15 599	26.0	36 394	26.2	691 950	13.5
100-499	5 016	8.4	18 755	13.5	1 019 649	19.9
500-4999	1 216	2.0	12 513	9.0	1 513 669	29.5
5000 and more	87	0.1	6 115	4.4	1 658 631	32.4

StatLink http://dx.doi.org/10.1787/336677172303

Source: Italian Statistical Office.

BASIC CONCEPTS, DEFINITIONS AND CLASSIFICATIONS 2

Table 2.5 (b) – **Groups, enterprises and employees belonging to groups, by number of enterprises involved in the group**
Italy, 2003

Number of enterprises involved in the group	Groups		Enterprises		Employees	
	Number	%	Number	%	Number	%
1	22 799	38.0	22 799	16.4	631 833	12.3
2	24 116	40.2	48 232	34.7	854 685	16.9
3-4	9 852	16.4	31 942	23.0	829 308	16.2
5-9	2 472	4.1	14 968	10.8	839 705	16.4
10-49	652	1.1	11 025	7.9	1 133 322	22.1
50 or more	72	0.1	9 966	7.2	824 272	16.1
Total	56 963	100.0	138 932	100.0	5 123 125	100.0

StatLink ⟶ http://dx.doi.org/10.1787/336677172303

Source: Italian Statistical Office.

Although the activity of multinationals grew dramatically over the last decade, much of international trade is still conducted by enterprises independent of one another and a very substantial number of enterprises produce goods and services for the domestic market alone. Consequently, another important distinction must be made between enterprises that have relations with the rest of the world (*exporting/importing enterprises*) and enterprises only oriented towards the domestic market. As can be seen in Table 2.6, in France there are approximately 19 000 exporting enterprises with more than 20 employees. Naturally, the percentage of exporting enterprises grows as the size of the enterprise increases, reaching a percentage of 40% for enterprises with 2 000 employees or more. It should also be pointed out that the difference between exporting and non-exporting enterprises is extremely interesting from an analytical standpoint, since the economic indicators (productivity, profitability, etc.) for exporters are normally better than for non-exporters, given the same size and activity sector.

Table 2.6 – **Exporting enterprises, employees and exports by number of employees**
France, 2005

Number of employees	Enterprises		Employees	Exports	
	Number	Exports rate (exports/turnover)		Value (million euros)	Share of total exports (percentage)
20-49	10 409	16.5	320 156	8 591.2	3.3
50-99	4 155	22.0	261 576	10 638.9	4.1
100-249	2 872	30.7	406 080	23 802.3	9.2
250-499	1 031	34.6	321 495	25 309.9	9.7
500-999	523	33.1	320 564	35 306.7	13.6
1 000-1999	213	39.1	271 194	33 016.1	12.7
2 000 and more	134	40.3	781 244	123 079.7	47.4
Total	19 337	34.7	2 682 309	259 744.8	100.0

StatLink ⟶ http://dx.doi.org/10.1787/336765200553

Source: Enquête annuelle d'entreprise 2005, Ministère de l'Économie.

2 BASIC CONCEPTS, DEFINITIONS AND CLASSIFICATIONS

The classification of enterprises by their legal form varies with each country's legislation, making international comparisons rather difficult. For example, Table 2.7 shows the data available for Italy and Norway.

Table 2.7(a) – **Enterprises and employees by legal form**
Norway, December 2004

Legal forms	Enterprises	Employees	Number of employees per enterprise
General partnership	7 739	10 401	1.3
Limited company	128 745	1 096 705	8.5
Public limited company	417	59 203	142.0
General partnership with shared liability	6 205	6 363	1.0
Sole proprietorship	155 505	61 438	0.4
Other legal forms	19 194	159 290	8.3
Total	317 805	1 393 400	4.4

StatLink http://dx.doi.org/10.1787/336776126426

a) Employees in the stock of enterprises per 1 January 2005, employees by December 2004.
Source: Statistics Norway.

Table 2.7(b) – **Enterprises and employees by legal form**
Italy, December 2001

Legal forms	Enterprises	Employees			Number of employees per enterprise
		Self-employed	Dependent	Total	
Sole proprietorships (a)	2 667 160	3 079 521	1 129 363	4 208 884	1.6
Partnerships	824 627	1 548 403	1 426 911	3 011 314	3.6
Corporations	531 590	692 343	6 892 706	7 585 049	14.3
Co-operatives (b)	47 719	114 869	671 218	786 092	16.5
Other forms	12 870	14 686	106 883	121 569	9.4
Total	4 083 966	5 485 822	10 227 081	15 712 908	3.8

StatLink http://dx.doi.org/10.1787/336780633170

a) Also includes self-employed workers and members of liberal professions.
b) Excluding social co-operatives.
Source: Italian Statistical Office.

The *intended use of goods* is another important classification criterion. For many years, several European countries published the production index and other cyclical indicators for industry according to the economic use of the goods (consumption, investment, etc.), aggregating the basic indices according to a scheme defined at the national level. Since 2001, however, cyclical indicators have been aggregated into "Main Industrial Groupings (MIGs)" defined at the Community level. The groupings are as follows: consumer durables, consumer non-durables, capital goods, intermediate goods and energy. The indices concerning groups and/or divisions of economic activity are assigned to each grouping according to the criterion of prevalence, *i.e.* according to whether the goods in that group/division are mainly intended for durable consumption, non-durable consumption, etc.

BASIC CONCEPTS, DEFINITIONS AND CLASSIFICATIONS 2

Classification by the *technology intensity* of goods and of the relevant sectors of economic activity is also interesting. This classification, originally proposed by the OECD and also adopted by Eurostat, distinguishes among four groupings of goods/sectors: high technology, medium-high, medium-low and low technology. The various manufacturing sectors are classified in one of the four groupings based on the specific technological level of the sector, the intensity of R&D spending, and on the technology embodied in the sector's purchases of intermediate and capital goods. This classification is often used to analyse export/import flows and to evaluate the *performance* of the various sectors of economic activity.

For agricultural holdings, the main classification criteria refer to the economic size of the holding, the type of occupancy, the type of farming and the territorial location (mountains, hills, etc.). Two criteria have been adopted to evaluate the economic size of the farm: the amount of labour employed; and the utilised agricultural area (UAA). Given the specific organisation of agricultural production and the fact that the farmer's family members are frequently involved in the farm's activities in various ways and extents, the labour provided is not measured by number of employees but in terms of full-time equivalent units (FTE). A FTE is defined as "total hours worked divided by average annual hours worked in full-time jobs" and makes it possible to define the various types of work actually provided using a standard measurement that can be used to evaluate the size of farms in a way that is analogous to that used for industrial and service enterprises. Typically, farms are subdivided according to whether the labour employed is less than one FTE, between one and 10 FTE, or more than 10 FTE. An alternative measure is the size of the agricultural area used, expressed in hectares and consisting of land used specifically for farming.

Agricultural holdings can also be classified based on the type of occupancy. Of course, the types of occupancy depend on the legal framework, uses and traditions. For example, in Italy (Table 2.8) the following categories are used:

- *those directly farmed by the owner*, with a further distinction depending on whether only family labour is used or also salaried labour. It is this type of occupancy when the owner himself provides manual labour on the agricultural holding;
- *those farmed by employees*: when the owner exclusively employs third parties to perform manual labour, while his work (and that of family members) normally consists of managing the agricultural holding;
- *share farming of complete holdings*: when a natural or legal person entrusts a holding to the head of a family, who undertakes with the aid of his family to carry out all work required on the holding and to bear some of the expenses himself.
- *other forms of occupancy*: this category includes the share farming of individual parcels of land (when the concession does not concern the entire holding, but only several parcels of land and the work is carried out without the aid of family members) and the lease of livestock (a form of stock farming based on an agreement between the owner of the pasture and the owner of the livestock).

2. BASIC CONCEPTS, DEFINITIONS AND CLASSIFICATIONS

Finally, agricultural holdings are classified either as specialised or non-specialised. The former include those specialising in the production of seeds, fruits and vegetables, permanent crops, grazing livestock and grain-fed livestock; the latter are subdivided into farms that practice either field crop combination or livestock combination and those that combine crop and livestock farming.

Table 2.8 – **Farms (including publicly owned holdings) and total area by total area class and type of occupancy (area in hectares)**
Italy, 2003

Type of occupancy	Total area class								
	Less than 1	1 - 2	2 - 5	5 - 10	10 - 20	20 - 50	50 - 100	100 and more	Total
Direct farming by owner	538 187	395 797	459 838	232 384	139 163	99 526	29 408	14 427	1 908 730
• Only family labour	455 831	334 230	385 686	190 982	110 226	76 641	19 491	7 159	1 580 246
• Predominantly family labour	64 303	47 726	54 055	30 150	20 204	15 780	6 503	4 101	242 822
• Predominantly labour from outside family	18 053	13 841	20 097	11 252	8 733	7 105	3 414	3 167	85 662
Farming with employees only	10 209	5 276	10 045	5 879	5 479	5 973	2 775	5 380	51 016
Share farming of complete holdings	-	402	-	142	207	72	47	69	939
Other forms of occupancy	390	221	242	603	244	214	115	549	2 578
Total	548 786	401 696	470 125	239 008	145 093	105 785	32 345	20 425	1 963 263

Source: Italian Statistical Office.

StatLink http://dx.doi.org/10.1787/336781812148

2.2.3. General government

The general government sector comprises:

- all institutional units that produce non-market goods and services intended for collective and individual consumption and financed primarily by compulsory payments by units belonging to other sectors;

- all institutional units whose main function is to redistribute the country's income and wealth.

In particular, the institutional sector of general government is subdivided into the following subsectors:

- *central government*: this includes all the administrative bodies of the central State and the other central bodies whose authority normally extends to the entire economic territory, except for central social security funds;

- *local government*: this includes public bodies (except for social security funds) whose authority extends only over part of the economic territory;

- *social security funds*: this includes all central, state and local institutional units whose main activity consists of granting social benefits funded wholly, or in part, by specific groups of the population, according to legislative or regulatory provisions. This subsector includes government administrations responsible for

BASIC CONCEPTS, DEFINITIONS AND CLASSIFICATIONS 2

setting, or approving, contributions and benefits, independently from their role as a supervisory or employing body.

The process for classifying each institutional unit resident in the national territory within the general government sector or in other institutional sectors is relatively complex and conducted in logically successive steps. These steps, shown in Figure 2.1, are based on the legal nature and ownership structure of each unit and on the relevant annual budget data. The process begins with the identification of the unit being analysed (in principle any of the units within the system included in the country's statistical records). The first question is whether this unit engages in a productive activity or not: if it does not, its main function is consumption, and it must be classified in the household sector. If it is a production unit, however, it must be determined whether it is private or public (in the sense that it is owned or controlled, directly or indirectly, by a central or local government body included in the general government sector). If it is private, the institutional unit will be included in one of the other institutional sectors.

If the unit is public, however, it must be determined whether it is market-oriented (market unit) or not (non-market unit), *i.e.* whether the goods or services it produces are traded on the market at economically meaningful prices, or if they are provided to consumers completely or virtually free of charge; only in the latter case, in fact, can the unit be classified in the general government sector. To solve this problem, the ESA considers the unit as non-market if the potential proceeds from the sale of goods and services cover at least 50% of the production costs (expenditure on staff, inputs of goods and services, etc.). This condition must be met for an appropriate number of years to ensure stability in the medium term and avoid having to continually reclassify units from one economic sector to another for purely cyclical reasons.

Once it has been established that the public institutional unit is non-market, it is necessary to determine whether it is a non-profit social institution (foundation, association, etc.). In other words, it must be determined whether, in addition to being controlled by a government (a condition already met in one of the preceding steps), it is also primarily financed by government (through unrecoverable transfers): only if this is the case, in fact, should the social institution be included in the general government sector. If its main sources of income are from capital or transfers of private funds (membership fees, donations, etc.), the unit must be classified in the sector of non-profit institutions serving households (NPISHs).

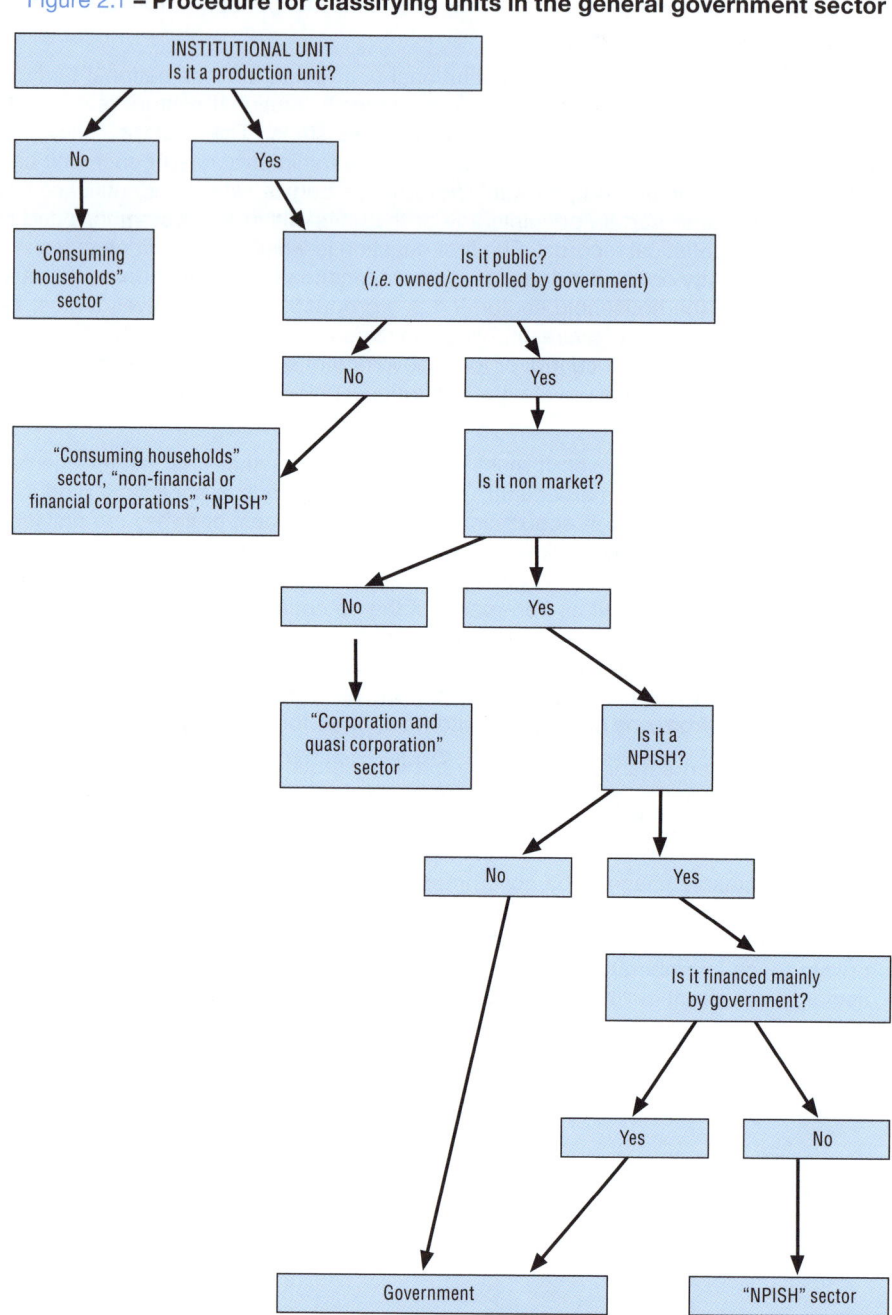

2 BASIC CONCEPTS, DEFINITIONS AND CLASSIFICATIONS

Figure 2.1 – **Procedure for classifying units in the general government sector**

```
                    INSTITUTIONAL UNIT
                    Is it a production unit?
                    /                \
                  No                  Yes
                  ↓                    ↓
          "Consuming           Is it public?
          households"          (i.e. owned/controlled by government)
            sector             /                \
                             No                 Yes
                             ↓                   ↓
          "Consuming households"          Is it non market?
          sector, "non-financial or        /          \
          financial corporations", "NPISH"  No        Yes
                                            ↓          ↓
                                "Corporation and      Is it a NPISH?
                                quasi corporation"    /         \
                                    sector          No          Yes
                                                                 ↓
                                                      Is it financed mainly
                                                      by government?
                                                       /          \
                                                     Yes           No
                                                      ↓             ↓
                                                  Government    "NPISH" sector
```

BASIC CONCEPTS, DEFINITIONS AND CLASSIFICATIONS 2

The rationale behind this admittedly complex procedure for classifying institutional units is based on the importance of defining correctly the boundaries of the general government sector. Firstly, the distinction between market and non-market production units has numerous implications for measuring national income and GDP. In fact, two important economic aggregates – production and value added – are quantified differently, depending on the type of unit: for market services units, these two aggregates are measured using the turnover; for non-market services units, they are based on the sum of production costs. This means that if a non-market unit were classified in the corporate sector, its value added would be undervalued.

Secondly, correctly defining the general government sector is important to ensuring the greatest possible international comparability (or inter-regional comparability if the statistics refer to sub-national territorial levels) and can have consequences not only for economic analysis, but also for policy making and institutional operations. For the European countries, for example, the financial resources levied by Community institutions from member countries and those distributed to these countries through structural funds are determined proportionally based on the measurement of the national (and regional) income produced by the various countries (and regions). The implications are even more obvious if we refer to the measurement of the deficit or public debt, two basic parameters for European economic and monetary policy.

Table 2.9 shows the territorial distribution of the over 15 000 units surveyed and classified as public institutions in the 2001 Italian census, with the relevant employment. It also shows the territorial distribution of the more than 235 000 non-profit institutions, *i.e.* those units, with or without a legal personality, public or private, that produce goods or services and that by law or under their own statutory rules cannot distribute profits or other gains except to compensate persons working on behalf of the institution's founders and its members. Consequently, non-profit institutions include associations, whether they are recognised or not, foundations, voluntary and non-governmental organisations, social co-operatives, political parties, trade unions, etc., which in 2001 had some 500 000 employees and nearly 3.5 million volunteers.

Table 2.9 – **Institutions, local units and employees by geographical distribution**
Italy, 2001

Geographical distribution	Public institutions			Non-profit institutions		
	Legal-economic units	Employees	Other forms*	Legal-economic units	Employees	Other forms*
North	8 710	762 345	71 910	120 884	271 606	1 918 298
Centre	2 343	1 913 539	167 969	48 808	110 186	675 959
South	4 527	533 241	32 582	65 540	106 731	825 338
Italy as a whole	15 580	3 209 125	269 461	235 232	488 523	3 419 595

StatLink http://dx.doi.org/10.1787/336784120254

* Includes project staff, temporary workers and volunteers.

Source: Italian Statistical Office.

2 BASIC CONCEPTS, DEFINITIONS AND CLASSIFICATIONS

2.3. Economic aggregates

As we have already mentioned, in an economic system a virtually infinite number of economic transactions take place between economic agents. These transactions, which may encompass a very wide range of purposes (such as the purchase or sale of goods, services, financial activities, income redistribution, etc.) and be carried out between different institutional sectors, result in changes in the situation of individual agents. Based on the reasons for these changes, individual transactions are classified (according to the rules of the SNA) into homogeneous groups, defined as *economic aggregates*. These aggregates measure the overall outcome of the transactions conducted by all units of the economic system. The aggregates include *private consumption*, consisting of all expenditures by households to purchase goods and services that satisfy their personal needs (food, clothing, etc.); *investment*, represented by expenditures to purchase goods to be used to generate income in one or more successive periods; *production*, *i.e.* the result of the economic activity of production units, etc.

Consequently, a single transaction can contribute to a specific economic aggregate, depending on why it was carried out and the economic agents involved. For example, the cash purchase of a new vehicle can be classified as consumption, if it is carried out by a household to transport the family, or as an investment (or gross fixed capital formation) if it is made by a salesman (*i.e.* an incorporated enterprise) in order to visit customers scattered over the territory. Similarly, the dealership that sells the vehicle will enter the amount received into its turnover, and this will contribute to determining the value of the total production of the economic system.

Economic aggregates (or variables) can be classified on the basis of various criteria, but the most relevant distinction is between *stock variables* and *flow variables*. Flows refer to activities and the effects of events that occur within a certain period of time, while stocks refer to situations at a specific time. To explain in greater detail, flows reflect the creation, transformation, exchange, transfer or extinction of economic value that takes place during a certain period of time; stocks represent the value of *non-financial assets* (also called "real assets", such as dwellings, capital goods, etc.) and/or *financial assets/liabilities* (such as means of payment, securities, etc.) at a particular moment in time. It is important to point out that, by their nature, flows can only be expressed with reference to a certain period of time (a year, a quarter, etc.), while stocks refer to a specific moment in time (last day of the year, of the quarter, etc.). Flows can also be expressed as the total value (amount) of the flows generated during the time period, or as an average value, *i.e.* by dividing the sum of the flows by the amount of time (number of days, months, etc.) included in the period being considered.

Real assets can either be *produced* or *non-produced*: produced assets are non-financial assets that have come into existence as outputs of processes that fall within the production boundary of the SNA (such as the vehicle referred to in the previous example): they consist of fixed assets, inventories and valuables. Non-produced assets are non-financial assets that come into existence other than through processes of production: they include both tangible assets (for example a forest) and intangible assets and also include costs of ownership transfer on, and major improvements to, these assets.

2.3.1. Production, intermediate costs and value added

As we have already seen, production represents the flow of goods and services generated under the control of an institutional unit, using goods, services and inputs of factors of production, such as labour and capital. A good represents a physical object used to satisfy a certain need, that can be traded between various agents and over which property rights can be held. Services are heterogenous produced outputs that change the conditions of the consuming unit who requested the service. In this case, the entity to which the property right refers is not a specific physical good, but the possibility of using the service.

Although production activity can concern an infinite number of goods and services, the SNA clearly defines the *boundaries of production*. Since these boundaries are defined conventionally, they may change over time. For example, the 1993 SNA includes as production some activities that were not contained in the previous version (developed in 1968). According to the 1993 SNA, the boundaries of production encompass, in addition to the products of economic activities in the strict sense, the following types of products:

- the production of all individual or collective goods or services supplied to units other than their producers, or intended to be so supplied, including the production of goods or services used up in the process of producing such goods or services;
- the own-account production of all goods retained by their producers for their own final consumption or gross capital formation;
- the own-account production of housing services by owner-occupiers and of domestic and personal services produced by employing domestic staff.

The 1993 SNA included in the production boundary the creation and use of literary and artistic originals and improvements to historic monuments created through a production process, even if that process took place in antiquity. The SNA also requires that the growth that occurs during the cultivation of crops and the rearing of animals be recorded over time, and not only when the products reach final maturity.

Lastly, it should be pointed out that the boundaries of production also encompass the so-called underground economy, *i.e.* the production of economic agents who evade requirements of an administrative nature. For example, the following are included in production: the activity of craft workers who repair or renovate buildings without declaring this to the administrative and tax authorities; goods produced by an enterprise that is not registered with the authorities and that uses workers not declared to social security agencies. Consequently, the fact that a productive activity is conducted illegally does not mean that it is excluded from the boundaries of production. Even though the statistical quantification of these activities is fraught with difficulties, statistical institutes have developed methods for including the valuation of the "non-observed economy" in official data.

According to the SNA, production should also include illegal activities that produce goods and services paid for by buyers voluntarily, such as smuggling, prostitution, the production and marketing of illegal drugs, etc. Production does not include illegal

2 BASIC CONCEPTS, DEFINITIONS AND CLASSIFICATIONS

activities that involve involuntary payments, such as thefts, which are an involuntary transfer between different agents. However, given the enormous difficulties involved in measuring production derived from illegal activities, only a few statistical institutes include such valuations, while others prefer to publish them in special studies.

Production may be valued in various ways, depending on the prices used. Firstly, it can be measured in *market prices* (or purchase prices), which represent the actual price agreed upon by the transactors. This therefore includes transport costs, trade margins and indirect taxes (such as value added tax), less subsidies for products, *i.e.* minus transfers made by governments (or by EU institutions) to influence, generally in a downward direction, the price charged by the producer/vendor. In the absence of market transactions, valuation is made according to costs incurred (non-market services produced by government) or by reference to market prices for analogous goods or services (services of owner-occupied dwellings).

If we exclude from the market price any tax payable and the transport costs invoiced separately by the producer, and we add any receiveable subsidies, we obtain the price actually received by the producer, *i.e.* the *basic price*. This price is particularly important for analysing the enterprise sector since it is the relevant price for decision-making by an enterprise, *i.e.* it is the price on the basis of which the enterprise's actual income and profitability are measured.

To obtain a certain amount of output, the producing unit must use the various original factors of production (labour and capital) as well as the goods and services produced by other units. The value of the goods and services consumed as inputs during the production process, excluding fixed assets whose use is recorded as consumption of fixed capital, constitutes the aggregate known as *intermediate consumption*. Intermediate consumption is always valued at purchase prices; it does not include *depreciation*, which is the decrease in the value of the fixed capital (such as industrial equipment) used during intermediate consumption.

The difference between production at basic prices and intermediate consumption is called *value added at basic prices*: this represents the value that has been added (output) by the production process to the pre-existing value of the goods and services used (input) during this process.

By totalling the value added at basic prices by individual homogeneous production units, we obtain the value added by industry. A special case is represented by the banking sector, which among its services provides financial intermediation to enterprises, households, general government, etc. Since the costs associated with this service are not normally measurable on the basis of specific commissions, national accounting prefers to measure the total of these costs indirectly, leading to the concept defined as "financial intermediation services indirectly measured" (FISIM).

If we aggregate the value added by individual branches, add to this the value of the indirect taxes on production (less subsidies) and subtract FISIM, we obtain the gross domestic product *at market prices* (GDP), which represents the aggregate of production processes within the national territory. If we subtract from GDP net taxes on production and imports, and compensation of employees and property income payable to the rest of the world, and we add the corresponding items receivable from the rest of the world (in other words, GDP less primary incomes payable to non-resident units plus primary incomes receivable from non-resident units), we obtain the gross national income (GNI), which represents the final result achieved only by units resident in the country from activity carried out both within the national territory and abroad. The table that presents these aggregates in the SNA is known as the *production account* (Table 2.10).

Table 2.10 – **Production account**
Value in current prices (million euros) – Italy, 2002-2005

Aggregates	2002	2003	2004	2005
RESOURCES				
Production at basic prices	2 514 947	2 587 887	2 690 677	2 752 042
Taxes less subsidies on products	129 807	131 614	139 712	144 479
USES				
Intermediate consumption	1 349 528	1 384 147	1 441 518	1 479 280
Gross domestic product	1 295 226	1 335 354	1 388 870	1 417 241

StatLink http://dx.doi.org/10.1787/336870088018

Source: Italian Statistical Office.

2.3.2. Consumption, capital formation and net foreign demand

The production achieved by an economic system, expressed in terms of GDP at market prices (Y), constitutes, together with imports of goods and services (M), the overall resources available for final consumption (C), gross capital formation (I) and exports of goods and services (X):

$$Y + M = C + I + X \qquad [2.1]$$

This entity is known in national accounts as the *goods and services account* (or also the *resources and uses account*).

Final consumption represents expenditure for goods and services aimed at satisfying human needs. Depending on the type of need met, final consumption can be broken down into *individual consumption*, carried out for the benefit of households, and *collective consumption*, which is done for the benefit of households, enterprises or other institutions. The individual consumption of households (which also includes the consumption of agricultural products they have produced themselves) can also be financed by NPISHs and general government, especially in the areas of health, education, social security and culture. This makes it necessary to distinguish between "final" consumption and "actual" consumption. The former represents the viewpoint of those financing the consumption, while the latter reflects the viewpoint of those benefiting from the consumption. Actual consumption represents the total goods and services used up by individual households; it corresponds to the households' consumption expenditure plus the individual consumption expenditure of general government and NPISHs.

Consumption can also be calculated as *national consumption*, *i.e.* the consumption within the national territory and abroad by the units resident in the national territory, or as *domestic consumption*, *i.e.* the consumption within the national territory both by resident and non-resident units (Table 2.11).

Final consumption is always valued in market prices and is calculated using consumption "functions", *i.e.* by aggregating expenditures for goods and services according to homogeneous categories (food, beverages, transport services, etc.). However, a different classification distinguishes between various types of consumption, based on the type and durability of the good. This leads to the distinction between services and goods, further distinguishing between "non-durable" goods, which are consumed immediately after purchase (food, pharmaceuticals, etc.) or within a limited amount of time (clothing), and "durable" goods, which are purchased to be used over a number of years (furniture, motor vehicles, household appliances, etc.).

Table 2.11 – **National final consumption and domestic final consumption**
Values in current prices (billion yen) – Japan, 2003-2005

	2003	2004	2005
National consumption	370 294	373 896	377 273
Expenditure of general goverment (–)	88 503	89 468	90 684
Expenditure of NPISHs (–)	5 877	6 118	6 396
Expenditure of resident households	275 915	278 310	280 193
Acquisitions abroad by residents (–)	2 783	3 409	3 320
Acquisition in Japan by non-residents (+)	646	804	923
Final domestic household comsumption	273 778	275 706	277 795

StatLink ⟶ http://dx.doi.org/10.1787/336874201116

Source: *National Accounts of OECD Countries*, OECD.

Final households' consumption also includes "actual" rent, *i.e.* the rent actually paid by households for the use of dwellings, and the "imputed" rent of homeowner-occupiers. This latter kind of rent is said to be "imputed" since it is estimated based on the rent that owner-occupiers would have to pay to occupy their dwellings, even if the owner-occupiers do not actually make any monetary payments.

Capital formation represents the value of acquisitions less disposals of produced non-financial assets, *i.e.* of assets derived from a production process. It can be broken down into gross fixed capital formation, changes in inventories and acquisitions minus disposals of valuables. *Gross fixed capital formation* consists of the total value of a producer's acquisitions (less disposals) of fixed assets during the accounting period plus certain additions to the value of non-produced assets (such as subsoil assets or major improvements to the quantity, quality or productivity of land) realised by the productive activity of institutional units. Gross fixed capital formation includes physical goods (machinery, equipment, etc.) as well as intangible products (such as software), obtained through a specific production process and used in other production processes for a period longer than one year. The components of gross fixed capital formation are always valued at market prices and can be aggregated by

2. BASIC CONCEPTS, DEFINITIONS AND CLASSIFICATIONS

industry of production, *i.e.* according to the characteristics of the goods (machinery, equipment and various products; buildings; intangible goods), or by owner or user industry, *i.e.* according to the characteristics of the purchaser, in which case the classification by institutional sector is used (households, businesses, general government).

Inventories consist of stocks of outputs still held by the units that produced them prior to their being further processed, sold, delivered to other units or used in other ways, as well as stocks of products acquired from other units intended to be used for intermediate consumption or for resale without further processing. Inventories can be raw materials and intermediate goods, work-in-progress or finished goods. Their purpose is to promote the economically efficient management of the production and distribution processes, making it possible to synchronise better the fluctuations of supply and demand. Consequently, inventories are considered one of the possible uses of the goods produced; the value for the term "I" in the identity [2.1] is the variation in the overall stock of inventories recorded during the reference period. In turn, this variation equals the value of goods intended for inventories minus the value of those that leave inventories to be used in the production process or sold, minus losses of value due to physical deterioration, accidental damage or theft.

Lastly, the term *net acquisitions of valuables* refers to "stores of value" (such as precious stones and metals), acquired mainly by households for purposes other than consumption. The resources and uses account naturally does not enter the amount of the stock of valuables, but its variation during the reference period.

The flow of gross fixed capital formation contributes to determine the evolution of the capital available to the economic system: in particular, if in a given year gross fixed capital formation (GFCF) is higher than depreciation (D), *i.e.* higher than the loss in the value of capital due to its physical deterioration during the production processes, the net fixed capital formation is positive, and this leads to an increase for that year in the "net" capital available to the economic system (NK):

$$NK_t = NK_{t-1} + (GFCF_t - D_t) \qquad [2.2]$$

In other words, depreciation can be considered as that portion of capital formation necessary to preserve unchanged the existing production capacity. What is important for the development of an economic system in the long term is therefore *the trend* of net capital formation. In order to emphasise this aspect, an important measurement of a country's actual economic growth is *net domestic product* (NDP), which is equal to the gross domestic product minus depreciation.

The trend of the NDP may be significantly different from that of the GNP, especially when the average life of capital goods changes significantly over time. This is a trend seen in virtually all industrialised countries since the 1990s when the "computer revolution" caused accelerated depreciation of existing equipment, as it was replaced by new equipment with a higher technology content but a significantly lower average life (*e.g.* the average life of a personal computer is much shorter than that of large industrial machinery). This means that countries that have invested more heavily in the new economy to remain competitive, have seen their gross capital formation (and

2. BASIC CONCEPTS, DEFINITIONS AND CLASSIFICATIONS

thus their GDP) increase, without this being reflected in an overall increase in the country's production capacity (*i.e.* in an equivalent increase in the NDP).

Lastly, with regard to trade in goods and services with the rest of the world, it must be emphasised that in the system of national accounts, both imports and exports are valued *free on board*, *i.e.* without considering the cost of transport and insurance between the border of the exporting country and that of the importing country. The difference between exports and imports is also known as *net foreign demand* and represents the contribution that foreign trade makes to Gross domestic product. In fact, another way of expressing the relationship [2.1] is as follows:

$$Y = C + I + (X - M) \qquad [2.3]$$

The above equation shows how a decrease in the net foreign demand reduces GDP, other conditions being the same.

Exports and imports concern not only goods, but also services such as personal, cultural and recreational services, financial services, communication services, etc. By convention, imports and exports of services comprise respectively the expenditures abroad of residents and the expenditures of foreigners within the national territory.

2.3.3. From gross domestic product to national income

The gross domestic product represents the summary measurement of the income produced over a given period of time (generally one year) by a specific economic system. However, to be used by the various institutional units (households, corporations, general government, etc.) for consumption, capital formation or trade in goods and services with the rest of the world, the income must be transferred from the centres of production to the places where it is used. This is achieved through the remuneration of the two factors of production considered in the SNA: labour and capital.

Labour is remunerated through the payment of compensation to individuals, to which must be added what are known as social charges, which simply represent deferred compensation. The sum of *wages and salaries* (payable in cash or in kind) and the value of the *social contributions* payable by employers (actual social contributions payable by employers to Social Security schemes or to private funded social insurance schemes to secure social benefits for their employees; or imputed social contributions by employers providing unfunded social benefits) constitutes the *compensation of employees*, *i.e.* the portion of income that is paid directly or indirectly to those who have contributed to the production process by providing their labour as employees. The difference between the gross value added and the compensation of employees determines the *gross operating surplus*, *i.e.* the portion of the income produced intended to compensate the labour provided directly by the entrepreneur and the other original factor of production (capital).

As we have seen, the GDP reflects the remuneration of labour and capital used for production purposes: therefore, the *gross national income* (GNI) is also equal to the aggregate value of the balances of gross primary incomes for all sectors. Naturally, it is also possible in this case to obtain the *net national income* by subtracting the value of depreciation from the gross national income.

Lastly, by deducting from the gross national income the net taxes paid to general government and the net current transfers paid to the rest of the world, the *gross national disposable income* is obtained, which can be used by resident units for the purpose of final consumption. The difference between national disposable income and final consumption (in both cases, after taking into account of an adjustment for pension funds) constitutes *saving*.

2.4. Values at current prices and constant prices

The value of economic transactions is expressed in terms of a specific common currency (dollars, euros, etc.). At the conceptual level, the value (said to be "nominal") of many transactions is determined by multiplying the quantity of the product involved in the transaction by its price, which is in turn defined as the amount of money that must be paid in exchange for a unit of the product. In this way, the value of the transaction is expressed *in current prices*, *i.e.* using the price agreed upon by the parties for that particular transaction at that specific time.

However, as we know, prices vary over time, so economic aggregates expressed in current prices do not enable us to determine to what extent the variations observed over a certain historical period (year, month, etc.) are due to variations in quantities or variations in prices. Consequently, economic statistics focuses not only on aggregates expressed in current prices, but also on the trend of the volumes and the associated price variations. For this purpose, many aggregates are calculated either in current prices or net of the price movements that occurred during the period under consideration. This is done by expressing the value of the various transactions using the prices prevailing during a certain period, taken as a reference. In this case, the resulting economic aggregates are said to be expressed *in constant prices,* and their variations over time are said to be defined "in real terms", in opposition to those "in nominal terms", calculated on the basis of values in current prices.

Let us take the example of the sale of automobiles, and let us assume that in the year 2000 a dealership sold 40 identical cars, with the same qualitative characteristics (model, options, etc.) at a price of 11 000 euros each. Next, let us assume that in 2001 the number of cars (again with the same qualitative characteristics) rose to 45, at a unit price of 11 500 euros. Consequently, the value in current prices of the sales realised by that dealer will be 440 000 euros (40 * 11 000) in 2000 and 517 500 euros (45 * 11 500) in 2001, with a percentage increase of 17.6% [(517 000 – 440 000) /440 000) * 100]. In reality, only part of the increase is due to a variation in the quantities acquired, *i.e.* an increase in sales in real terms, while the remainder is due to a variation in prices. In particular, the increase in sales at constant prices (of 2000) is equal to 12.5% [(45 * 11 000 – 40 * 11 000)/(40 * 11 000) * 100].

The relationship between an economic aggregate expressed in current prices and the same aggregate expressed in constant prices is know as a *deflator*. Thus, it is possible to have deflators of the gross domestic product, private consumption, gross fixed capital formation, etc. Valuations in constant prices can also be made either at the prices of a certain base year or at the prices of the previous year. As we shall see in Chapter 4, at the end of 2005 several EU countries changed to a system that deflates national accounting aggregates based on the previous year's prices.

2.5. Index numbers

The deflator reflects a typical statistical ratio, *i.e.* a quotient of two statistical terms, both of which refer to the same phenomenon measured at different times: this type of statistical relationship is called an *index number*. Index numbers may be calculated in reference to either time or space. In official economic statistics, index numbers (or, more briefly, "indices") are more often used for time comparisons. In this case, the index is constituted by the ratio between the measurement of a phenomenon at a given moment in time, and the measurement at another moment taken as a reference (the base of the index). Let us, for example, calculate the ratio between the value of private consumption at current prices for 2000-2005 and its value in 2000 prices. The resulting index (expressed in "base 2000", given that in this year the numerator and denominator are equal) will measure the trend of the implicit prices of private consumption during 2001-2005, in relation to price levels observed in 2000.

We can distinguish between *simple index numbers* and *complex index numbers*: within a time frame, the former make it possible to compare the variation over time of an individual phenomenon in relation to the base; the latter, however, can express the variation of a group of phenomena in relation to their value during the period chosen as the base of the index. A particularly important element is also the distinction between *fixed base* index numbers and *moving base* index numbers. The former always use as a reference (*i.e.* in the denominator) the same quantity (in the preceding example, the value of consumption in 2000), while the latter use in the denominator an element that varies over time. The indices used for time comparisons normally have the value 100 in the reference (or base) period.

The calculation of simple fixed base indices (IF) is relatively easy. Using V_t to indicate the value over time t (for t = 1, 2, ... n) of the relevant economic aggregate, the index expressed in base 0 ($_0IF_n$), for the periods from 0 to n is:

$_0IF_0 = V_0/V_0 * 100$

$_0IF_1 = V_1/V_0 * 100$

$_0IF_2 = V_2/V_0 * 100$

....

$_0IF_n = V_n/V_0 * 100$

In the case of a simple moving base index (IM), with previous period used as base ("chain" index), the values of the index for the periods from 1 to n are:

$IM_1 = V_1/V_0 * 100$

$IM_2 = V_2/V_1 * 100$

BASIC CONCEPTS, DEFINITIONS AND CLASSIFICATIONS 2

$IM_3 = V_3/V_2 * 100$

....

$IM_n = V_n/V_{n-1} * 100$

Given that the percentage variation VP_t is

$$VP_t = [(V_t - V_{t-1})/V_{t-1}] * 100$$

and also that $\quad VP_t = [(V_t/V_{t-1}) - 1] * 100$

and that $\quad VP_t = [(V_t/V_{t-1}) * 100] - 100$,

then $\quad VP_t = IM_t - 100$.

In this way, we see that the simple moving-base indices in each period only express the percentage variations in relation to the previous period.

The fixed-base indices expressed in a given base can easily be converted into another base. To go from one fixed-base index referring to period w to a fixed-base index referring to period z, it suffices to divide the index $_wIF_t$ by the value of the index expressed in base w, but referring to a new base period $_wIF_z$, and to multiply the result by 100:

$$_zIF_t = {_wIF_t}/{_wIF_z} * 100$$

It is slightly more complicated to convert a simple fixed-base (expressed in base w) to a moving-base index and vice versa: in the former case, it is necessary to divide each term $_wIF_t$ by its preceding $_wIF_{t-1}$ and multiply the result by 100. In fact, given that the generic term $_wIF_t$ is given by $(V_t/V_w * 100)$, it follows that:

$$IM_t = (V_t/V_w * 100)/(V_{t-1}/V_w * 100) * 100$$

which becomes:

$$IM_t = (V_t/V_w * 100) * (V_w/V_{t-1} * 100) * 100$$

that is:

$$IM_t = (V_t/V_{t-1}) * 100$$

When converting from a moving-base index IM_t into a fixed-base index $_0IF_t$ (where 0 refers to the first term of the series being considered), each term IM_t must be multiplied by the product of all the moving base indices included between the time 0 and the time t-1. For example, to calculate $_0IF_5$, the following operation must be performed:

$$_0IF_5 = (IM_1 * IM_2 * IM_3 * IM_4 * IM_5) * 100$$

If we now wish to express the fixed-base index with reference to a term different from 0, such as z, after calculating the series $_0IF_t$ we can, as previously described, change the base by dividing all the terms $_0IF_t$ (for t = 1, 2, ... n) by the value $_0IF_z$ and multiply the result by 100.

2 BASIC CONCEPTS, DEFINITIONS AND CLASSIFICATIONS

As already indicated, complex index numbers are able to express, in a single synthetic value, the variation of many phenomena with respect to a period chosen as the base of the index. The synthesis of the basic information is made by calculating its weighted average using weighting schemes selected in accordance with the objective being pursued. Consequently, the construction of a complex index number requires that the following elements be determined: the statistical data on the phenomena to be considered in the index; the base of the index; and the weighting scheme.

There is an extraordinary variety of indices, which differ mainly in the weighting scheme used: there are indices that use arithmetic, geometric, harmonic means, etc., and weight schemes that give greater importance to the base period or to the period for which the index is being calculated. The following index numbers are widely used in the field of economic statistics: Laspeyres (IL), Paasche (IP) and Fisher (IF) indices: the first two use arithmetic means and differ in the schemes of weights adopted, while the Fisher index is equal to $\sqrt{IL \cdot IP}$, *i.e.* the geometric mean of the Laspeyres and Paasche indices.

Let us now consider the Laspeyres index, assuming that we wish to construct a synthetic index of the prices of a given set of consumer goods for the period from 1 to t. To calculate a synthetic index that expresses the variation in the general level of prices observed, we must naturally attribute to each price a weight that expresses the importance of the relevant good in the overall consumption expenditure. Let us assume that we choose as a weight the value of the consumption of the good i during the time t (v_{it}) equal to:

$$v_{it} = p_{it} \, q_{it}$$

where p_{it} is the price of that particular good and q_{it} is the relevant quantity consumed. Let us also assume that we choose the period 0 as a reference base: thus, for the period 0 we shall have the price of the individual good p_{i0} and the relative value consumed v_{i0}. The Laspeyres index, which represents a weighted mean of basic price indices for the period t in base 0 is therefore:

$$_0IL_t = \frac{\sum_{i=1}^{n} \frac{p_{it}}{p_{i0}} p_{i0} q_{i0}}{\sum_{i=1}^{n} p_{i0} q_{i0}} = \frac{\sum_{i=1}^{n} p_{it} q_{i0}}{\sum_{i=1}^{n} p_{i0} q_{i0}} \qquad [2.4]$$

As can be seen, both the numerator and the denominator contain the quantity consumed during the time 0 (q_{i0}): consequently, the index is not affected by the changes that occurred in the pattern of consumption during the periods after the base period; it is affected only by the basic price variations (p_{it}/p_{i0}).

BASIC CONCEPTS, DEFINITIONS AND CLASSIFICATIONS 2

However, the Paasche index for the period t in base 0 is expressed by:

$$_0IP_t = \frac{\sum_{i=1}^{n} \frac{p_{it}}{p_{i0}} p_{i0} q_{it}}{\sum_{i=1}^{n} p_{i0} q_{it}} = \frac{\sum_{i=1}^{n} p_{it} q_{it}}{\sum_{i=1}^{n} p_{i0} q_{it}} \qquad [2.5]$$

In this case, the weighting structure is provided by the quantities consumed q_{it} during period t, and not during the base period, as for the Laspeyres index. Consequently, the Paasche index is affected by the changes due both to the variation in prices (p_{it}/p_{i0}) and in the pattern of consumption between the period chosen as the base of the index and period t.

Laspeyres and Paasche indices are widely used to construct price, volume and value indicators. When Laspeyres and Paasche formulae are used to construct price indices, the results obtained show a systematic bias. If, as is shown by economic theory, the quantity consumed falls as the price rises (all other conditions being the same), then use of the Laspeyres index tends to overestimate the general price trend of the products included in the index: in fact, if the pattern of consumption is kept unchanged during the base period, the substitution effect for products whose prices increase more than average is not taken into account. In other words, the index measures the variation in the general level of prices that would have occurred if consumers had not "adjusted" their own behaviour to price increases, thereby reducing the quantities consumed of those products whose prices rose more than others. Consequently, the Laspeyres index will always indicate a variation in the average level of prices that is greater than that measured with the Paasche index. On the other hand, the Paasche index will have a negative "bias", giving less-than-average weight to those products whose prices increased the most during the period considered. The Fisher index, as a geometric mean of the two indices, does not have these biases.

It should also be pointed out that, in ordinary practice, the Paasche index can be difficult to use because of the lag in the availability of information on the structure ofweights. This is the case, for example, when calculating a monthly consumer price index for the 2000-2005 period, in base 2000 = 100. While the prices p_{it} can be observed monthly, the quantities consumed q_{i2005} can only be evaluated at the end of the year: consequently, the Paasche index (and the Fisher index) for 2005 can only be calculated in 2006, a problem that does not arise for a Laspeyres index calculated for 2000-2005 and expressed in base 2000.

2. BASIC CONCEPTS, DEFINITIONS AND CLASSIFICATIONS

2.6. Time series

A substantial portion of economic statistics are finalised by comparing economic aggregates over time, and these comparisons are generally conducted using time series. In intuitive terms, a *time series*

$$Y_t = y_1, y_2, y_3, \ldots y_n \qquad [2.6]$$

is a succession of numerical data arranged on the basis of time t. Given that time is a continuous variable, but that statistical observations of economic phenomena are normally carried out with a certain periodicity (year, quarter, month, etc.), economic time series are generally "discrete", *i.e.* composed of a finite number of observations made with reference to conventionally defined time periods.

The trend of time series is naturally influenced by many factors: some of these cause temporary movements in time series, while others have an underlying influence on trends. Very schematically, we can imagine a time series as being composed of three basic "components" (Figure 2.2):

- the *trend-cycle* (CT_t) represents the underlying trend of the series, which is typically determined by intrinsically economic factors. In turn, the trend-cycle can be broken down into the long-term trend (the trend) and the fluctuations, which are not necessarily regular, observed in relation to the trend over a multi-year period (the cycle);

- *seasonality* (S_t), determined by climatic, cultural and organisational factors that cause movements in the time series, which are repeated with some regularity from year to year;

- *irregularity* (A_t), determined by an infinite series of temporary and random phenomena that cannot be identified either with the trend-cycle or seasonal variation.

There are many ways of representing how these components determine the evolution of a time series, although it should be emphasised that in all cases these representations are only a statistical abstraction constructed for the purpose of measurement and analysis. For example, we can imagine that the time series is the result of the sum of the three components just described (additive model):

$$Y_t = CT_t + S_t + A_t \qquad [2.7]$$

or of their product (multiplicative model):

$$Y_t = CT_t * S_t * A_t \qquad [2.8]$$

or of a mixed scheme:

$$Y_t = CT_t * S_t + A_t \qquad [2.9]$$

BASIC CONCEPTS, DEFINITIONS AND CLASSIFICATIONS 2

Figure 2.2 – **Components of a time series:
trend-cycle, seasonal variation, irregular variation**

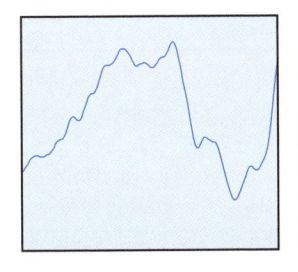

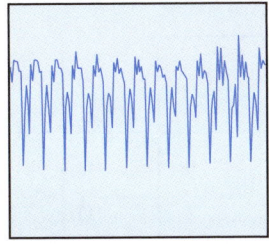

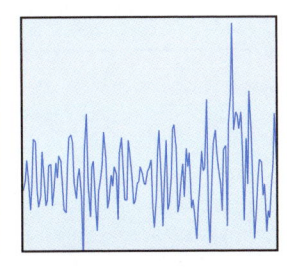

The decomposition of a time series into basic components can be extremely useful for understanding some economic phenomena better. For example, let us look at the index that measures industrial production in Germany (Figure 2.3). As can easily be seen, the movements of the index are dominated by fluctuations that are repeated annually because of the closing of industrial establishments during the summer months and the Christmas holidays, while the trend-cycle is difficult to read. In the case of the consumer price index of Spain (Figure 2.4), the dominant component is the trend, making it difficult to assess the role played by seasonality, which is nevertheless important for the prices of many products (such as fresh food products), or by the cycle.

To isolate the most significant components for the purposes of economic analysis, many methods for decomposing a time series have been developed; of particular importance are "seasonal-adjustment" methods, which make it possible to isolate the seasonal component and produce series "net" of this component and/or the irregular component. For example, Figure 2.5 shows the seasonally adjusted series of the Italian industrial production index obtained by applying the TRAMO-SEATS procedure, which together with the X12-ARIMA procedure is most frequently used by statistical institutes to produce seasonally adjusted economic time series. The analysis of Figure 2.5 clearly shows a phase of expansion between the beginning of 2000 and the initial months of 2001, followed by a phase of recession (until the end of 2001), and then substantial stagnation that continued throughout 2002, and later a slow slippage in production following a moderate negative trend.

2 BASIC CONCEPTS, DEFINITIONS AND CLASSIFICATIONS

Figure 2.3 – **General industrial production index – Raw data**
Germany, 2000-2005

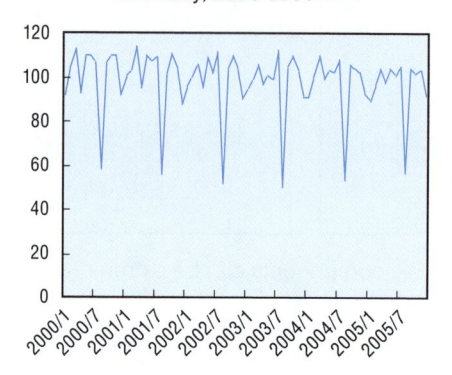

Source: OECD, Main Economic Indicators.

Figure 2.4 – **Consumer price index – All items**
Spain, 2000-2005

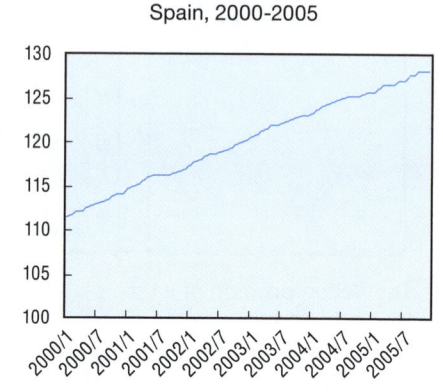

Source: OECD, Main Economic Indicators.

Figure 2.5 – **General industrial production index – Seasonally adjusted data**
Italy, 2000-2005

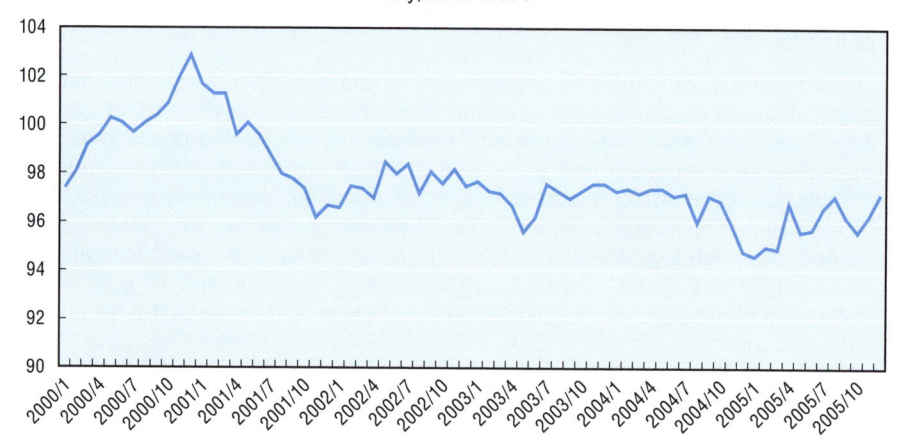

Source: OECD, Main Economic Indicators.

2.6.1. Measuring the movements of a time series

The graphic analysis of a time series, even though it provides useful information for understanding the evolution of the phenomenon being analysed, cannot by itself estimate the intensity of its movements. To do so, we must use statistical measurements capable of comparing the values of the phenomenon at various moments in time; but to make a "significant" time comparison, *i.e.* one which is able to provide the user with a sensible result in economic terms, it is necessary

BASIC CONCEPTS, DEFINITIONS AND CLASSIFICATIONS 2

to make some choices. Firstly, we must specify the period of time to which we are referring, *i.e.* the *time interval (or horizon)* of the analysis. The time interval is typically defined by two specific observations (the beginning and end of the interval), and the time comparison can be made by comparing contiguous periods (years, quarters, months, days, weeks, etc.) or periods that are separated from each other in the time frame. Secondly, we must identify the *frequency* at which we wish to measure the phenomenon over time, a choice closely linked to the characteristics of the economic variable being analysed and to the cognitive objectives of this analysis. If, for example, an analyst wishes to understand the current or future economic situation, he/she will tend to observe the trend of economic aggregates over the most recent quarters or months, while if the objective is to evaluate the changes that have occurred in an economic system following major legislative changes, the comparison will presumably be based on annual data referring to a long time interval. Furthermore, the choice of comparable time units is a necessary but not sufficient condition for making meaningful comparisons. In fact, as we have already mentioned, economic time series are influenced by climatic, cultural and organisational factors that tend to introduce into these series movements that are of little interest to economic analysis.

To measure the intensity of the movements of a time series, various indicators can be used. Percentage variations are very frequently used. Given a time series I_t, where t indicates the generic period of observation, the following percentage variations can be defined:

$$\text{month-on-month growth rate: } M_t = \frac{I_t - I_{t-1}}{I_{t-1}} * 100 \qquad [2.10]$$

$$\text{year-on-year growth rate: } Y_t = \frac{I_t - I_{t-z}}{I_{t-z}} * 100 \qquad [2.11]$$

Where z = 1 for annual series, z = 4 for quarterly series and z = 12 for monthly series. For monthly and quarterly series the following relation is then valid:

$$M_t \gtreqless M_{t-z} \Leftrightarrow Y_t \gtreqless Y_{t-1} \quad \forall t \qquad [2.12]$$

Therefore, if for monthly series the cyclical variation for the month t is higher (lower) than that recorded 12 months earlier, the trend variation for the month t will necessarily be higher (lower) than that recorded in month t-1. With a few changes, it can also be shown that:

$$Y_t - Y_{t-1} = (M_t - M_{t-12}) * (I_{t-1}/I_{t-12}) \qquad [2.13]$$

and that:

$$Y_t = M_t (I_{t-1}/I_{t-12}) + M_{t-1} (I_{t-2}/I_{t-12}) + \ldots + M_{t-11} (I_{t-12}/I_{t-12}) \qquad [2.14]$$

i.e. that the year-on-year variation at time t is equal to the weighted sum of the last 12 month-on-month variations.

If we define as A_T the simple annual average for year T of the monthly values I_t for year T:

$$A_T = (I_{tT} + I_{t+1T} + \ldots + I_{t+11T})/12 \qquad [2.15]$$

we can calculate the average annual growth (AA_T) as:

$$AA_T = (A_T - A_{T-1})/A_{T-1} * 100 \qquad [2.16]$$

that is:

$$AA_T = (\{[(I_{tT} + I_{t+1T} + \ldots + I_{t+11T})/12] - A_{T-1}\}/A_{T-1}) * 100 \qquad [2.17]$$

This equation shows us how the average annual variation for the year T depends on the relationship that is established between each month of year T and the average for year T-1. In the case of time series that increase from month to month (*i.e.* positive monotonic series, such as nominal contractual wages), the level of the average of year T will be located approximately around the value recorded during the central months of that year, and the average annual growth AA_T will depend on the dynamic of the time series during the second part of year T-1 and the first part of year T.

Lastly, let us define as *cyclical gain* at month t of year T (AC_{tT}) the relationship:

$$AC_{tT} = [(S_{tT} - A_{T-1})/A_{T-1}] * 100 \qquad [2.18]$$

where the quantity S_{tT} expresses the average value of year T that would result if for the rest of the year the time series remained at the level recorded during month t:

$$S_{tT} = \left[\sum_{i=1}^{t} I_{iT} + (12-t) I_{tT} \right] / 2 \qquad [2.19]$$

The quantity S_{tT} expresses the average of two terms: the values of the time series actually observed in the first t months of year T and their extrapolation to the remaining part of the year obtained, assuming that the level reached in month t remains unchanged for the months from t+1 to 12. The cyclical gain at March of year T will then express the average annual variation that would be seen in year T if the series remained unchanged for the months April to December at the level reached in March. Similarly, the cyclical gain calculated from December of year T-1 expresses the variation that would occur in year T if the time series remained unchanged at the level reached in December of the previous year, *i.e.* the part of the growth that would be attributed "arithmetically" to year T, but which in reality occurred during the previous year.

It can also be shown that:

$$AA_T = AC_{12T-1} + [M_1 (I_1 + AA_{T-1}) * 12/12] + [M_2 (I_2 + AA_{T-1}) * 11/12] + \ldots +$$
$$+ [M_{12} (I_{12} + AA_{T-1}) * 1/12] \qquad [2.20]$$

i.e. that the average annual growth in year T is equal to the cyclical gain of December of year T-1, plus the weighted sum of the 12 month-on-month variations (from January to December) of year T.

BASIC CONCEPTS, DEFINITIONS AND CLASSIFICATIONS 2

Lastly, let us point out that the average annual growth cannot simply be obtained as the average of 12 monthly trend variations. In fact, the relationship between these two measurements is as follows:

$$AA_T = [Y_{1,T} * (I_{1,T-1}/A_{T-1})] + [Y_{2,T} * (I_{2,T-1}/A_{T-1})] + \ldots +$$
$$+ [Y_{12,T} * (I_{12,T-1}/A_{T-1})] \qquad [2.21]$$

From above formula, it is seen that AA_T is a weighted (and not a simple) average of the year-on-year variations, with weights provided by the level of the time series reached at time t-12 with respect to the annual average T-1.

2.6.2. Seasonal adjustment procedures

Although many seasonal adjustment procedures based on different methodological approaches have been proposed over time, two procedures are currently most widely used: X12-ARIMA and TRAMO-SEATS. The former performs the decomposition between the trend-cycle (CT_t), seasonality (S_t) and irregularity (A_t) through the successive application of different-sized moving averages, while the latter does so using the ARIMA (Auto Regressive Integrated Moving Average) models.

Given a time series y_t, the series y_t^* obtained by applying a moving average of "order" m (=n1+n2+1) is given by:

$$y_t^* = \sum_{i=-n1}^{n2} \vartheta_i y_{it} \qquad [2.22]$$

In other words, a moving average represents an operator that transforms the original series into a linear combination, with weights ϑ_i. There is a potentially infinite variety of moving averages. For example, if all weights ϑ_i are equal, the moving average is said to be "simple", but if they are different, the average is said to be "weighted". If n1=n2, the moving average is said to be "centred", and when the order of a centred moving average is uneven, the resulting individual values of the series y_t^* necessarily refer to the same time periods of y_t. If, however, the order is even, this correspondence is lost. If we assume, for example, that we have a monthly series y_t, and we apply a moving average of order 4 (i.e., considering $y_t, y_{t+1}, y_{t+2}, y_{t+3}$), the result obtained can no longer refer to the months to which the original series referred, but to theoretical periods that "straddle" them. To obtain a result referring to the original months, we must calculate the arithmetic mean of two successive terms of the moving average obtained in the first step.

Lastly, a moving average is said to be "symmetric" if its order is uneven, then n1 = n2 and the value of the weights ϑ_i are identical for each of the terms t+i and t-i, $\forall i$. However, if the weights are not identical, or if n1 is different from n2, the moving average is said to be "asymmetric".

Moving averages are particularly important because they make it possible to approximate complex mathematical functions through which some of the

2 BASIC CONCEPTS, DEFINITIONS AND CLASSIFICATIONS

components of time series can be represented. For example, the trend-cycle (CTt) can be represented by a polynomial function f(t) of time t:

$$CT_t = a_0 + a_1 t + a_2 t^2 + \ldots + a_n t^n \qquad [2.23]$$

which can be approximated by a centred moving average with weights appropriately selected on the basis of the order of the polynomial to be approximated. A third-grade polynomial can in fact be approximated by a five-term moving average with weights [-0.086, 0.343, 0.486, 0.343, -0.086], or by a seven-term average with weights [-0.095, 0.143, 0.286, 0.332, 0.286, 0.143, -0.095].

It is not only the trend-cycle that can be approximated through moving averages but also the seasonal component. This means that by applying moving averages, it is possible to "filter" the various components of a time series and this is exactly what the X12-ARIMA procedure makes possible. In very schematic terms, the X12-ARIMA procedure (derived from X11-ARIMA developed by Statistics Canada on the basis of the procedure originally proposed by the U.S. Census Bureau) performs the seasonal adjustment of a monthly time series $Y_t = CT_t \cdot S_t \cdot A_t$ through the following steps:

1. Elimination of outliers from the time series that are due to purely accidental factors (strikes, floods, etc.) and preliminary processing of data for corrections due to holidays, different numbers of working days in each month, etc.

2. Calculation of the preliminary estimate of the trend-cycle (CT_t') through the use of a centred 25th-order moving average. The relationship $(S_t A_t)' = Y_t / CT_t'$ then provides a preliminary estimate of the product of the seasonal and irregular components.

3. For each term of the series $(S_t A_t)'$ a five-term weighted moving average is calculated (with weights 1/9, 2/9, 3/9, 1/9, 2/9) that is "vertical", i.e. the datum of each month is "mediated" with the data on the same month of the two previous years and the two following years. In this way a preliminary estimate of the seasonal component is obtained (S_t'), which is later completed through a 13-term weighted moving average. By dividing $(S_t A_t)'$ by the preliminary estimate S_t', the preliminary estimate of the component A_t' is obtained and thus the preliminary estimate of the seasonally adjusted series $D_t' = Y_t / S_t'$.

4. Once the first phase has been completed, i.e. when the preliminary estimates of the various components have been obtained, an "intermediate" estimate of the trend-cycle (CT_t'') is calculated by applying to the preliminary seasonally adjusted series D_t' the five-term Henderson moving average with weights -21/286, 84/286, 160/286, 84/286, -21/286, thereby obtaining an intermediate estimate of the series $(S_t A_t)'' = Y_t / CT_t''$.

5. Calculation of the final estimate S_t^* of the seasonal component by applying a "vertical" seventh-order moving average to the series $(S_t A_t)''$, with weights 1/15, 2/15, 3/15, 3/15, 3/15, 2/15, 1/15, later adjusted through a 13-term moving average, making it possible to obtain the intermediate seasonally adjusted series $D_t'' = Y_t / S_t^*$.

BASIC CONCEPTS, DEFINITIONS AND CLASSIFICATIONS 2

6. Final calculation of the trend-cycle (CT_t^*) by applying to the intermediate seasonally adjusted series D_t" a Henderson moving average of variable size (9, 13 or 23 terms), selected on the basis of the size of the irregular component in the specific time series (the greater the irregularity, the longer the moving average recommended).
7. Calculation of the final estimate of the irregular component $A_t^* = D_t"/CT_t^*$.
8. Evaluation of the quality of the seasonal adjustment by calculating statistical tests.

Stochastic processes and ARIMA models

As we have seen, although a moving average can approximate an n-grade polynomial, *i.e.* a deterministic function, the time series x_t may also be written as the sum of two components:

$$x_t = f(t) + u_t \qquad [2.25]$$

where f(t) represents a generic function of time and u_t represents a random component. In reality, the separation between the deterministic and the random component, as well as their relative importance, is much less clear than what one might imagine intuitively. In 1921, the English statistician Yule observed that the successive application of moving averages to a series of purely random values produced a result characterised by pseudo-periodic movements, while a few years later the Russian statistician Slutsky observed that as the number of moving averages applied increased, the pseudo-periodic movements tended to assume a clearly sinusoidal form. If then, by applying moving averages, we go from a purely random process to one of a pseudo-deterministic type, then we can also imagine phenomena, such as the trend-cycle or seasonality, as the linear combination of purely random elements.

Let us define the "stochastic process" X_t as a family of random variables arranged according to a parameter t (*i.e.* time) belonging to a parametric set T. In other words, let us define X_t as a process that is evolving over time following probabilistic laws. Let us now assume that, as t varies, the process generates infinite realisations, which are distributed according to the characteristics of the random variables that make up the process. This means that a time series x_t can be imagined as the succession over time of specific realisations of a stochastic process observed at time t = 1, 2, ..., n. The time series x_t therefore represents a sample drawn from the infinite probability distributions that make up the process, and by studying its characteristics we can try to identify the characteristics of these distributions, *i.e.* the characteristics of the stochastic process X_t that generated the observed time series.

While in theory there is an infinite quantity of stochastic processes, in practice the modern analysis of time series is concentrated on stationary processes (in the weak sense), *i.e.* those processes that have a mean, variance and covariance that are not dependent on time t:

Stochastic processes and ARIMA models (cont.)

$$\mu(t) = E(X_t) = \mu \qquad \sigma^2(t) = E(X_t - \mu)^2 = \sigma^2 \qquad \gamma(t, \tau) = E(X_t - \mu)(X_{t-\tau} - \mu) = \gamma(\tau) \quad [2.26]$$

If a stochastic process ε_t is stationary and:

$$\mu(t) = E(\varepsilon_t) = 0 \qquad \sigma^2(t) = E(\varepsilon_t - \mu)^2 = \sigma^2 \qquad \gamma(t, \tau) = E(\varepsilon_t - \mu)(\varepsilon_{t-\tau} - \mu) = 0 \quad [2.27]$$

i.e. if the process has zero mean, constant variance and covariance equal to zero, it is said to be a *white noise*.

Any stationary stochastic process can be decomposed into two parts:

$$X_t = D_t + ND_t \quad [2.28]$$

a deterministic component (D_t); and a non-deterministic component (ND_t). And it can be represented as follows (Wold's decomposition):

$$X_t = D_t + \sum_{i=0}^{\infty} \vartheta_i \, \varepsilon_{t-i} \quad [2.29]$$

in which ε_t represents a white noise process, with $\vartheta_0 = 1$ and $\sum_{i=0}^{\infty} \vartheta_i^2 < +\infty$.

Consequently, [2.28] indicates that any stationary stochastic process can be decomposed into a deterministic component and into a weighted moving sum (or average) of white noises in relation to "past" times. If we leave aside the deterministic component, under specific conditions it can be shown that an infinite moving sum (average)

$$\sum_{i=0}^{\infty} \vartheta_i \, \varepsilon_{t-i}$$

can be approximated by a process of the type $\sum_{i=0}^{\infty} \phi_i X_{t-i}$.

This means that a time series x_t, the finite realisation of a stationary stochastic process X_t, can be represented as follows:

$$\sum_{i=0}^{\infty} \phi_i x_{t-i} = \mu + \sum_{i=0}^{\infty} \vartheta_i \, \varepsilon_{t-i} \quad [2.30]$$

i.e.:

$$x_t + \phi_1 x_{t-1} + \phi_2 x_{t-2} + \phi_3 x_{t-3} + \ldots = \mu + \varepsilon_t + \vartheta_1 \varepsilon_{t-1} + \vartheta_2 \varepsilon_{t-2} + \vartheta_3 \varepsilon_{t-3} + \ldots \quad [2.31]$$

Stochastic processes and ARIMA models *(cont.)*

said to be an "autoregressive moving average" in that it is a combination of two components: the first in which the variable x_t is regressed upon itself lagged in time, and the second composed of an infinite moving sum (average) of white noise processes. By introducing the "lag" operator B, so that $x_t - x_{t-h} = (1 - B^h) x_t$, then [2.31] can be written as:

$$x_t + \phi_1 B x_t + \phi_2 B^2 x_t + \phi_3 B^3 x_t + \ldots = \mu + \varepsilon_t + \vartheta_1 B \varepsilon_t + \vartheta_2 B^2 \varepsilon_t + \vartheta_3 B^3 \varepsilon_t + \ldots \quad [2.32]$$

i.e.

$$(1 + \phi_1 B^1 + \phi_2 B^2 + \phi_3 B^3 + \ldots) x_t = \mu + (1 + \vartheta_1 B^1 + \vartheta_2 B^2 + \vartheta_3 B^3 + \ldots) \varepsilon_t \quad [2.33]$$

which, in compact form, can be written as:

$$\phi(B) x_t = \mu + \vartheta(B) \varepsilon_t \quad [2.34]$$

with $\phi(B)$ and $\vartheta(B)$ polynomials in lag operator B. As we said earlier, all this requires that the time series (as well as the stochastic process from which it was generated) be stationary. When the series is non-stationary in variance, the use of logarithmic transformation (or other similar transformations) makes it possible to overcome this problem. However, when the time series x_t is non-stationary in mean, this stationarity can be obtained by applying differences of the type $\nabla = (x_t - x_{t-1})$. This means that the general form of an ARIMA model is as follows:

$$\phi(B) \nabla x_t = \mu + \vartheta(B) \varepsilon_t \quad [2.35]$$

Estimating opportunely the parameters ϕ' and ϑ' and resolving the model with regard to the variable x, it is possible to obtain forecasts $x_{t+1}, x_{t+2}, \ldots$ to lengthen the historical series and then apply the centred moving averages used in the X12-ARIMA procedure.

In conclusion, the decomposition of the time series is conducted by the X12-ARIMA procedure according to the following expression:

$$Y_t = CT_t^* \cdot S_t^* \cdot A_t^* \quad [2.24]$$

i.e. by applying the results obtained in steps 5, 6 and 7.

As was indicated earlier, the application of moving averages is a relatively easy method for approximating rather complex functions. Unfortunately, the calculation of moving averages involves the loss of important data at both ends of the time series, with the data being increasingly numerous the higher the order of the moving average (a 13-term centred moving average, for example, involves the loss of six data at the beginning and six data at the end of a time series). Although the loss of data at the beginning of the series can be a relatively minor drawback, the loss of final data, *i.e.* those that show the most recent trend of the phenomenon being studied, can be particularly problematic, as this is normally the subject that interests economic analysts. Two solutions are most frequently used to overcome this problem: to adopt for the final part of the series asymmetric moving averages, *i.e.* based only on past data, or to lengthen the time series by forecasting future data. However, both methods present risks of distortion: in fact, the application of asymmetric moving averages tends to produce phase shifts in the estimation of the trend-cycle, with negative effects on the accuracy of the estimate of the seasonally adjusted series. In addition, the quality of the forecasting of future data strongly affects the accuracy of the estimate of the seasonally adjusted series, which may require substantial revisions if there are significant forecasting errors. The X12-ARIMA procedure makes it possible to adopt both approaches, using ARIMA models to forecast the missing data (see box).

On the other hand, the TRAMO-SEATS procedure is based on the following steps:

1. Estimation of the ARIMA model, elimination of outliers and other preliminary processing.

2. Identification of the ARIMA models for the trend-cycle and seasonal variation components, having hypothesised orthogonals between them and with regard to the irregular component.

3. Estimation, through what is known as "canonical decomposition" (which tends to maximise the variance of the irregular component), of the trend-cycle, seasonality and irregularity, and calculation, through appropriate transformations, of the seasonally adjusted series.

4. Evaluation of the quality of the decomposition by calculating statistical tests.

Although they are based on rather different theoretical approaches, the two procedures tend, for many time series, to produce fairly similar results. However, if the time series has special characteristics (high irregularity, changes of level, etc.) the results may differ significantly.

Chapter 3

The Main Producers of Economic Statistics

Who produces economic statistics? How is the international statistical system organised? Which are the main databases available on the Internet? This chapter outlines the institutional and organisational features of the main producers of economic statistics, starting with international organisations and moving on to review the European and the OECD statistical systems. The division of work between the international organisations and the bodies responsible at the national level for producing statistics (national statistical institutes, other government bodies and central banks) has a significant influence on the availability, and most of all, the quality of the data in existence. Of particular importance during the past 20 years has been the role played by Eurostat and other European institutions, both in setting objectives for the national production of economic statistics, and in making these increasingly comparable internationally. This chapter also contains references to the databases available from international and supranational organisations other than OECD.

3. THE MAIN PRODUCERS OF ECONOMIC STATISTICS

3.1. The international statistical system

As noted in Chapter 1, the modern system of national accounting was born out in the years immediately following the Second World War. The call for a comparable system for measuring the economic development of the various countries arose directly out of the decision-making needs of national authorities and international institutions. Over the years, international organisations and national statistical authorities have developed new methodological approaches and databases in many other fields (education, health, the environment, etc.), that go beyond the sectoral aspects of economic statistics. Cooperation between international organisations and national statistical institutes led to the creation of what is called the "international statistical system".

Given the large number of international organisations in existence worldwide, the sources of international statistics now available are very numerous. Their sheer number represents an unprecedented wealth of information, but this requires a capacity on the part of users to be able to select, from sources that are diverse and sometimes contradictory, the data most relevant to their own needs. In practice, cooperation between international organisations has not yet reached the point where overlap or duplication of activities has been eliminated, while the availability of new information and communication technologies (ICT) has made it easier to build databases, which have proliferated. Quite frequently, the databases of different international bodies contain references to the same variables, but attach a different value to them. In some cases, these variations are simply the result of differences in the frequency with which data are updated, in others they are due to differences in

---

The UN Fundamental Principles of Official Statistics

The Statistical Commission,

- Bearing in mind that official statistical information is an essential basis for development in the economic, demographic, social and environmental fields and for mutual knowledge and trade among the States and peoples of the world;
- Bearing in mind that the essential trust of the public in official statistical information depends to a large extent on respect for the fundamental values and principles which are the basis of any society which seeks to understand itself and to respect the rights of its members;
- Bearing in mind that the quality of official statistics, and thus the quality of the information available to the Government, the economy and the public depends largely on the cooperation of citizens, enterprises, and other respondents in providing appropriate and reliable data needed for necessary statistical compilations and on the cooperation between users and producers of statistics in order to meet users' needs;
- Recalling the efforts of governmental and non-governmental organisations active in statistics to establish standards and concepts to allow comparisons among countries;
- Recalling also the International Statistical Institute Declaration of Professional Ethics;
    … redacted …

3 THE MAIN PRODUCERS OF ECONOMIC STATISTICS

> **The UN Fundamental Principles of Official Statistics** *(cont.)*
>
> Adopts the present principles of official statistics:
>
> **Principle 1.** Official statistics provide an indispensable element in the information system of a democratic society, serving the Government, the economy and the public with data about the economic, demographic, social and environmental situation. To this end, official statistics that meet the test of practical utility are to be compiled and made available on an impartial basis by official statistical agencies to honour citizens' entitlement to public information.
>
> **Principle 2.** To retain trust in official statistics, the statistical agencies need to decide according to strictly professional considerations, including scientific principles and professional ethics, on the methods and procedures for the collection, processing, storage and presentation of statistical data.
>
> **Principle 3.** To facilitate a correct interpretation of the data, the statistical agencies are to present information according to scientific standards on the sources, methods and procedures of the statistics.
>
> **Principle 4.** The statistical agencies are entitled to comment on erroneous interpretation and misuse of statistics.
>
> **Principle 5.** Data for statistical purposes may be drawn from all types of sources, be they statistical surveys or administrative records. Statistical agencies are to choose the source with regard to quality, timeliness, costs and the burden on respondents.
>
> **Principle 6.** Individual data collected by statistical agencies for statistical compilation, whether they refer to natural or legal persons, are to be strictly confidential and used exclusively for statistical purposes.
>
> **Principle 7.** The laws, regulations and measures under which the statistical systems operate are to be made public.
>
> **Principle 8.** Coordination among statistical agencies within countries is essential to achieve consistency and efficiency in the statistical system.
>
> **Principle 9.** The use by statistical agencies in each country of international concepts, classifications and methods promotes the consistency and efficiency of statistical systems at all official levels.
>
> **Principle 10.** Bilateral and multilateral cooperation in statistics contributes to the improvement of systems of official statistics in all countries.

definitions, or errors in the way the data have been gathered or processed. Lastly, unclear indications about the methods used to compile the data can lead the user to confuse one variable with another. The result is that users often find it impossible or difficult to identify which statistics are most appropriate for their requirements, and they run the risk of using data that are in fact not comparable, thus making mistakes in their interpretation.

3. THE MAIN PRODUCERS OF ECONOMIC STATISTICS

The international organisations most active in the statistical field are, together with the OECD (Organisation for Economic Co-operation and Development), the UN (United Nations), the IMF (International Monetary Fund) and the WB (World Bank). The United Nations, founded in 1945, now numbers over 190 countries, and in spite of the problems in recent years, represents the fulcrum of the system of international relations developed over the past 50 years. In the field of statistics, too, the UN fulfils a pivotal function, through its Statistical Commission. Comprising 24 member states of the UN, elected for a period of four years, the Commission (which celebrated its 60th anniversary in 2007) meets annually in plenary session that is open to all UN member states (which are usually represented by the presidents or director-generals of their national statistical institutes) as well as to international organisations, admitted to meetings as observers. The Commission is called upon to approve all the main standards in the field of statistical methodology (classifications, handbooks, etc.).

In 1994, the Statistical Commission also approved a declaration on the "Fundamental Principles of Official Statistics" (see box above), which has become a key reference in the drawing up of national statistical laws and regulations, as well as the rules of conduct of national statistical institutes. The "Principles" underline the fundamental value of statistical information in the democratic development of modern society; they require producers of official statistics to adopt measures to ensure that their statistics are produced on the basis of purely scientific criteria, disseminated on an impartial basis, drawn up with guarantees for the confidentiality of the information received, and so on. Over time, the Principles have been fully absorbed by several national statistical systems, giving direction both to the rules governing national statistical institutes and the operating procedures they follow, and thus contributing to the development of the statistical function according to values shared at the international level.

The Secretariat of the Statistical Commission is provided by the Statistics Division of the UN, which regularly publishes statistics gathered by the member states (available on the Internet website, *www.un.org*), and contributes to the development of international statistical methodology through the work of various working groups that bring together statisticians from the member states and from other international organisations. It also fulfils the important function of providing technical assistance to less-developed countries, and supplies the other divisions of the UN with the necessary data enabling them to compile analytical reports on specific phenomena (poverty, economic development, etc.) and to debate and discuss political issues.

Particularly significant among the activities of the Statistical Division is the production of the 48 indicators for monitoring the progress of the less-developed countries towards the Millennium Development Goals, the objectives defined in 2000 by the UN General Assembly in terms of level of *per capita* income, reduction of mortality rates, improving levels of education, etc. (see box below). These indicators are produced by a large number of organisations coordinated by the UN Statistical Division.

THE MAIN PRODUCERS OF ECONOMIC STATISTICS   3

The Millennium Development Goals

Goal 1. Eradicate extreme poverty and hunger
- Target 1. Reduce by half the proportion of people whose income is less than $1 a day
- Target 2. Reduce by half the proportion of people who suffer from hunger

Goal 2. Achieve universal primary education
- Target 3. Ensure that all boys and girls complete a full course of primary education

Goal 3. Promote gender equality and empower women
- Target 4. Eliminate gender disparity in primary and secondary education, preferably by 2005, and at all levels by 2015

Goal 4. Reduce child mortality
- Target 5. Reduce by two-thirds the mortality rate among children under five

Goal 5. Improve maternal health
- Target 6. Reduce by three-quarters the maternal mortality ratio

Goal 6. Combat HIV/AIDS, malaria and other diseases
- Target 7. Halt and begin to reverse the spread of HIV/AIDS
- Target 8. Halt and begin to reverse the incidence of malaria and other major diseases

Goal 7. Ensure environmental sustainability
- Target 9. Integrate the principles of sustainable development into country policies and programmes; reverse loss of environmental resources
- Target 10. Reduce by half the proportion of people without sustainable access to safe drinking water
- Target 11. Achieve significant improvement in lives of at least 100 million slum dwellers, by 2020

Goal 8. Develop a global partnership for development
- Target 12. Develop further an open trading and financial system that is rule-based, predictable and non-discriminatory, includes a commitment to good governance, development and poverty reduction – nationally and internationally
- Target 13. Address the least developed countries' special needs. This include tariff- and quota-free access for their exports; enhanced debt relief for heavily indebted poor countries; cancellation of official bilateral debt; and more generous official development assistance for countries committed to poverty reduction
- Target 14. Address the special needs of landlocked and small island developing States
- Target 15. Deal comprehensively with developing countries' debt problems through national and international measures to make debt sustainable in the long term
- Target 16. In cooperation with developing countries, develop decent and productive work for youth;
- Target 17. In cooperation with pharmaceutical companies, provide access to affordable essential drugs in developing countries
- Target 18. In cooperation with the private sector, make available the benefits of new technologies - especially information and communications technologies

3 THE MAIN PRODUCERS OF ECONOMIC STATISTICS

The International Monetary Fund (IMF), founded in 1944 to promote international cooperation in the field of finance, ensure the stability of the international monetary system and sustain economic growth, today has 185 member states, normally represented by their economics ministries and/or national central banks, and is one of the main providers of international statistical information. In the division of statistical labour amongst international organisations, the IMF has responsibility for specific areas, such as financial statistics, balance of payments and the public sector. Through its Statistics Department, the IMF gathers numerous statistics on all the countries in the world, issues various publications and databases (www.imf.org), contributes to the development of international statistical standards and provides technical assistance to less developed countries. Of particular importance is evaluation of the quality of the statistics produced by individual countries (see Chapter 5), undertaken by the IMF as part of its multilateral monitoring of the economic conditions in member countries.

The World Bank, which currently has 185 member states, was founded in 1944 to combat poverty and improve the standard of living in developing countries. In the field of statistics, the World Bank contributes to the development of standards in methodology, and gathers and publishes certain statistics for analytical and political purposes (www.wb.org), with special emphasis on the less-developed countries. Through its various lines of credit, the World Bank plays a fundamental role in the development of statistical systems in the poorest countries, as well as in compiling statistics on major economic and social phenomena.

To strengthen the statistical capacity of developing countries, in 1999 the OECD, the IMF, the European Commission, the WB and the UN founded the *Partnership in Statistics for Development in the 21st Century* (PARIS21). The mission of PARIS21 (www.paris21.org) is to act as a catalyst for promoting a culture of evidence-based policymaking and monitoring in all countries, and especially in developing countries, and to foster more effective dialogue among those who produce development statistics and those who use them, through facilitating international events, supporting country-based activities, regional workshops, and subject matter task teams. The activities of PARIS21 are organised by a Secretariat based in OECD and supervised by a Steering Committee, an international group of stakeholders with representatives from developing countries from each region of the world, bilateral donors, and multilateral institutions.

3 THE MAIN PRODUCERS OF ECONOMIC STATISTICS

The main statistical databases of international and supranational organisations other than OECD

Millennium Indicators Database (UN). An overall framework of 48 indicators for measuring the progress of developing countries under the Millennium Development Goals was put in place by experts from the United Nations, the IMF, the OECD, the World Bank and other international institutions. The database contains the indicators and the associated metadata.

Monthly Statistical Bulletin (UN). The database contains a selection of monthly, quarterly and yearly economic indicators for the member states.

Commodity Trade Statistics Database (UN). Contains annual data on foreign trade for more than 130 countries (in some cases going back to 1962), disaggregated by type of goods and trading partner country. Values are expressed in US dollars.

International Financial Statistics (IMF). This is the main database of the IMF, containing economic and financial data produced on an annual, quarterly and monthly basis, with a total of around 32,000 series of historical data covering more than 200 countries.

World Development Indicators (WB). Contains annual data on approximately 800 indicators relating to economic, demographic, social and environmental themes. The data, which are available in some cases as far back as 1960, cover 152 countries.

New Cronos (Eurostat). This is the most important Eurostat database, and it contains an enormous amount of data covering a variety of economic, social and environmental fields. Freely accessible via the Internet, it contains monthly, quarterly and annual data.

Euroindicators (Eurostat). Contains a selection of the main monthly and quarterly indicators, which is updated in real time. It allows an immediate comparison to be made of current developments in the individual European countries as well as data on the Euro area and the European Union.

Structural indicators (Eurostat). Presents annual data based on a selection of indicators covering five areas of interest: employment; innovation and research; economic reform; social cohesion; the environment and economic conditions, as well as detailed information on their methodological features and on international comparability. It also contains data on the United States and Japan.

Regio (Eurostat). This is the database of reference for sub-national analysis concerning the countries of the European Union. It contains a number of series of historical data of an economic or social nature. The detail given is by region and, in some cases, by province.

Monthly Bulletin (ECB). The statistical appendix to the Monthly Bulletin contains a number of series giving actual monetary and financial data. In addition, the Internet website offers various data sets that contain series of historic data on the Euro area.

3 THE MAIN PRODUCERS OF ECONOMIC STATISTICS

3.2. The OECD statistical system

The Organisation for Economic Co-operation and Development was founded in 1961, and its current members are 30 of the world's most developed countries. The aim of the Organisation is to assist in the achievement of sustainable economic development, the improvement in standards of living, and the growth of international trade. Where statistics are concerned, the OECD is active in the economic, social and environmental fields, with a total of over 100 various activities. The OECD plays a part in the development of international standards by producing statistics on a variety of subjects, and compiling and publishing a wide range of statistical data, produced mostly by national authorities (*www.oecd.org/statistics*), and promoting the gathering in member countries of the statistics needed to produce its analytical reports and draw up guidelines on economic, social and environmental policy. The OECD co-operates in the statistical field with the major non-member countries (Russia, China, Brazil, India and South Africa), various geographical regions (principally Asia and Latin America) and almost all international organisations producing statistical data and metadata.

The organisation of statistical activities at the OECD is based on a "decentralised model", whereby various statistics are developed both by the Statistics Directorate and by substantive Directorates responsible for analytical studies and policy analyses and recommendations. The Statistics Directorate (STD) was created in 1992 with the mandate: *a)* to improve the supply of relevant and timely statistical information to analysts and policy makers inside and outside the Organisation; *b)* to develop international statistical standards, systems and classifications in collaboration with other international statistical agencies; *c)* to improve co-ordination between the statistical activities of the OECD and those of other agencies; and *d)* to provide a mechanism for co-ordinating statistical activities within the Organisation.

From a substantive point of view, STD is responsible for macroeconomic statistics (national accounts, short-term economic indicators, international trade, etc.) and for some social (*i.e.* labour force) and business statistics. In addition, STD plays a key role in promoting internal co-ordination and co-operation with other international organisations. The majority of other statistical activities are carried out in eight OECD Directorates: Development Co-operation (DCD); Economics (ECO); Education (EDU); Employment, Labour and Social Affairs (ELSA); Environment (ENV); Financial and Enterprise Affairs (DAF); Centre for Tax Policy and Administration (CTP); Public Governance and Territorial Development (GOV); Science, Technology and Industry (STI).

The Information Technology and Network Services (ITN) and the Public Affairs and Communications Directorate (PAC) play an important role in supporting the development, implementation and dissemination of OECD statistics. The former co-operates with STD and other Directorates to develop statistical databases and other IT infrastructures for conducting statistical activities, while the latter is responsible for the dissemination of all OECD products, including statistical data and publications.

The governing board of the OECD is the Council, which comprises the official representatives of member countries and establishes the general policy and priorities of the Organisation in close contact with the Secretary-General. Directorates also

3. THE MAIN PRODUCERS OF ECONOMIC STATISTICS

support one or more Committees, which represent national governments and establish work programme priorities in their respective areas of responsibility, evaluate reports prepared by the Secretariat, develop recommendations, etc. To deal with technical or specific issues, Committees establish working parties or task forces. Accordingly, several statistical bodies have been established over time, including the Committee on Statistics, created in 2004.

OECD statisticians are committed to implementing the "Principles for Statistical Activities Carried out by International Organisations" prepared in 2006 by the Committee for Co-ordination of Statistical Activities (CCSA). In addition, OECD statisticians are committed to carry out their work according to the International Statistical Institute's declaration on professional ethics. The actual implementation of these principles and quality dimensions described in the "Quality Framework for OECD Statistics" (see Chapter 5) is undertaken through the guidelines and procedures provided in the Framework for all OECD statistical activities.

To face new challenges, such as the evolution of the international statistical system and especially the increase and diversification of users' needs, the OECD Statistics Strategy was launched in 2001, with the ultimate goal of improving the overall quality of OECD statistics. Since then, several initiatives have been undertaken to address technical, managerial and organisational issues. Especially important here have been increases in the efficiency of OECD statistical activities and on-line access to OECD statistics, in the context of the OECD Publishing Policy. For example, the OECD Statistics Portal, which provides users with access to selected statistics and methodological publications produced by the Organisation, is by far the most accessed theme of the OECD web site, with a high growth over the last few years. A similar picture emerges when looking at the number of visits to statistical databases available in *SourceOECD*, the OECD e-library through which all OECD products are made available to registered users. The number of institutions with access to all statistical publications and databases via *SourceOECD* also rose to 800. This means that over 10 million academics, students, government officials, researchers and corporate users now have unrestricted access to all databases via *SourceOECD*.

3.3. The European Statistical System and the European System of Central Banks

The European institutions play an increasingly important role in international statistics, especially the European Commission and the European Central Bank. The process of European integration began in the 1950s and advanced progressively over the next 30 years, to be re-launched in the 1990s with the construction of the European Union, and most recently extended from 2004 with the accession of 12 new member countries. Integration has had a significant influence on the statistical activities of the European countries, producing major changes both in the internal organisation of the Commission, and in its relations with the national statistical authorities.

First among the European institutions in the field of statistics is the Statistical Office of the European Communities (Eurostat), one of the Directorates General into which

3 THE MAIN PRODUCERS OF ECONOMIC STATISTICS

the Commission is broken down. Eurostat gathers and disseminates large quantities of data produced by the national statistical institutes and various other public bodies (www.ec.europa.eu). Eurostat also supervises the production of "Community statistics" according to agreed upon definitions and classifications, coordinating the other Directorates General of the European Commission active in the statistical field.

To underline the importance that the European Community attaches to rules on the statistical function, one need only recall that the Treaty of Amsterdam (Art. 285) provides that:

> *"Without prejudice to Article 5 of the Protocol on the Statute of the European System of Central Banks and of the European Central Bank, the Council, acting in accordance with the procedure referred to in Article 189b, shall adopt measures for the production of statistics where necessary for the performance of the activities of the Community.*
>
> *The production of Community statistics shall conform to impartiality, reliability, objectivity, scientific independence, cost-effectiveness and statistical confidentiality; it shall not entail excessive burdens on economic operators."*

In the European Union, the principle of "subsidiarity" also operates in the field of statistics, which means that a national function may be transferred to the European level only when this is absolutely necessary to achieve the desired result, or if by so doing, the result could be achieved more efficiently. The need to have access to statistical data that are fully comparable between the member states has meant that the concepts, definitions and classifications used in the production of Community statistics are increasingly frequently laid down in norms (Regulations, Decisions and Directives) adopted by the European Council, the European Parliament or the European Commission, while national statistical institutes (or other public bodies, such as ministries and public sector entities) are called upon to produce the data required by autonomously managing the organisational, financial and methodological aspects. For example, these national bodies are normally free to use either an administrative source or carry out a statistical survey in order to provide a specific item of data, provided the ultimate characteristics of the statistics produced correspond to those laid down at European level. In other words, the production of European statistics is based on the principle of harmonisation of the output and not of the input. There are certain exceptions to this, such as data for consumer prices or the labour force, for which data-gathering procedures are very carefully specified in legislation.

The drafting of legislation in the field of statistics is a long and complex process, sometimes too long to satisfy the ends for which it is required. In practice, once a new need for information has been identified, Eurostat draws up, using its own theme-based working groups (in which the representatives of the national statistical institutes take part), the text of a regulation that identifies the variables to be passed on to Eurostat on behalf of the member states, the timetable for transmission, the definitions and classifications to be adopted, etc. Once the text is ready, it is sent to the Statistical Programme Committee (SPC), in which the countries are represented

THE MAIN PRODUCERS OF ECONOMIC STATISTICS 3

by the presidents or directors general of their national statistical institutes. After the SPC has given its approval, Eurostat forwards the proposal to the European Council and the European Parliament, which are obliged to reach agreement on a final text based on what is known as the "co-decision" procedure.

In the most hotly disputed cases, it can take several years for the entire decision process to be completed, while continuing growth in demand for the information calls for a rapid response on the part of the producers. This is why in some cases the European Commission (most of all the Directorates General in charge of specific policies) prefers to turn to private-sector institutions to gather statistics on an *ad hoc* basis, rather than to embark upon a decision-making process that is complex and potentially long. On the other hand, precisely in order to speed up the legislative process, there is a tendency for only very general legislative texts to be subjected to the approval procedure described above, thus leaving it to the European Commission alone (without involving the Council or the Parliament) to do the work of approving, in collaboration with the SPC, documents covering mostly technical or detailed aspects.

Much of the work of Eurostat is directed at verifying the quality of the statistics submitted by the member states, which are obligated to follow Eurostat recommendations for improving the comparability and quality of the data. In the event this is not done, Eurostat (in its capacity as part of the European Commission) can institute proceedings for breach before the European Court of Justice to oblige the country to adopt the measures requested.

The second pillar of European statistics is the European Central Bank (ECB) and the European System of Central Banks (ESCB or Eurosystem), comprising the ECB itself and the national central banks. In the statistical field, the ESBC has powers analogous to those of the European Commission, and thus the production of information on monetary and financial phenomena in the area of the European Monetary Union, too, is mostly defined through special regulations and other legal instruments. The ECB, through its Statistics Directorate General, fulfils the role of gathering and publishing monetary and financial statistics and balance of payments statistics, drawn not only from the euro area as a whole, but also from individual countries. The "systemic" perspective that typifies statistical activities within the European Commission has thus come to be used as well in the ESBC, though the latter has faster decision-making processes and more flexible resources than the European Statistical System.

Despite the numerous advances of the past decade, and the good coordination that exists between the ESCB and the European Statistical System, maintained by Eurostat and the Statistical Directorate General of the ECB, it has to be said that the two "systems" appear very different, and function at quite different speeds. In the case of the European Statistical System, the key organisation (Eurostat) is one of the Directorates General of the European Commission and does not have the same full autonomy and independence (including for its budget) as the European Central Bank. On the other hand, the national statistical institutes (in contrast with the national central banks) are under the legal control of the governments, and their

3. THE MAIN PRODUCERS OF ECONOMIC STATISTICS

independence is hardly ever constitutionally guaranteed (as is the case for the ESCB, thanks to the Maastricht Treaty), and their budgets are decided annually by the national political authorities, while Central Banks have their own resources.

To conclude, the development of a true European Statistical System is still encountering some problems. However, it must be acknowledged that the spirit of partnership that exists between Eurostat, national producers of statistics, the European Central Bank and ESCB has resulted in European financing for the development of statistics at Community and national levels, and in the adoption of new technologies. As a result, the position of statistics in the Community has improved considerably over the last 10 years. European statistics have underpinned fundamental political and economic processes, such as the European Monetary Union and the enlargement of the Union to include new countries.

In particular, the requirement for economic information on both structural and short-term aspects that is full, prompt and above all internationally comparable, has given an extraordinary boost to the work of the national statistical systems, with major repercussions in terms of the quality of national statistics and independence of the national statistical institutes. That said, the recent history of European statistics, especially the crisis surrounding erroneous data on the basis of which Greece was allowed to join the European Monetary Union (see Chapter 5), has highlighted the limitations of the current situation.

Chapter 4

An Overview of OECD Economic Statistics

How can we compare the economic structure of OECD countries? Are small and medium enterprises more efficient than the large ones? How can we measure innovation or globalisation? Are the official measures of inflation reliable? This chapter shows how economic statistics published by the OECD can help in answering these and other questions relevant both for analytical and policy purposes. In particular, for each topic (statistics on agriculture, energy, industry and services, national accounts, etc.) the key definitions used to compile internationally comparable statistics are presented, together with the sources. The chapter also describes some of the activities already underway or planned to improve the quality of OECD statistics. Finally, charts and tables are used to highlight just a subset of data available in OECD databases and publications.

4 AN OVERVIEW OF OECD ECONOMIC STATISTICS

4.1 Agriculture and fishery statistics

The OECD collects and compiles a wide range of data used to support its agricultural policy analysis (see Box 1) and long-term forecasts. These activities are carried out in co-operation with other international organisations, notably the Food and Agriculture Organisation (FAO) and UNCTAD.

OECD agriculture statistics are focused, first of all, on current developments in agricultural markets for major temperate zone agricultural commodities. Detailed information for production, consumption, trade, stocks and prices are collected for OECD countries and a large number of other countries (including China, Argentina, Brazil, India, South Africa, Russia and other CIS independent states and many smaller countries in Africa, Asia and Latin America). Most series cover the period from 1970 to the most current year and include updated annual projections for up to 10 years in the future.

Fisheries statistics include the collection and dissemination of annual data concerning landings (harvest) and processing, fleet, fishers, employment, trade, aquaculture and government financial transfers. The data are used for analytical purposes and serve as reference for other international organisations and as a means for cross-checking and reconciling information from national sources. At the international level, co-ordination takes place among agencies involved in fisheries statistical programmes. Furthermore, analytical work on the economics of fisheries asks for a number of specialised datasets to be created in support of such work.

A major database is maintained with essential information for the assessment of agricultural market access (AMAD). It contains a common dataset on tariffs, tariff-rate quotas and imports so that researchers, policy makers and others can analyse the levels of tariff protections in agriculture among members of the World Trade Organisation (WTO). The development and use of a common dataset can assist in improving international transparency of agricultural trade as covered by multilateral rules and disciplines.

4 AN OVERVIEW OF OECD ECONOMIC STATISTICS

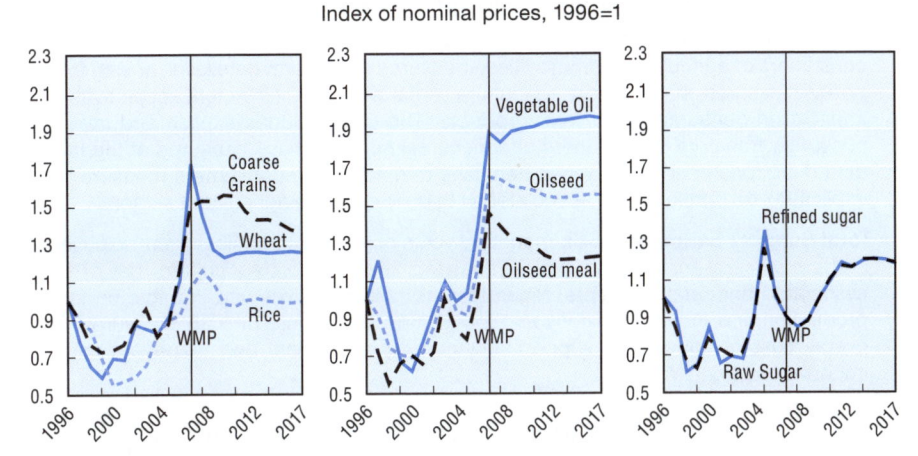

Figure 4.1.1 – Outlook for world crop prices to 2017
Index of nominal prices, 1996=1

StatLink http://dx.doi.org/10.1787/335406334811
Source: OECD (2008), *OECD-FAO Agricultural Outlook 2008-2017*, OECD Publishing

The OECD Producer and Consumer Support Estimates

To support its policy work, the OECD also compiles a unique set of statistics called Producer and Consumer Support Estimates. Compiled since 1987, these statistics present the monetary value of transfers associated with all policy measures affecting agriculture. These are classified into a number of major groups that relate to the implementation criteria of the measures. The most important distinctions relate to whether measures are based on commodity output, on input use, on other criteria such as land area, animal numbers, income or revenue, or finally on non-commodity criteria. Whether production is required or not in order to benefit from a measure is another important criterion identified for all measures. With the reform of agricultural policies in OECD countries, the number and complexity of policy measures has increased significantly and the classification and nomenclature evolves in response. Currently, the indicators most commonly used in policy monitoring and analysis are:

- **Producer Support Estimate (PSE):** annual monetary value of gross transfers from consumers and taxpayers to support agricultural producers, measured at farm gate level, arising from policy measures that support agriculture, regardless of their nature, objectives or impacts on farm production or income. The PSE measures support arising from policies targeted at agriculture relative to a situation without such policies, i.e. one in which producers are subject only to the general policies (including economic, social, environmental and tax policies) of the country.

- **General Services Support Estimate (GSSE):** monetary value of gross transfers to general services provided to agriculture collectively, arising from policy measures that support agriculture, regardless of their nature, objectives and impacts on farm production, income or consumption of farm products. These payments for eligible private or public general service are provided to the agricultural sector collectively and not individually to farmers.

4 AN OVERVIEW OF OECD ECONOMIC STATISTICS

The OECD Producer and Consumer Support Estimates *(cont.)*

- **Consumer Support Estimate (CSE):** monetary value of gross transfers to (from) consumers of agricultural commodities, measured at the farm gate level, arising from policy measures that support agriculture, regardless of their nature, objectives or impacts on consumption of farm products. The CSE includes explicit and implicit consumer transfers to producers of agricultural commodities, measured at the farm gate (first consumer) level. When negative, transfers from consumers measure the implicit tax on consumption associated with policies to the agricultural sector.

- **Total Support Estimate (TSE):** monetary value of all gross transfers from taxpayers and consumers arising from policy measures that support agriculture, net of the associated budgetary receipts, regardless of their objectives and impacts on farm production and income, or consumption of farm products. The TSE measures the overall cost of agricultural support financed by consumers and taxpayers net of import receipts.

Figure 4.1.2 – **Total Support Estimates for OECD countries**
As percentage of GDP, 1986-2007

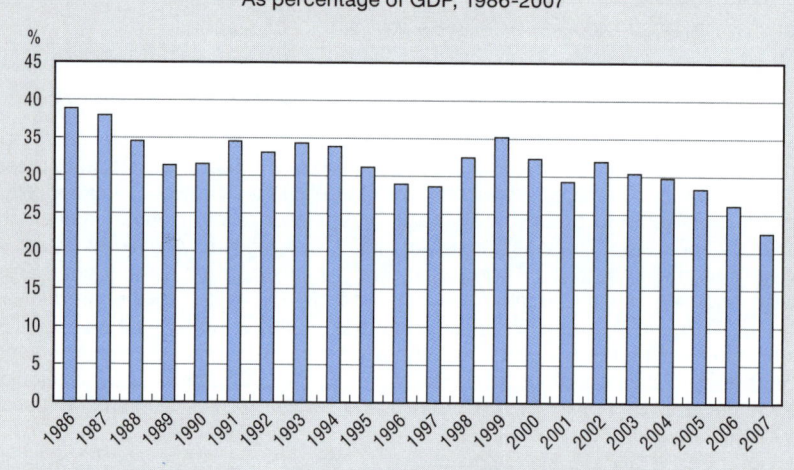

StatLink http://dx.doi.org/10.1787/335411615202

Source: OECD (2008), "PSE/CSE" in *OECD Agricultural Statistics – online database.*

AN OVERVIEW OF OECD ECONOMIC STATISTICS 4

Further information

Publications
OECD (2008), *Agricultural Policies in OECD Countries: At a Glance,* OECD Publishing

OECD (2007), *Agricultural Policies in OECD Countries: Monitoring and Evaluation*, OECD Publishing

OECD (2007), *Agricultural Policies in Non-OECD Countries: Monitoring and Evaluation*, OECD Publishing

OECD (2008), *OECD-FAO Agricultural Outlook 2008-2017*, OECD Publishing

OECD (2006), *Review of Fisheries in OECD Countries: Vol. 2 - Country Statistics, 2002-2004*, OECD Publishing

OECD (2005), *Review of Fisheries in OECD Countries: Volume 1: Policies and Summary Statistics*, OECD Publishing

Websites
www.agri-outlook.org
www.oecd.org/agr/support/
www.oecd.org/agr/fish/
www.amad.org

4 AN OVERVIEW OF OECD ECONOMIC STATISTICS

4.2 Energy statistics

Data for energy statistics are compiled by the International Energy Agency (IEA), an autonomous Agency of the OECD. The IEA acts as energy policy advisor for its member countries in their effort to ensure reliable, affordable and clean energy for their citizens. Founded during the oil crisis of 1974, its initial role was to coordinate measures in times of oil supply emergencies. But during recent decades, the energy markets have changed, and so has the IEA. It now focuses well beyond oil crisis management on broader energy issues, including climate change policies, market reform, energy technology collaboration and outreach to the rest of the world.

The IEA collects, processes and publishes data and information on energy production, trade, stocks, transformation, consumption, prices and taxes as well as on greenhouse gas emissions for the 30 OECD member countries and over 100 non-OECD countries worldwide. The statistics are published in 10 annual and two quarterly publications; they also are available on CD-ROMs and Internet services. The annual publications include:

- *Energy Statistics of OECD Countries:* contains data on energy supply and consumption in original units for coal, oil, natural gas, combustible renewables/wastes and products derived from these primary fuels, as well as for electricity and heat for the 30 OECD member countries.

- *Energy Statistics of Non-OECD Countries:* a similar publication to the Energy Statistics of OECD Countries but for over 100 non-OECD countries all around the world.

- *Energy Balances of OECD Countries:* presents standardised energy balances expressed in "million tonnes of oil equivalent" for the 30 OECD member countries. Energy supply and consumption data are presented by main fuel: coal, oil, gas, nuclear, hydro, geothermal/solar, combustible renewables/wastes, electricity and heat. This allows for easy comparison of the contributions each fuel makes to the economy and their interrelationships through the conversion of one fuel to another. All of this is essential for estimating total energy supply, forecasting, energy conservation and analysing the potential for interfuel substitution.

- *Energy Balances of Non-OECD Countries:* a similar publication to the Energy Balances of OECD Countries but for over 100 non-OECD countries all around the world.

- *Electricity Information:* provides essential statistics on electricity and heat for each OECD member country by bringing together information on production, installed capacity, input energy mix for electricity and heat production, input fuel prices, consumption, end-user electricity prices and electricity trades. The document also presents selected non-OECD country statistics on the main electricity and heat flows.

- *Coal Information:* provides detailed information on the past and current evolution of the world coal market. It presents country specific statistics for OECD member countries and selected non-OECD countries on coal production, demand, trade and prices.

AN OVERVIEW OF OECD ECONOMIC STATISTICS 4

- *Natural Gas Information:* presents a detailed gas supply and demand balance for each individual country and for the three OECD regions (North America, Europe and Asia-Pacific), as well as a breakdown of gas consumption by end-user. Import and export data are reported by source and destination. It also contains essential information on LNG (liquefied natural gas) and pipeline trade, gas reserves, storage capacity and prices not only for the OECD countries but also for the rest of the world.

- *Oil Information:* contains key data on world production, trade, prices and consumption of major oil product groups, with time series back to the early 1970s, as well as more detailed and comprehensive picture of oil supply, demand, trade, production and consumption by end-user for each OECD country individually and for the OECD regions. Trade data are reported extensively by origin and destination.

- *Renewables Information:* presents a detailed and comprehensive picture of developments for renewable and waste energy sources for each of the OECD member countries, encompassing energy indicators, generating capacity, electricity and heat production from renewable and waste sources, as well as production and consumption of renewable and waste products. It also includes a selection of indicators for non-OECD countries.

- *CO_2 Emissions from Fuel Combustion:* provides a basis for comparative analysis of CO_2 emissions from fossil fuel combustion, a major source of anthropogenic emissions. The data cover the period from 1971 onwards for more than 140 countries and regions, by sector and by fuel. Emissions were calculated using IEA energy databases and the default methods and emissions factors from the Revised 1996 IPCC Guidelines for National Greenhouse Gas Inventories.

In addition, two quarterly publications are made available to users:

- *Energy Prices and Taxes:* contains up-to-date information on prices and taxes in national and international energy markets, such as import prices, industry prices and consumer prices. The statistics cover the main petroleum products, gas, coal and electricity, giving for imported products an average price both for the importing country and country of origin. Every issue includes full notes on sources and methods and a description of price mechanisms in each country.

- *Oil, Gas, Coal and Electricity:* provides quarterly statistics on oil, coal, natural gas and electricity for the OECD countries. Oil statistics cover production, trade, refinery intake and output, stock changes and consumption. Statistics for electricity, natural gas and coal show supply and trade. Import and export data are reported by origin and destination.

Monthly oil and gas data services are also available on the Internet. The IEA Monthly Oil Data Service comprises the detailed databases of historical and projected information used in preparing the IEA's monthly Oil Market Report. The databases include supply, demand, balances, stocks, trade and field-by-field supply. The IEA Monthly Gas Data Service provides historical and current data on natural gas supply and demand for OECD countries, as well as detailed information on trade origins and destinations.

4. AN OVERVIEW OF OECD ECONOMIC STATISTICS

Figure 4.2.1 – **Total primary energy supply per unit of GDP**
Tonnes of oil equivalent (toe) per thousand 2000 US dollars of GDP calculated using PPPs, 2007

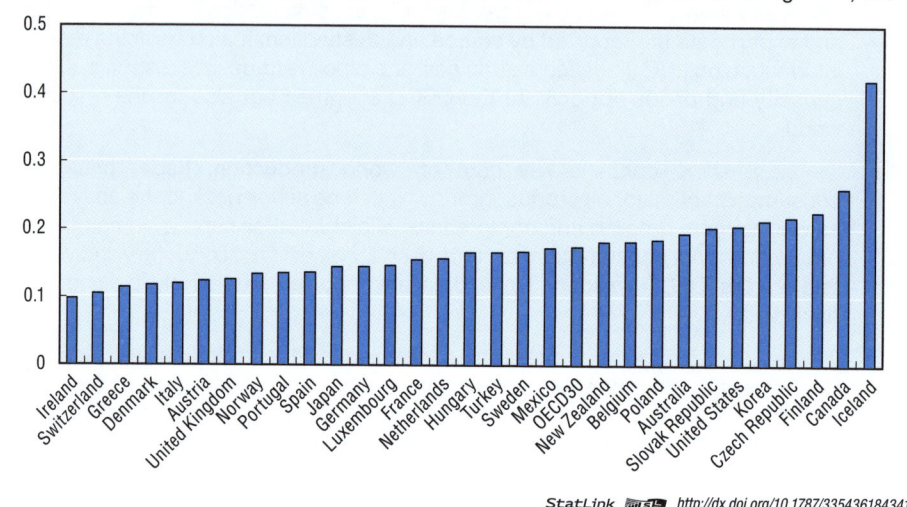

Sources: IEA (2007), *Energy Balances of OECD Countries*, IEA.

StatLink http://dx.doi.org/10.1787/335436184341

Figure 4.2.2 – **Crude oil spot prices**
US dollars per barrel

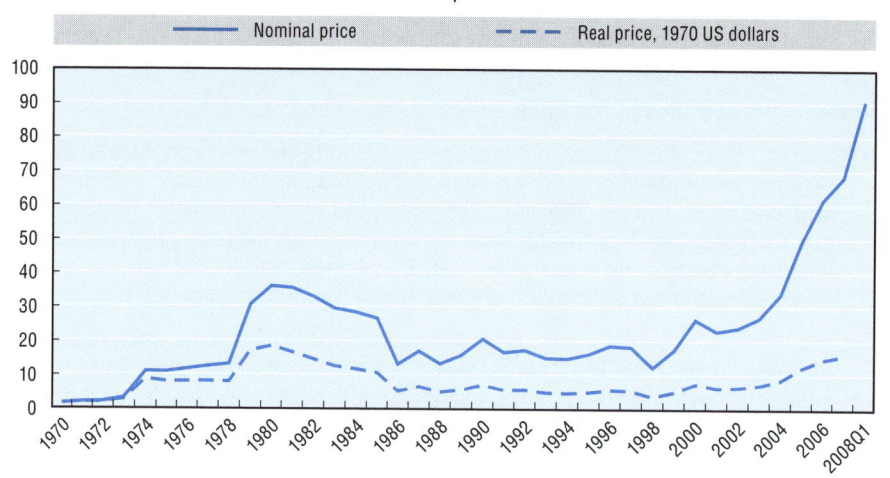

Sources: IEA (2007), *Energy Prices and Taxes*, IEA.

StatLink http://dx.doi.org/10.1787/335440844175

AN OVERVIEW OF OECD ECONOMIC STATISTICS 4

Further information

Publications
IEA (2006), *China's Power Sector Reforms: Where to Next?*, IEA.
IEA (2006), *Optimising Russian Natural Gas: Reform and Climate Policy*, IEA.
IEA (2007), *Energy Policies of IEA Countries, series*, IEA.
IEA (2007), *Energy Use in the New Millennium: Trends in IEA Countries*, IEA.
IEA (2007), *Mind the Gap: Quantifying Principal-Agent Problems in Energy Efficiency*, IEA.
IEA (2007), *Natural Gas Market Review 2007: Security in a Globalising Market to 2015*, IEA.
IEA (2007), *World Energy Outlook 2007: China and India Insights*, IEA.

Online databases
Energy Prices and Taxes.
World Energy Statistics and Balances.

Websites
www.iea.org

4 AN OVERVIEW OF OECD ECONOMIC STATISTICS

4.3 Industry and services statistics

This section describes statistics used for the structural and sectoral analyses of business behaviour in the industrial and services sectors. In particular, it presents data concerning: business demography (*i.g.* the creation and destruction of enterprises); structural business statistics by size-class; statistics concerning two specific economic sectors that provide financial services (insurance and pension funds); and indicators tracking the impact of regulatory reforms on the market efficiency of industrial and services activities.

Compared to other domains of economic statistics, the collection of these data is relatively recent and therefore their international comparability is still an issue. Moreover, the differences in laws and institutional frameworks make the production of internationally harmonised statistics extremely difficult (for example, the legal definition of an enterprise depends on national legislation, as well as the registration of its birth or death). Nevertheless, with the growing importance of structural economic policies and policies aimed at fostering economic and employment growth, policy makers and analysts are paying growing attention to these data, and statisticians are making efforts to improve the timeliness and comparability of business statistics.

Business demography

The creation of new businesses and the decline of unproductive ones are often regarded as key to business dynamism in OECD economies. Understanding business behaviour and "creative destruction" (in the Schumpeterian sense), and identifying successful and failing businesses, as well as fostering entrepreneurship and innovation have become increasingly important objectives for policy makers in many OECD economies in recent years. Business churn (i.e. entry plus exit rates) is commonly viewed as a measure of the ability of economies to expand the boundaries of economic activity, to shift resources towards growing areas and away from declining areas, and to adjust the structure of production to meet consumers' changing needs. Moreover, higher rates of business creation and churning are generally held to benefit economic growth, job creation and poverty alleviation via increased productivity and innovation.

Many national statistical offices now provide official statistics on the exit, entry and turnover of businesses. Eurostat has recently developed an enterprise demography database typically using data sourced from business registers or administrative tax sources, which has greatly improved the comparability of business demography data from European countries.

Since comparison of these statistics across non-EU countries is a more complex undertaking the OECD Statistics Directorate has recently developed a framework that provides definitions for a number of key business demography indicators and which has served as the basis of a joint Emostat-OECD *Manual on Business Demography Statistics*. To improve international comparability this framework now forms the basis for formal data collection from OECD countries. However, the data presented below were produced by NSOs prior to adoption of this framework, so differences remain.

AN OVERVIEW OF OECD ECONOMIC STATISTICS 4

▶ **Key definitions**

Enterprise: is a legal entity possessing the right to conduct business on its own. It may consist of one or more local units or establishments corresponding to production units situated in a geographically separate place and in which one or more persons are employed

Number of employees: includes all persons, covered by a contractual arrangement, who receive compensation for their work, whether full-time or part-time. It excludes working proprietors, active business partners, unpaid family workers and home-workers, irrespective of whether or not they are on the payroll.

Employer enterprise birth: occurs when an enterprise records employees greater than zero for the first time. The corollary to a birth is an **employer enterprise death**, which occurs when a business that previously had one or more employees and ceases to trade or have employees.

Figure 4.3.1 – **Birth and death rates**
As a percentage of total number of enterprises, 2003 or latest available year

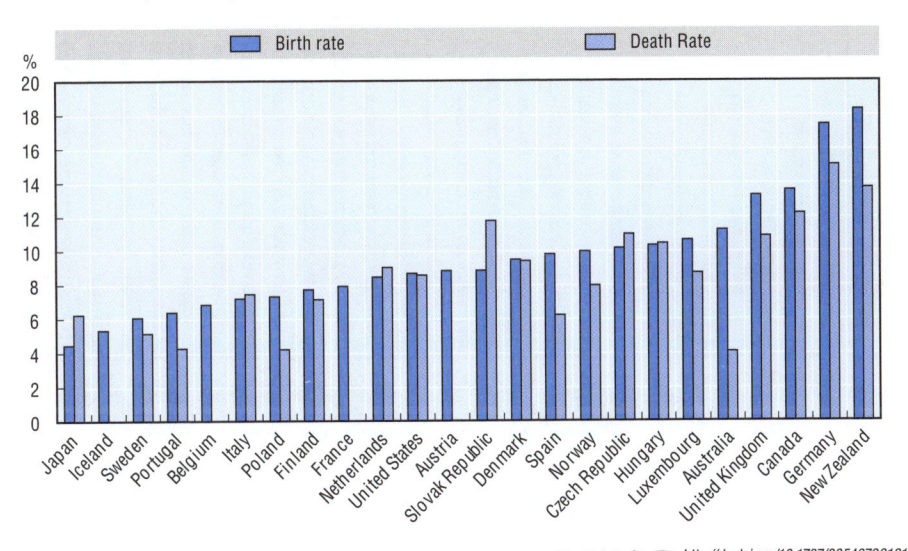

StatLink http://dx.doi.org/10.1787/335467001810
Source: OECD (2006), *Structural and Demographic Business Statistics*, OECD Publishing.

Enterprises by size classes

Statistics showing the distribution of enterprises by size class help to analyse the potential, and actual, contribution of small enterprises to economic growth. Potential, because the data used here cannot show the contribution small enterprises make to economic and employment growth over time as they move from the start-up phase to some optimal size. Still, many studies have used longitudinal datasets to establish their important contribution in this context.

4 AN OVERVIEW OF OECD ECONOMIC STATISTICS

Unfortunately, the international comparability of enterprise statistics is still an issue. A majority of OECD countries presents business statistics using the enterprise as the statistical unit, while others (Japan, Korea and Mexico) use the concept of establishment. However, because most enterprises are also establishments, this is not expected to significantly affect comparability. An area where considerable differences do arise, however, is the coverage of businesses. In many countries, this information is based on business registers and economic censuses or surveys whose coverage of businesses varies across countries depending on the administrative thresholds, registration requirements, tax legislation and permissible business burdens in place. For example, US data reflects only businesses with employees. For Ireland and Korea, only businesses with more than three or more than four employees, respectively, are represented.

Figure 4.3.2 – **Enterprises with less than 20 persons engaged**
As a percentage of total number of employees or total number of enterprises
2005 or latest available year

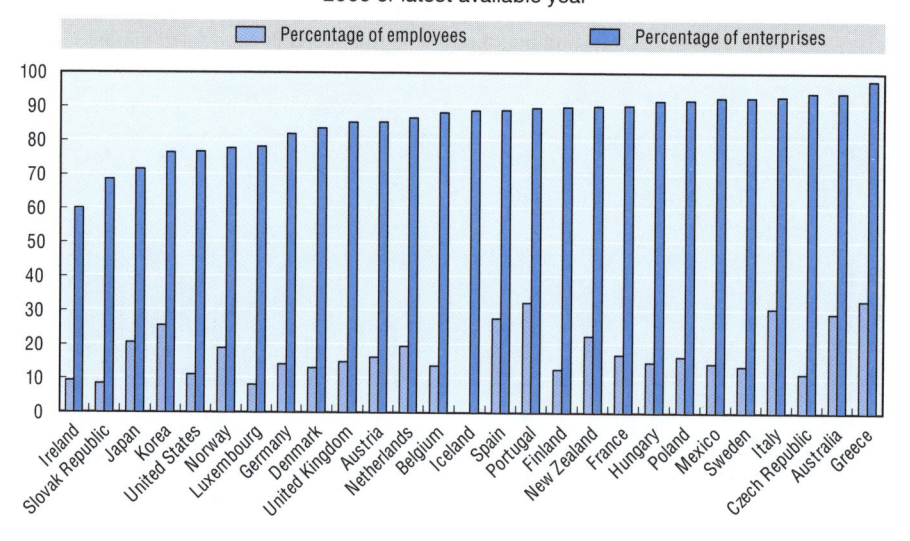

Source: OECD (2005), *OECD SME and Entrepreneurship Outlook*, OECD Publishing.

AN OVERVIEW OF OECD ECONOMIC STATISTICS 4

Entrepreneurship indicators

Internationally comparable measures of the amount and type of entrepreneurship, as well as the key determinants of entrepreneurship, represent an important new area of statistical activity. Several indicators of overall entrepreneurship levels, based on measures of self-employment or firm creation, exist but harmonisation of definitions is required to make them comparable. Furthermore, policy makers wish to focus on the subset of entrepreneurs that create high-growth, innovative firms.

New data collections based on framework and definitions developed by the OECD-Eurostat Entrepreneurship Indicators Program (EIP) have been recently initiated to produce the information required by policy makers.

Insurance

Since 1982, the OECD has collected and analysed various insurance statistics. The data are reported on a yearly basis from all the OECD governments' relevant authorities. The set of statistics and indicators contains not only general information on insurance activities (number of companies, number of employees, gross premiums, net premiums, etc.), but also data related to major trends of the international insurance industry, such as the market share by foreign companies in each country, business written abroad, premiums in terms of risk destination (foreign or domestic risks), foreign and domestic investments. The scope of the datasets also includes gross claims payments, gross operating expenses and commissions.

▶ **Key definitions**

Total gross premiums: represent total insurance premiums written in the reporting country. It is a major indicator of the importance of the insurance industry in the economy of each country.

Market share in the OECD: measures the importance of the national insurance market of each OECD country compared to the whole OECD insurance market, based on total gross premiums.

Density of insurance industry: the ratio of direct gross premiums to the population. It represents the average insurance spending per capita in a given country.

Penetration of insurance industry: the ratio of direct gross premiums to gross domestic product. It represents the relative importance of the insurance industry in the domestic economy.

Life insurance share: the ratio of gross life insurance premiums to total gross premiums. It measures the relative importance of life insurance as compared to non-life insurance.

Premiums per employee: ratio of the direct gross premiums to the number of employees in insurance companies. It is an indicator of the relative efficiency of the national insurance industry.

4 AN OVERVIEW OF OECD ECONOMIC STATISTICS

Retention ratio: the ratio of net written premiums to total gross premiums. It represents the proportion of retained business, and thus, indirectly, the importance of reinsurance for domestic insurance companies.

Ratio of reinsurance accepted: ratio of reinsurance accepted to total gross premiums. It provides an indication of the significance of reinsurance accepted in the national insurance market.

Foreign companies' market share in the domestic market: this figure describes the importance of foreign companies in the domestic insurance market and is measured through the following indicators:

a) market share of foreign-controlled companies and branches and agencies of foreign companies in total gross premiums;

b) market share of branches and agencies of foreign companies in total gross premiums.

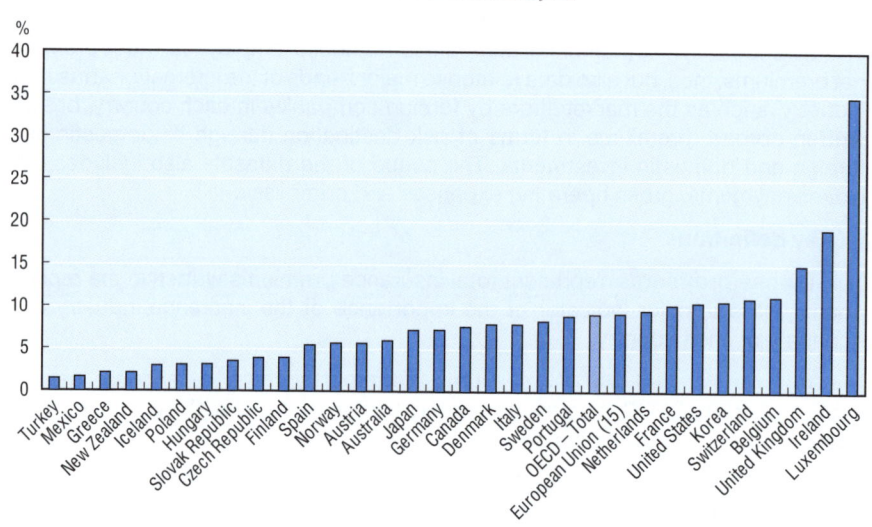

Figure 4.3.3 – **Penetration of insurance industry**
2005 or latest available year

StatLink http://dx.doi.org/10.1787/335503632317
Sources: OECD (2007), *Insurance Statistics Yearbook, 1996-2005*, OECD Publishing.

Funded pensions

Recent years have witnessed intense pension reform efforts in OECD countries, which have often involved an increased use of funded pension programmes managed by the private sector. There is a growing need among policy makers and the regulatory community, as well as among private-sector participants, to compare their programme developments and experiences with those of other countries. Because funded arrangements are likely to play an increasingly important role in delivering retirement income security in many countries, and because the investment of pension assets will increasingly affect securities markets in future years, an accurate, comprehensive, comparable and up-to-date body of international statistics is a necessary tool for policy makers, regulators and market participants.

In 2002, the OECD launched the Global Pension Statistics project (GPS), which intends to provide a valuable means of measuring and monitoring the pensions industry, and permit inter-country comparisons of current statistics and indicators on key aspects of retirement systems across OECD and non-OECD countries. Data are collected on a yearly basis so that trends can be readily analysed.

The statistics cover an extensive range of variables (assets, asset allocation, liabilities, contributions, benefits, members) and include funded pension plans for both public and private sector workers according to the OECD classification (see the Glossary available at *www.oecd.org/dataoecd/0/49/38356329.pdf*).

Following this classification, data are split between different financing vehicles (*i.e.* autonomous pension funds, book reserves, pension insurance contracts and investment companies/banks managed funds) and different pension plan types (*i.e.* occupational vs. personal pension plans, defined benefit vs. defined contribution plans).

▶ **Key definitions**

Pension fund assets as a share of GDP: the ratio of the absolute size of total investments to gross domestic product. It represents the importance of private pensions relative to the size of the economy. It also gives an indication of the maturity of the system.

Pension fund asset allocation: asset allocation data can be used to assess the extent of diversification of investments and the degree of matching of liabilities. Investment products are cash and deposits, bills and bonds issued in public and private sectors, loans, shares, lands and buildings, mutual funds, unallocated insurance contracts, private investment funds and other investments.

Active members as a percentage of the working population: ratio of the total number of active members of pension funds to the working population (total civilian employment).

Total members by type of status: the proportion of active and passive members in the total number of pension fund members. This allows calculation of the dependency ratio given by the ratio of active to passive members.

Contribution as a percentage of GDP: the ratio of total pension fund contributions to gross domestic product. It is an indicator of the rate of contribution to pension funds in each country, or "gross pension saving rate".

Total contributions by type of status: the proportion of payments made to pension plans by employers and employees in the total payments made to pension funds.

Benefits as a percentage of GDP: an indicator of economic output dedicated to paying pension fund benefits. It can be compared with public pension expenditure.

Average annual private retirement pension: an indicator of the benefits per person, calculated as a percentage of average salary. This ratio cannot be taken as a proxy of the quasi-replacement rate because benefits can be paid as lump sums

4 AN OVERVIEW OF OECD ECONOMIC STATISTICS

to the individual or paid out from the pension fund to an insurance company in order to be transformed into annuities.

Assets by type of plans: total assets breakdown by occupational and personal plans; defined benefit vs. defined contribution plans.

Figure 4.3.4 – **Importance of pension funds relative to the size of the economy in OECD countries**
As percentage of GDP, 2006

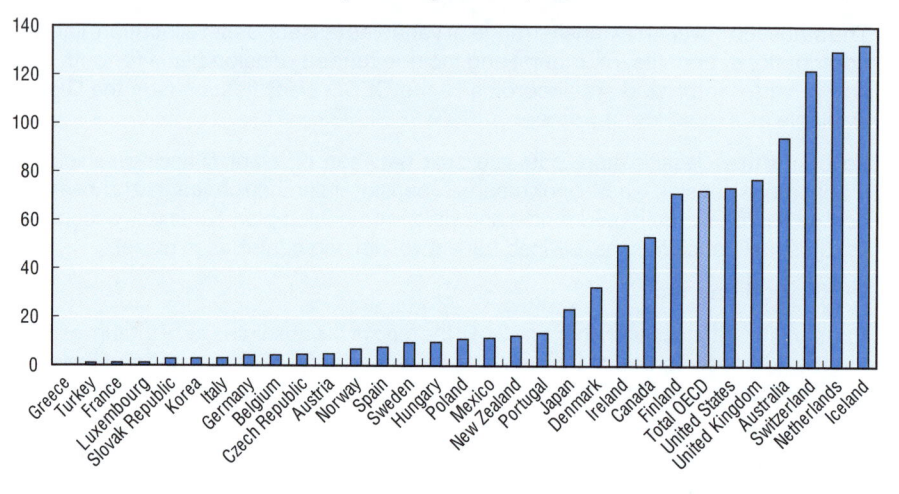

Sources: OECD (2006), *Pension Market in Focus,* October 2006, Issue 3, http://www.oecd.org/daf/pensions/pensionmarkets

Bank profitability

To assess the changes in the state of the health of national banking systems of OECD countries and to be able to determine their operating performance, policy makers, business managers, investors, lenders and analysts need detailed information on the financial statements of banks and on national financial systems. Statistics on bank profitability provide long basic data on the income statement and the balance sheet of a number of bank groupings in the OECD countries, as well as a number of financial ratios based on selected financial statement items over several years, so that comparisons between countries are made and important trends are spotted. This source also gives structural information of a general nature on the national financial systems and some additional data classified according to residence and currency (domestic or foreign).

Because of some differences in the structural and regulatory features of national banking systems, specific accounting rules and practices and various reporting methods, the statistics are not integrated in the System of National Accounts. However, they are based on a standard framework in which national data are grouped and/or re-classified.

AN OVERVIEW OF OECD ECONOMIC STATISTICS 4

▶ Key definitions

Bank groupings: institutions that conduct ordinary banking business, such as commercial banks, savings banks and co-operative banks; *i.e.* institutions that primarily take deposits from the public at large and provide financing for a wide range of purposes.

Income statement: otherwise known as a profit and loss statement, it is one of the major financial statements that all banks are required to prepare annually. It provides a record of an institution's revenues and expenses for a given period of time, and thus serves as the basic measuring stick of profitability.

Balance sheet: also known as the statement of financial position, it is a snapshot of a bank's financial condition at a single point in time. It presents a summary listing of the institution's assets, liabilities and owners' equity.

The OECD Product Market Regulation Database

The Product Market Regulation (PMR) Database contains a comprehensive and internationally comparable set of indicators about the state of regulation and market structures in OECD countries on the economy-wide and sectoral level. The term "regulation" here covers the diverse set of instruments by which governments impose requirements on enterprises and citizens, including laws, formal and informal orders, subordinate rules, administrative formalities and rules issued by non-governmental or self-regulatory bodies which have been delegated regulatory power by the government. Therefore, the PMR indicators measure the extent to which policy settings promote or inhibit competition in areas of the product market where competition is viable. The main sources of information used to construct the PMR indicators are the responses of OECD Member governments to the Regulatory Indicators Questionnaire and data published by the OECD and other international organisations.

The indicators included in the PMR indicator system are:

- **Indicators of economy wide regulation:** the indicators of product market regulation (PMR) are economy wide indicators of policy regimes in OECD countries and have been estimated for 1998 and 2003. These indicators summarise a wide array of different regulatory provisions across OECD countries.

- **Indicators of regulation in professional services:** the professional services indicators cover entry and conduct regulations in the legal, accounting, engineering and architecture professions and have been estimated for 1996 and 2003.

- **Regulation in retail trade:** The retail indicators have been estimated for 1998 and 2003.

- **Regulation in energy, transport and communications:** the indicators summarise regulatory provisions in seven sectors: electricity, gas, post, telecom, rail, air passenger transport and road. These indicators have been estimated for 21 OECD countries for the period 1975 to 2003.

4 AN OVERVIEW OF OECD ECONOMIC STATISTICS

- **Regulation impact:** sectoral indicators that measure the "knock-on" effects of regulation in non-manufacturing sectors on all sectors of the economy. These indicators have been estimated for the period 1975 to 2003 for 36 sectors in 21 OECD countries.

Figure 4.3.5 – **Product market regulation**
Restrictiveness of economy-wide product market regulation, 2003
Indicator scale of 0-6 from least to most restrictive

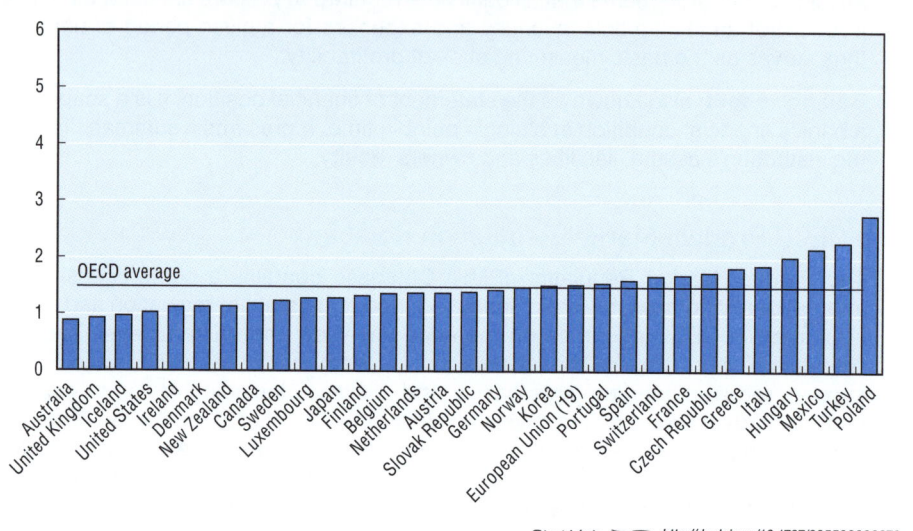

Source: OECD (2008), *Economic Policy Reforms: Going for Growth 2008*, OECD Publishing.

4. AN OVERVIEW OF OECD ECONOMIC STATISTICS

Further information

Publications

Ahmad, N. (2006), "A Proposed Framework for Business Demography Indicators", *OECD Statistics Directorate Working Papers*, OECD Publishing.

Birch, D. (1979), *The Job Generation Process*, MIT Program on Neighborhood and Regional Change, Cambridge.

Conway P. and Nicoletti G. (2006), "Product Market Regulation in Non-Manufacturing Sectors of OECD Countries: Measurement and Highligths", *OECD Economics Department Working Papers, No. 350*, OECD Publishing.

Eurostat, OECD (2007), *Eurostat-OECD Manual on Business Demography Statistics*, OECD Publishing.

OECD (2005), *Entrepreneurship: A Catalyst for Urban Regeneration*, Local Economic and Employment Development (LEED), OECD Publishing.

OECD (2005), *OECD SME and Entrepreneurship Outlook*, 2005 Edition, OECD Publishing.

OECD (2005), "Product Market Regulation in OECD Countries: 1998 to 2003, in *Econmic Policy Reforms: Going for Growth 2005*, OECD Publishing.

OECD (2006), *Structural and Demographic Business Statistics:1996-2003*, OECD Publishing.

OECD (2006), The *SME Financing Gap (Vol. I): Theory and Evidence*, OECD Publishing.

OECD (2007), *SMEs in Mexico: Issues and Policies*, OECD Publishing.

Vale, S. (2006), "The International Comparability of Business Start-Up Rates", *OECD Statistics Working Papers*, 2006/4, OECD Publishing.

Online databases

OECD Banking Statistics
OECD Global Pension Statistics
OECD Insurance Statistics
Available at *www.sourceoecd.org/database/oecdstat*

Websites

www.oecd.org/daf/pensions/gps
www.oecd .org/eco/pmr

4 AN OVERVIEW OF OECD ECONOMIC STATISTICS

4.4 General government

This section illustrates statistics available to describe some of the fundamental functions carried out by governments and other public institutions. It starts with the description of general government accounts, which provide a comprehensive picture of economic and financial flows created by the public sector's activities and represent a fundamental tool to guide the fiscal and the monetary policies. More detailed statistics compiled to analyse specific activities are also presented: the social expenditure database, which provides a detailed view of the government's expenditures for pensions, health and social assistance; the databases on revenues and taxing wages, which represent a fundamental tool for analysing how the fiscal policy is financed; finally, the central government debt database, which allows detailed evaluations of the impact of the government's operations on financial markets and on the sustainability of fiscal conditions in the long run.

General government accounts

General government accounts are an elaboration of the national accounts for the general government sector and are compiled from government finance statistics in accordance with the System of National Accounts 1993 (SNA 93). The accounts are presented by sub-sector: central government, state government, local government and social security funds. Note that public enterprises are excluded since they are not part of the general government sector.

The SNA 93 recommends that transactions be recorded on an accrual basis. This means that claims and liabilities, revenues and expenditure should be recorded according to their due amounts at the time when they are due, which is not necessarily when the cash flows occur. The OECD collects general government sector data from countries in the form of three harmonised tables: "main aggregates of general government"; "detailed taxes and social contributions receipts"; and "expenditure of general government by function".

The main indicator calculated using these data is the net borrowing/net lending of general government as a percentage of GDP. For EU countries, the deficit (or surplus) is defined as the balancing item "net lending/net borrowing" as per the EU's adaptation of SNA 93, the European System of Accounts 1995. Two other indicators are also often calculated: general government total expenditure as a percentage of GDP, and general government total revenue as a percentage of GDP.

▶ **Key definitions**

Final consumption expenditure: consists of expenditure earmarked for the non-market production of goods and services for collective consumption (security, justice, etc.) and for individual consumption (health care, housing, education, etc.), to which must be added government expenditure to finance goods and services provided to households by market producers.

Total revenue: equal to total sales (market output and output for own final use) and payments for non-market output plus subsidies (receivable) plus property income

AN OVERVIEW OF OECD ECONOMIC STATISTICS 4

(receivable) plus total taxes (receivable) plus total social contributions (receivable) plus other current transfers and capital transfers (receivable).

Total expenditure: calculated as intermediate consumption plus compensation of employees plus subsidies (payable) plus interest (payable) plus taxes (payable) plus social benefits and social transfers in kind (via market producers) plus current transfers and capital transfers (payable) plus an adjustment for the net equity of households in pension funds reserves plus gross capital formation and net acquisition of non-financial, non-produced assets.

Net borrowing/net lending: the final balancing item of the sequence of economic, "non-financial" accounts, resulting basically from current transactions and investment (gross capital formation). It is also equal to total revenue minus total expenditure. This is the most commonly referred to aggregate. In principle, it should be equal to the balancing item of the financial account. In practice, being calculated from different accounting sources, there is always a discrepancy. For the last few years, a discrepancy has existed between this variable and the European Union's (EU) corresponding variable called "excessive deficit procedure" deficit/surplus for EU Members of the OECD. In the latter, settlements on swap transactions are recorded as property income (interest), whereas they are recorded as financial transactions in the SNA.

Figure 4.4.1 – **Government net borrowing/net lending**
As a percentage of GDP, average 2004-2006

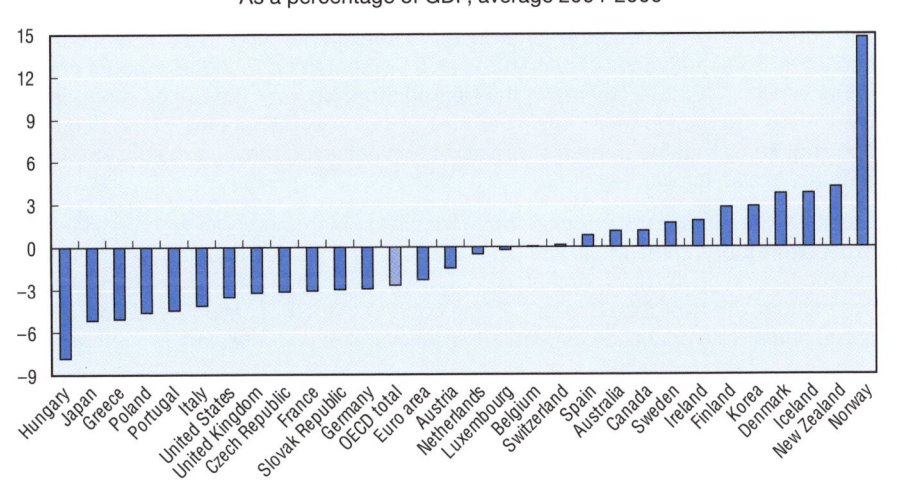

StatLink http://dx.doi.org/10.1787/335541273454

Source: OECD (2007), *OECD Economic Outlook*, Vol. 2007/2, No. 82, OECD Publishing.

Social expenditure

In principle, the SNA93 provides a comprehensive accounting framework for social expenditure and its financing. In practice, however, the aggregate nature of data in the SNA93 proved inadequate for analysis of social policies. As a result, the *OECD*

4. AN OVERVIEW OF OECD ECONOMIC STATISTICS

Social Expenditure Database (SOCX) was developed in the 1990s. The database includes reliable and internationally comparable statistics on public and (mandatory and voluntary) private social expenditure at the programme level. The 2007 version also includes, for the first time, estimates of net total social spending for 24 OECD countries. SOCX provides a unique tool for monitoring trends in aggregate social expenditure and analysing changes in its composition. The main social policy areas are as follows: old age, survivors, incapacity-related benefits; health; family; active labour market programmes; unemployment; housing; and other social policy areas.

Across OECD countries, gross public social expenditure has increased from about 16% of GDP in 1980 to 21% of GDP in 2003, on average. In Sweden, public social spending is about 31% of GDP, while it is 5% to 6% of GDP in Mexico and Korea. The largest categories of social spending are pensions (7% of GDP, on average), health (6%) and income transfers to the working-age population (5%). Spending on pensions accounts for more than 12% of GDP in Austria, France, Greece, Italy and Poland, and less than 4% in Australia, Iceland, Ireland, Korea, Mexico and Turkey.

From the perspective of society, net social expenditure (i.e. after tax), from both public and private sources, gives a better indication of the total resources used to pursue social goals than simply looking at gross public spending alone. On average, total net social expenditure accounted for 23% of GDP in 2003, ranging from more than 30% in France, Germany and Sweden to less than 10% in Korea and Mexico.

If private social benefits and the impact of the tax system are also taken into account, this considerably reduces the differences in social spending-to-GDP ratios across countries. Total net social expenditures as a percentage of national income are then rather similar in Austria, Denmark, the Netherlands, Norway, the United Kingdom and the United States. However, a similar size of net social spending across countries does not imply that the degree of redistribution achieved through the tax and benefit systems is also similar.

Other OECD databases provide more detailed information about specific public expenditure programmes. For example, in the context of the Health Database, data on total expenditure on health as a percentage of GDP or per capita, as well as pharmaceutical expenditure, are available. Similarly, in the context of the Education Database, data on public and private education expenditures are available. In particular:

- *The dataset on the expenditure by funding source and transaction type* consists of data concerning all entities that provide funds for education, either initially or as final payers, that are classified as either governmental (public) sources or non-governmental (private) sources, the sole exception being "international agencies and other foreign sources", which are treated as a separate category. There are three types of financial transactions: direct expenditure on educational institutions; transfers to students or households and to other private entities; households' expenditure on education outside educational institutions.

- *The dataset on expenditure by nature and resource category* consists of data on the distribution of education expenditure by the nature of expenditure (current and capital expenditure) and service provider (public institutions, government-dependent private institutions, and independent private institutions, i.e. both educational and other institutions). These expenditure figures are intended to represent the total cost of services provided by each type of institution, without regard to sources of funds (whether they are public or private).

Figure 4.4.2 – **Public social spending**
Selected countries as percentage of GDP, 1980-2003

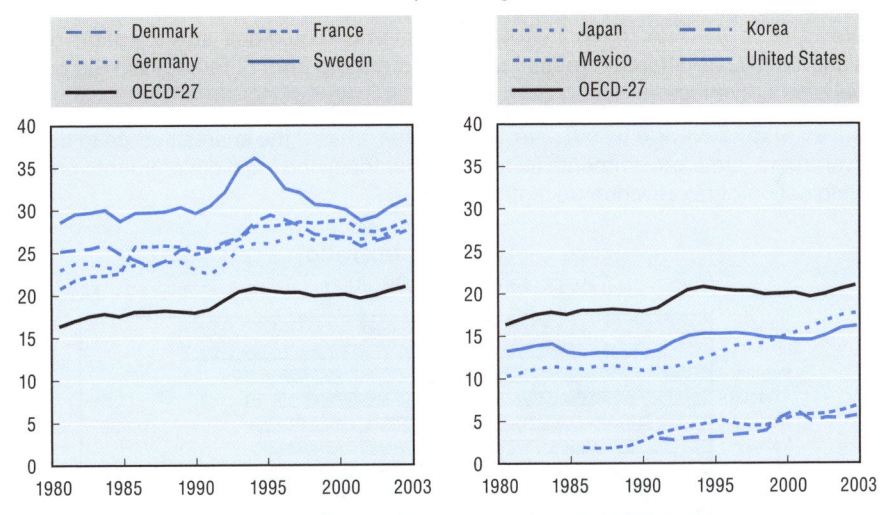

Note: Information for 1980 to 2003 is available for 22 countries, while information for the Czech Republic, Iceland, Korea, Mexico, and Poland is available from 1990 onwards. OECD-27 refers to an unweighted average of OECD countries, not including Hungary (data from 1999 onwards), Slovak Republic (data from 1995 onwards) and Turkey (no data since 2000).

Source: OECD (2007), *Social Expenditure Database 1980-2003*.

Revenue statistics

Statistics on tax revenues come from administrative sources, ultimately from tax administrations but usually transmitted through national statistical offices. Taxes are a form of payment to government but are distinguished from other payments by the fact that they are compulsory and unrequited (in the sense that the individual taxpayer does not receive something of equal value in exchange for the taxes paid). The OECD generally includes compulsory social security contributions in its measures of tax revenue because the link between an individual's contributions and benefits are not sufficiently strong to regard the contributions as requited. The OECD also includes taxes paid by government, such as social security contributions for government employees (but only if actual payments are made) and sales taxes on government purchases.

The OECD classifies taxes into six broad categories: taxes on income and profits; social security contributions; payroll taxes; property taxes; consumption taxes; other taxes. Each of these is further subdivided into more precise categories.

4. AN OVERVIEW OF OECD ECONOMIC STATISTICS

▶ **Key definitions**

Total tax to GDP ratio: provides an overall measure of the general level of taxation in the economy.

Ratios of revenues from individual taxes to GDP: provide useful detail that can be used to gauge, for example, if the impact of personal income tax is different from that of consumption taxes.

Shares of individual taxes in total tax revenue: provides an indication of the balance between different types of taxes, abstracting from differences in the overall level of tax revenues.

Shares of tax revenue by sub-sector of government: the shares that go to central government, state governments (in federal countries) and local governments provide an indication of tax revenue decentralisation.

Figure 4.4.3 – **Total tax ratio**
As percentage of GDP, 2005

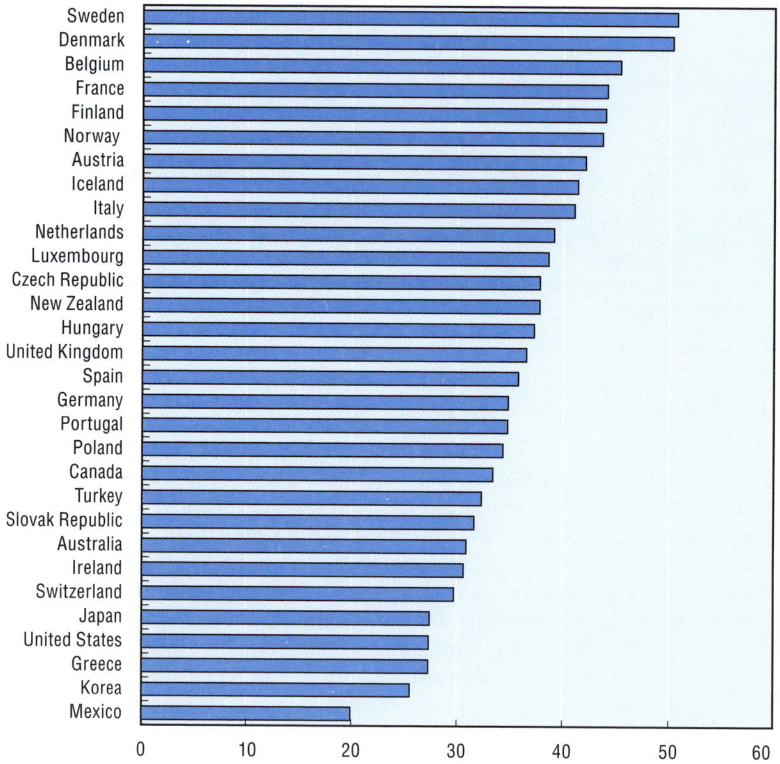

Source: OECD (2007), *Revenue Statistics 1965-2006*, OECD Publishing.

StatLink http://dx.doi.org/10.1787/335555122651

Taxing wages

The OECD's *Taxing Wages* data measure the tax burden on labour supplied by a small number of 'typical families'. The tax burden includes personal income tax, employers' and employees' social security contributions and payroll taxes. Universal family benefits paid in cash for dependent children are treated as negative taxes. The data are obtained by using the tax laws to calculate the taxes that are legally due for each family, based on its demographic composition and the earnings of its members.

There are eight household types: single individuals with no children earning 67%, 100% and 167% of average wages; a lone parent with two children earning 67% of average wages; a married couple with two children and a single earner at 100% of average wages; two-earner married couples, one partner earning 100% and the other 33% of average wages, with two children and without children; a two-earner married couple, one partner earning 100% and the other 67% of average wages, with two children.

▶ **Key definitions**

The tax wedge: personal income tax, social security contributions plus payroll taxes as a percentage of labour costs (the wage plus employers' social security contributions and payroll taxes). This represents the difference between the cost of labour to the employer and the amount that the worker receives after tax. The marginal rate of these taxes as labour costs increase is also calculated.

Personal tax: personal income tax and employees' social security contributions as a percentage of the wage. This represents the taxes levied directly on the worker. The marginal rate of these taxes as wages increase is also calculated.

Personal income tax: personal income tax as a percentage of the wage.

4 AN OVERVIEW OF OECD ECONOMIC STATISTICS

Table 4.4.1 – **Tax burden**
Income tax plus employee and employer contributions less cash benefits as a % of labour costs
Single persons without children at 100% of average earnings, 2000-2006

	2000	2001	2002	2003	2004	2005	2006
Australia	30.6	27.3	27.7	28.0	28.0	28.3	28.1
Austria	47.3	46.9	47.1	47.4	48.1	47.9	48.1
Belgium	57.1	56.7	56.3	55.7	55.4	55.4	55.4
Canada	33.2	32.0	32.1	32.0	32.0	31.9	32.1
Czech Republic	42.7	42.6	42.9	43.2	43.5	43.8	42.6
Denmark	44.3	43.6	42.6	42.6	41.3	41.1	41.3
Finland	47.8	46.4	45.9	45.0	44.5	44.6	44.1
France	49.6	49.8	49.8	49.8	49.9	50.1	50.2
Germany	54.0	53.0	53.5	54.2	53.2	52.4	52.5
Greece	38.4	38.1	37.7	37.7	39.5	40.4	41.2
Hungary	54.6	55.8	53.7	50.8	51.8	51.1	51.0
Iceland	26.1	26.9	28.4	29.2	29.4	29.0	28.6
Ireland[1]	28.9	25.8	24.5	24.2	25.0	23.5	23.1
Italy	46.4	46.0	46.0	45.0	45.4	45.4	45.2
Japan	24.8	24.9	30.5	27.4	27.3	27.7	28.8
Korea[1]	16.4	16.4	16.1	16.3	17.2	17.3	18.1
Luxembourg	38.6	37.0	34.2	34.7	35.1	35.9	36.5
Mexico	12.6	13.2	15.8	16.8	15.3	14.7	15.0
Netherlands	39.7	37.2	37.4	37.1	38.8	38.9	44.4
New Zealand	19.4	19.4	19.5	19.7	20.0	20.4	20.9
Norway	38.6	39.2	38.6	38.1	38.1	37.2	37.3
Poland	43.2	42.9	42.9	43.1	43.4	43.5	43.7
Portugal	37.3	36.4	36.6	36.8	36.8	36.3	36.3
Slovak Republic	41.8	42.8	42.5	42.9	42.5	38.3	38.5
Spain	38.6	38.8	39.1	38.5	38.7	38.9	39.1
Sweden	50.1	49.1	47.8	48.2	48.4	48.1	47.9
Switzerland	30.0	30.1	30.1	29.7	29.4	29.5	29.7
Turkey[1]	40.4	43.6	42.5	42.2	42.8	42.8	42.8
United Kingdom	32.2	31.9	32.0	33.5	33.6	33.7	33.9
United States	29.5	29.4	29.2	29.0	29.0	28.9	28.9
Unweighted average:							
OECD	37.8	37.4	37.4	37.3	37.4	37.2	37.5
EU-15	43.4	42.4	42.0	42.0	42.2	42.2	42.6
EU-19	43.8	43.2	42.8	42.7	42.9	42.6	42.9

StatLink http://dx.doi.org/10.1787/336464573762

1. Ireland, Korea and Turkey wage figures are based on the old definition of average worker (ISIC D, rev3.)

Source: OECD (2006), *Taxing Wages 2005-2006*, OECD Publishing.

Central government debt

To finance their deficits, governments issue via financial markets various debt instruments such as bonds, Treasury bills and commercial papers. Debt instruments attract both institutional and retail investors and represent an important share in the portfolios of fund managers. Raising funds through marketable instruments depends on factors like access to well-functioning primary and secondary markets (in particular market liquidity) and the presence of well-developed market segments – institutional and retail investors. The OECD Central Government Debt statistics refer to quantitative information on marketable central government debt instruments in all OECD member countries, excluding state and local government debt and the Social Security Fund. Sources of these statistics are the debt-management offices and the central banks of OECD member countries.

Data refer to both resident and non-resident holdings. The maturity structure of the debt instruments relates to residual maturity instead of initial maturity. The method of valuation is either nominal value or market value.

▶ **Key definitions**

Central government: consists of the institutional units making up the central government plus those NPIs (non-profit institutions) controlled and mainly financed by central government. The political authority of central government extends over the entire economy. Central government has therefore the authority to impose taxes on all resident and non-resident units engaged in economic activities within the country.

Market value: the actual price agreed upon by buyers and sellers. Assets and liabilities are valued at the prices prevailing at the time they were recorded on the balance sheet, not at their original prices.

Nominal value: value of a security at issue.

Maturity and residual maturity: maturity is the period of time until the redemption or expiration of a financial instrument. Residual maturity is the time remaining until the expiration or the repayment of the instrument.

Central government debt as a percentage of GDP: the ratio between the central government debt and the GDP is useful for comparing the level of central government debt across OECD countries.

Government-issued bonds as a percentage of total marketable debt: the share of central government-issued bonds in the domestic market for debt instruments. Around 90% of central government borrowing requirements are met through such financing.

Marketable central government debt by type of investor: share of marketable central government debt held by residents and non-residents.

4 AN OVERVIEW OF OECD ECONOMIC STATISTICS

Table 4.4.2 – **Central government debt**
As a percentage of GDP, 1995-2005

	1995	1996	1997	1998	1999	2000	2001	2002	2003	2004	2005
Australia	19.1	19.7	19.0	16.0	14.1	11.7	9.8	8.9	7.8	6.9	6.5
Austria	55.9	56.6	58.7	59.4	61.4	60.4	59.7	59.9	59.9	61.1	61.4
Belgium	113.7	112.6	109.9	105.4	103.6	99.7	99.3	98.2	95.8	93.6	93.2
Canada	56.8	56.3	52.7	50.1	46.7	40.9	39.7	38.1	35.8	32.1	30.4
Czech Republic	10.5	9.4	9.4	9.9	11.2	13.5	14.9	16.4	19.3	21.4	23.6
Denmark	74.9	72.9	69.1	64.0	60.9	54.8	52.0	51.6	49.3	46.9	39.1
Finland	62.5	66.6	64.7	59.5	56.3	48.5	45.3	42.1	44.0	42.6	38.7
France	41.5	44.0	45.6	46.3	47.8	47.4	48.4	49.9	51.9	52.6	53.8
Germany	21.1	22.9	24.3	26.1	34.1	34.1	34.6	36.0	37.7	39.1	40.3
Greece	114.9	118.5	115.3	113.6	113.4	119.3	120.7	119.2	117.3	119.5	119.0
Hungary	83.7	71.0	62.4	60.7	60.0	54.5	51.5	54.5	56.8	56.8	58.5
Iceland	52.3	49.8	46.3	41.0	35.5	34.1	39.6	36.0	33.9	28.6	20.0
Ireland	72.2	64.6	57.2	47.7	44.0	35.0	30.9	27.9	27.0	25.5	23.8
Italy	113.1	113.6	111.0	108.7	106.7	103.6	102.7	99.5	96.6	96.2	98.4
Japan	65.6	69.3	77.0	88.0	97.7	106.2	123.9	137.5	141.2	156.9	163.7
Korea	8.9	8.2	10.3	14.8	16.9	17.4	18.2	18.5	21.9	25.2	29.6
Luxembourg	2.6	3.4	3.7	4.1	3.5	3.2	3.1	2.7	1.7	1.5	0.9
Mexico	40.8	31.1	25.7	27.8	25.6	23.2	22.5	24.0	24.2	23.0	22.4
Netherlands	57.1	56.1	53.0	51.1	48.8	43.9	41.3	41.5	43.0	44.0	42.8
New Zealand	49.7	42.7	36.7	38.4	35.5	32.6	30.4	28.8	27.0	24.2	22.7
Norway	31.0	27.7	24.9	22.4	21.0	19.5	18.3	19.2	21.6	18.7	17.5
Poland	49.6	43.9	43.0	39.5	39.7	35.8	36.4	40.6	45.0	43.7	45.0
Portugal	61.9	61.3	58.0	54.8	55.2	54.1	56.0	58.7	60.6	63.5	69.1
Slovak Republic	19.1	18.5	21.0	22.7	22.8	24.0	36.4	35.4	35.7	39.4	34.2
Spain	52.4	56.1	54.7	52.9	51.7	49.9	46.3	44.0	40.8	39.4	36.5
Sweden	76.9	79.1	75.1	73.4	65.2	58.3	50.2	48.5	49.3	48.3	48.0
Switzerland	22.1	24.2	25.5	28.1	25.7	26.0	25.3	28.4	28.5	28.4	28.5
Turkey	17.5	45.0	44.2	41.7	53.8	50.5	99.7	87.4	78.6	73.5	67.8
United Kingdom	..	..	..	50.8	45.1	43.4	39.8	40.2	39.9	41.5	45.6
United States	49.2	48.0	45.5	42.8	39.4	34.4	33.0	33.8	35.4	36.5	36.5

StatLink http://dx.doi.org/10.1787/336476116034

Source: OECD (2006), *Central Government Debt: Statistical Yearbook 1996-2005*, OECD Publishing.

AN OVERVIEW OF OECD ECONOMIC STATISTICS   4

Further information

Publications
OECD (2007), *National Accounts of OECD Countries*, OECD Publishing.
OECD (2007), *OECD Economic Surveys*, OECD Publishing.
OECD (2007), *Revenue Statistics 1965-2006*, OECD Publishing.
OECD (2007), *Society at a Glance: OECD Social Indicators*, OECD Publishing.
OECD (2007), *Taxing Wages 2006-2007, 2007 Edition: Special Feature: Tax reforms and tax burdens 2000-2006*, OECD Publishing.

Online databases
National Accounts of OECD Countries.
OECD Economic Outlook Statistics.
Finance, available at *www.sourceoecd.org/database/oecdstat.*
OECD Social Expenditure, available at *www.sourceoecd.org/database/oecdstat.*
OECD Tax Statistics (Revenue Statistics and Taxing Wages).

Websites
www.oecd.org/eco/sources-and-methods
www.oecd.org/ctp/taxingwages
www.oecd.org/els/social/expenditure
www.oecd.org/std/finance

4.5 Science, technology and innovation

Over the last 20 years, the OECD has been extremely active in developing statistical standards in the area of science, technology and innovation. Through its working groups, the Organisation has co-ordinated the development of several handbooks, widely used in all continents by national statistical offices and other government agencies, and data collection on very innovative and policy relevant issues. This section provides an overview of areas for which developmental and data collection work started several years ago (research and development statistics, innovation statistics, ICT statistics) and areas where the work was launched more recently or is still in an exploratory phase (biotechnology and patents).

Research and development

Since research and experimental development (R&D) and innovation are increasingly recognised as key elements of the knowledge-based economy, the collection of reliable and comparable statistics to monitor the R&D efforts of countries and firms is of crucial importance. Statistics on R&D have been collected in OECD countries since the 1960s. They are used to measure inputs into the innovation process in terms of expenditure and personnel.

The collection of these statistics has been guided by the OECD *Frascati Manual*, which was first published in 1963 and is currently in its 6th edition (OECD, 2002). The *Frascati Manual* has become a worldwide standard for R&D surveys and is part of a wider family of methodological manuals covering a wide range of science and technology indicators, including manuals on R&D (*Frascati Manual*), innovation (*Oslo Manual*), human resources (*Canberra Manual*), and the technological balance of payments and patents.

R&D is defined as "creative work undertaken on a systematic basis in order to increase the stock of knowledge, including knowledge of man, culture and society, and the use of this stock of knowledge to devise new applications". The term R&D covers the following three activities:

- *Basic research:* experimental or theoretical work undertaken primarily to acquire new knowledge of the underlying foundation of phenomena and observable facts;

- *Applied research:* original investigation undertaken in order to acquire new knowledge, but directed primarily towards a specific practical aim or objective; and

- *Experimental development:* systematic work drawing on existing knowledge gained from research and/or practical experience which is directed to producing new materials, products or devices, to installing new processes, systems or services, or to improving substantially those already produced or installed.

The basic measure used is *intramural expenditure*, which refers to all expenditure for R&D performed within a statistical unit or sector of the economy. A secondary measure used is *extramural expenditure* which covers payment for R&D performed outside the statistical unit or sector of the economy. Both current costs and capital expenditure are included, while depreciation costs are excluded. In the case of the government sector, expenditures refer to *direct* rather than indirect expenditure, so for example, R&D tax credits are excluded.

In order to avoid double-counting, R&D surveys generally trace the flows of funds based on replies from R&D *performers* instead of relying on the sources of the funds, although in some cases, funder-based measures are used (for example, government R&D budgets). For international and temporal comparisons the *Frascati Manual* recommends using purchasing power parities (PPP) and the implicit gross domestic product (GDP) deflator, although it is recognized that these reflect the opportunity cost of the resources involved rather than the "real" amounts. Since the latest revision of the System of National Accounts (SNA 93) recommends that R&D be treated as capital formation (and no longer as current expenditure), capital measures for R&D (including R&D deflators and depreciation) are currently being constructed in many countries, although these are usually outside the scope of R&D surveys.

In addition to expenditure data, personnel data are used to measure the resources that go directly into R&D activities, although it is sometimes difficult to isolate the R&D activities of ancillary staff from those of other R&D staff. Three main approaches are used in the measurement of R&D personnel: headcounts; R&D activities in full-time equivalents; and the characteristics of personnel. Headcount data allow simple linkages with other series, such as education or employment data, or results from population censuses. Such data (with a breakdown by gender, age or nationality) are used for analytical studies and can support labour or education policies. Headcount data refer to the number of persons engaged in R&D at a given date (e.g. end of the calendar period), or to the average number of persons employed during the calendar year, or the total number of persons employed during that year.

Full-time equivalence (FTE) data constitute a preferred measure for assessing the volume of R&D performed in a country. R&D may sometimes be the primary function of some employees (e.g. a researcher in an R&D lab), while for others it could be a secondary activity (e.g. members of a design and testing establishment), or a part-time activity (e.g. university teachers or post-graduate students). To count only persons whose primary function is R&D would result in an under-estimate of true R&D efforts, while a headcount of all of those undertaking some type of R&D activity would result in an over-estimate. This is why FTE data is preferred for certain types of analysis. One FTE corresponds to one person-year; therefore, a person working 30% of his/her time on R&D would be counted as 0.3 FTE. In some cases, it may be more practical to survey the FTE of R&D personnel as of a specific date, but if there are significant seasonal variations, allowance should be made for this and data adjusted for a full year. Countries use different adjustment methods, such as R&D coefficients, to identify and allocate the R&D content of the work of various persons and produce aggregate figures.

In terms of the *characteristics* of R&D personnel, the *Frascati Manual* recommends that gender and age be collected, and to the extent possible, occupation and qualification, as well as region.

4 AN OVERVIEW OF OECD ECONOMIC STATISTICS

▶ **Key definitions**

Gross domestic expenditure on R&D (GERD): total intramural expenditure on R&D performed on the national territory during a given period. Similar measures are BERD (for R&D performed in the business sector), HERD (in the higher education sector) and GOVERD (in the Government sector).

Gross national expenditure on R&D (GNERD): total expenditure on R&D financed by a country's institutions during a given period. This includes R&D performed abroad but financed nationally and excludes R&D performed within a country but funded from abroad.

Government Budget Appropriations or Outlays for R&D (GBAORD): covers the budgets of central or federal government as well as those of provincial or state governments when these are significant, but excludes local government funds. It includes all government-funded R&D regardless of the sector of performance.

R&D intensity: measured by the ratio GERD/GDP.

AN OVERVIEW OF OECD ECONOMIC STATISTICS 4

Figure 4.5.1 – **R&D intensity**
Gross domestic expenditure on R&D as a percentage of GDP, 2005 or latest available year

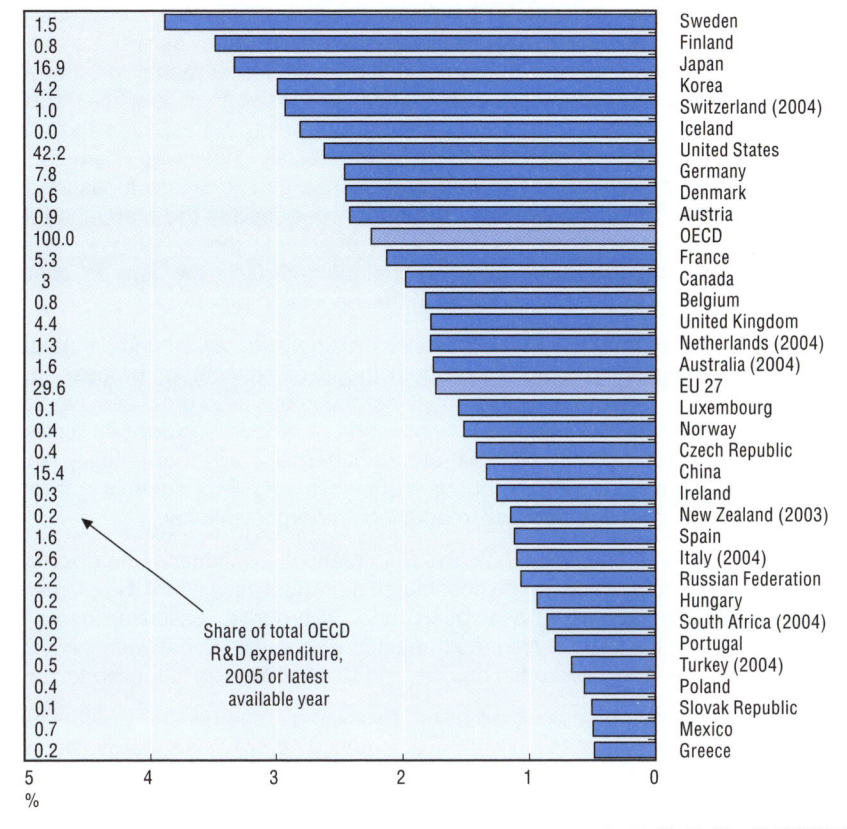

Share of total OECD R&D expenditure, 2005 or latest available year	Country
1.5	Sweden
0.8	Finland
16.9	Japan
4.2	Korea
1.0	Switzerland (2004)
0.0	Iceland
42.2	United States
7.8	Germany
0.6	Denmark
0.9	Austria
100.0	OECD
5.3	France
3	Canada
0.8	Belgium
4.4	United Kingdom
1.3	Netherlands (2004)
1.6	Australia (2004)
29.6	EU 27
0.1	Luxembourg
0.4	Norway
0.4	Czech Republic
15.4	China
0.3	Ireland
0.2	New Zealand (2003)
1.6	Spain
2.6	Italy (2004)
2.2	Russian Federation
0.2	Hungary
0.6	South Africa (2004)
0.2	Portugal
0.5	Turkey (2004)
0.4	Poland
0.1	Slovak Republic
0.7	Mexico
0.2	Greece

StatLink ⟶ http://dx.doi.org/10.1787/335582876018
Sources: OECD (2007), *Main Science & Technology Indicators 2007/1*, OECD Publishing.

Innovation

It has been long understood that the generation, exploitation and diffusion of knowledge are fundamental to economic growth, development and the well being of nations. Central to this is the need for reliable statistical measures of *innovation*. During the 1980s and 1990s, a considerable body of work was undertaken to develop models and analytical frameworks for the study of innovation. This led to the development of the *Oslo Manual*, the first edition of which was published in 1992 and focused on technological product and process (TPP) innovation in the manufacturing sector. The goal of the *Manual* has been to provide a harmonized set of concepts and tools for countries to develop their own innovation surveys in a comparable way. This became the reference for many large-scale surveys examining the nature and impacts of innovation in the business sector, in particular the European Community Innovation Survey (CIS), which was first undertaken in 1992.

The framework of the Oslo Manual has continued evolving. Its scope has been extended to better analyse innovation in the service sectors, as well as to "non-technological" innovation, and the latest edition includes an annex on innovation surveys in developing countries. The Manual proposes to follow the "subject" approach, which considers the firm as the central point and explores the various factors influencing its innovative behaviour (strategies, incentives, barriers, etc.) This is in contrast with "object"-based approaches that focus on measuring and characterizing individual innovations. The framework used in the Manual attempts to integrate insights from various schools of economic theory, ranging from the Schumpeterian "creative destruction" model centered on the firm to systemic approaches that focus on dynamic links in the innovation process.

The latest edition of the Oslo Manual defines an *innovation* as: "the implementation of a new or significantly improved product (good or service), or process, a new marketing method, or a new organizational method in business practices, workplace organisation or external relations". Innovation activities include all scientific, technological, organizational, financial and commercial steps that actually lead, or are intended to lead, to the *implementation* of innovations. Four types of innovations are distinguished: product, process, marketing and organizational.

When collecting data on innovations, the Oslo Manual recommends an observation period of 1-3 years, *i.e.* a firm will be considered a product innovator if it implements at least one innovation during the observation period. In order to measure an innovation's degree of novelty, the Manual also recommends distinguishing between innovations that are new to the firm, new to the market, and if possible, new to the world.

Several indicators can be calculated using, for example: the number of firms having introduced a product/process innovation, or a marketing/organizational innovation (as a percentage of innovative firms, or as a percentage of all firms); the expenditure on innovation by type of activity (intramural/extramural R&D, acquisition of machinery, training, etc.); the sources of knowledge and types of linkages (internal or external; open sources vs. acquisition vs. cooperation); the share of turnover from new-to-market product innovations; the impact of process innovation on costs; and the relative importance of different types of factors (cost, knowledge, market, institutional) for both innovators and non-innovators.

AN OVERVIEW OF OECD ECONOMIC STATISTICS 4

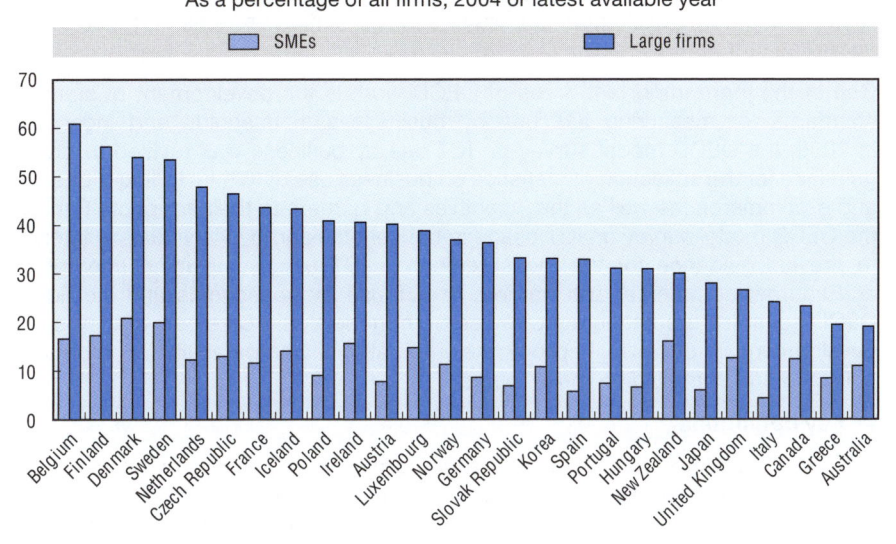

Figure 4.5.2 – **Firms collaborating in innovation activities, by size**
As a percentage of all firms, 2004 or latest available year

Sources: OECD (2007), *Science, Technology and Industry: Scoreboard 2007*, OECD Publishing.

Information and communication technology

For more than a decade, information and communication technology (ICT) has promoted profound economic and social change. The need for statistics and analysis to support and inform policy making in this area has grown in parallel. Since 1997, the OECD has been working to establish a set of definitions and methodologies that facilitate the compilation of internationally comparable data for measuring various aspects of the information society, the information economy and electronic commerce. Data for the ICT sector and other related phenomena are gradually becoming available for a growing number of countries, but the available time series are relatively short.

Correct measurement of ICT investment is crucial for estimating the contribution of ICT to economic growth and performance. Data availability and measurement of ICT investment based on national accounts (SNA93) vary considerably across OECD countries. In particular, it is only very recently that expenditure on software has been treated as capital expenditure in the national accounts, and methodologies still vary considerably across countries. To tackle the specific problems relating to software in the context of the SNA93 revision of the national accounts, OECD and Eurostat have jointly developed recommendations concerning the capitalisation of software. These are now being implemented by OECD countries.

A classification of ICT sector and products has also been developed to facilitate the construction of internationally comparable indicators on ICT consumption,

4. AN OVERVIEW OF OECD ECONOMIC STATISTICS

investment, trade and production. As far as ICT infrastructure is concerned, data cover areas such as telecommunication network, broadband diffusion, Internet network and traffic exchange, access to communication services and their quality, as well as tariffs.

One of the more important areas of OECD work is the development of statistical standards for measuring ICT use by businesses, households and individuals. In 2006, the OECD model survey on ICT use by business was revised to provide guidance for the collection of statistics on business use of ICT, including e-business and e-commerce, as well as the incentives and barriers to their adoption. Similarly, the OECD model survey on ICT usage in households and by individuals is intended to provide guidance for the measurement of ICT usage (including Internet use and Internet commerce) and barriers to ICT use by households and individuals. OECD countries are encouraged to use both models as a core part of their survey development in order to improve the international comparability of information collected and compiled on these topics.

▶ **Key definitions**

ICT sector: a combination of manufacturing and services industries whose products capture, transmit or display data and information electronically. The definition, originally based on the ISIC Rev. 3 industry classification, has just been revised according to ISIC Rev. 4.

ICT products: the guiding principles for defining ICT products are based on those for the ICT sector. However, ICT sector and ICT products are not in a one-to-one relationship: some enterprises classified to the ICT sector do not only produce ICT goods; conversely, ICT goods can originate from non-ICT industries.

ICT skills: although there is not any commonly adopted definition of ICT skills and there is no internationally agreed list of ICT related occupations, the OECD has adopted, as interim solution, a narrow and a broad definition of ICT-skilled employment, which includes ICT specialists, who have the capabilities to develop, operate and maintain ICT systems. In addition to ICT specialists, the broader definition comprises also advanced and basic users, for whom ICTs are not their main job but a tool.

E-commerce transactions: sale or purchase of goods or services, whether between businesses, households, individuals, governments and other public or private organisations, conducted over computer-mediated networks. The goods and services are ordered over those networks, but the payment and the ultimate delivery of the good or service may be conducted on or offline.

AN OVERVIEW OF OECD ECONOMIC STATISTICS 4

Table 4.5.1 – **Percentage of enterprises' total turnover from e-commerce**
2003-2006[1,2]

	2003	2004	2005	2006
Ireland	16.6	18.3	20.2	16.7
Denmark	7.5	12.2	..	17.5
United Kingdom	11.9	14.3	15.6	17.4
France	..	..	..	16.7
Norway	6.2	7.5	14.7	13.9
Finland[3]	10.6	12.7	14.2	14.3
Germany	..	11.3	13.0	13.9
Sweden	12.3	..	..	13.6
Austria	6.3	6.8	7.0	9.9
Belgium	7.0	6.5	8.8	7.9
Czech Republic	5.7	5.9	8.4	7.1
Portugal	1.6	4.9	..	8.2
Iceland	5.9	..	..	8.0
Hungary	..	..	..	7.0
Spain	2.1	2.9	2.7	6.9
Poland	..	2.8	4.4	5.9
Italy	1.9	3.4	2.1	2.0
Greece	0.9	1.6	2.1	2.8

StatLink ⟶ http://dx.doi.org/10.1787/336568367287

1. Enterprises in the following industries are included: Manufacturing, construction, wholesale and retail, hotels and restaurants, transport, storage & communication, real estate, renting and business activities, and other community, social and personal service activities.
2. Total sales via Internet or other networks during reference year, excluding VAT.
3. For 2006, networks other than Internet: only EDI.

Source: Eurostat, *Community Survey on ICT usage in enterprises*, April 2007

4. AN OVERVIEW OF OECD ECONOMIC STATISTICS

> **Measuring the information society**
>
> The last two decades have witnessed the widespread adoption of a great number of ICT technologies, notably the personal computer, the cell phone and the Internet. ICT permeates every aspect of life – economic, social, political, cultural and otherwise – and has created great interest regarding its actual and potential impact.
>
> The OECD's Guide to Measuring the Information Society proposes a comprehensive conceptual model for information society statistics. In particular, it considers three features:
>
> - **E-readiness:** preparing the technical, economic and social infrastructures necessary to support ICT. E-readiness indicators allow each country to construct a statistical picture of the state of readiness of the infrastructure necessary to engage in ICT-activities. Indicators of e-readiness include: access to computers and the Internet; telecommunication networks (fixed channels, mobile, DSL and cable) and prices; investment in ICT equipment and software; ICT occupations and skills; ICT-related patents and R&D.
>
> - **E-intensity:** the state of ICT use, volume, value and nature of the transactions. E-intensity indicators permit countries to profile who is exploiting ICT possibilities and who is not, and to identify leading sectors and applications. Internet subscribers, Internet hosts and domain names, Internet use by households and individuals; e-business; value of e-commerce sales are part of the e-intensity statistics.
>
> - **E-impact:** Policy makers need statistics to evaluate whether, and to what extent, ICT makes a difference in terms of efficiency and the creation of new sources of wealth. Macro-economic indicators measure the contribution of the ICT sector to growth in GDP, trade and employment. Several OECD projects have generated estimates for the impact of ICT investment on labour productivity and ICT diffusion on multi-factor productivity (MFP) growth. New statistical work is currently ongoing to measure the social impact of ICT, particularly through e-health, e-training, e-government and e-crime.

Biotechnology

Biotechnology consists of a collection of related technologies with pervasive applications in many different economic sectors, including agriculture, forestry, aquaculture, mining, petroleum refining, environmental remediation, human and animal health, food processing, chemicals, security systems, and many different industrial processes. It is precisely the range of current and potential applications of biotechnology, together with their economic, environmental and social impacts, that creates a policy interest in creating high-quality economic and innovation indicators for biotechnology.

However, unlike ICT or other technologies, biotechnology lacks a core "sector" that can be quickly identified and surveyed. This has created major challenges for developing comparable biotechnology indicators (for example, national differences in the definition of biotechnology, the fields of application for biotechnology and of a biotechnology firm). To address these issues, the OECD developed a *Framework*

AN OVERVIEW OF OECD ECONOMIC STATISTICS 4

for Biotechnology Statistics, which provides guidance for the collection of data on biotechnology. In particular, both a single and a list based definition of biotechnology have been developed. The single definition of biotechnology, deliberately broad, covers all modern biotechnology but also many traditional or borderline activities (for this reason, the single definition should always be accompanied by the list-based definition). The OECD definition of biotechnology is: the application of science and technology to living organisms, as well as parts, products and models thereof, to alter living or non-living materials for the production of knowledge, goods and services.

The OECD list-based definition of biotechnology includes seven categories, and respondents are usually given a write-in option for new biotechnologies that do not fit any of the categories. A firm that reports activity in one or more of the categories is defined as a biotechnology firm. The seven categories include: DNA/RNA, proteins and other molecules, cell and tissue culture and engineering, process biotechnology techniques, gene and RNA vectors, bioinformatics and nanobiotechnology. Most countries now use the OECD list-based definition of biotechnology or similar definitions that focus on modern biotechnologies. However, full comparability has not yet been reached, due to different methods of constructing sample frames and dealing with survey non-response. The methodological similarities and differences of the national biotechnology surveys are summarised in *OECD Biotechnology Statistics 2006*.

▶ **Key definitions**

Biotechnology-active firm: a firm engaged in key biotechnology activities, such as the application of at least one biotechnology technique (as defined in the OECD list-based definition of biotechnology techniques) to produce goods or services and/or the performance of biotechnology R&D. The number of biotechnology firms is the most widely available indicator, although it is not the best measure of a country's biotechnology effort, due to large differences in the size of individual firms.

Dedicated biotechnology firm: a biotechnology-active firm whose predominant activity involves the application of biotechnology techniques to produce goods or services and/or the performance of biotechnology R&D. These firms are a subset of the biotechnology active firms.

Biotechnology Research & Development: R&D into biotechnology techniques, biotechnology products or biotechnology processes, in accordance with both the OECD biotechnology definition and the Frascati Manual for the measurement of R&D.

Public sector biotechnology R&D: public R&D in biotechnology techniques, biotechnology products or biotechnology processes.

Biotechnology employment: employment involved in the generation of biotechnology products. Included are all employees that have biotechnology related responsibilities in R&D, production, administration or management.

Biotechnology sales: revenues generated from the sale (or transfer) of biotechnology products (including knowledge products). It is thus generally a subset of the total revenue earned by biotechnology firms.

4 AN OVERVIEW OF OECD ECONOMIC STATISTICS

Biotechnology applications: the field in which the firm applies biotechnology techniques, biotechnology products or biotechnology processes. Biotechnology has applications in many fields, including human and animal health, agriculture, fishing and forestry, food processing, industrial processing, and natural resource extraction, including energy. Although the definition of the fields of application differs across countries, it is possible to create three main fields of application that are generally comparable across countries: health, agro-food, and industrial-environmental applications. Health includes both human and animal health, agro-food includes all agricultural applications plus fishing, silviculture and food processing; and industry-environmental includes industrial processing, natural resources and environmental applications. In addition, an "other" category covers services and platform technologies, such as bioinformatics, plus other application fields not included in the three main categories in some countries.

Figure 4.5.3 – **Total expenditures on biotechnology R&D by biotechnology-active firms**

Millions of USD PPP (current), 2004 or latest available year

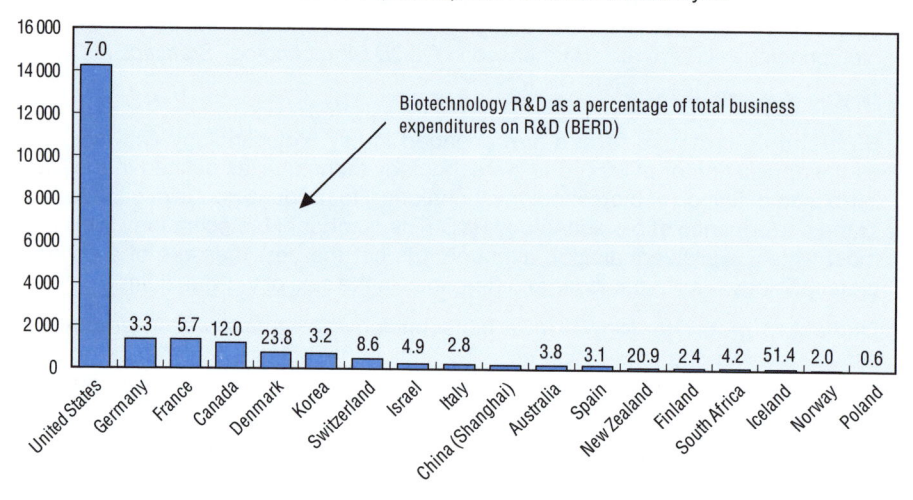

Biotechnology R&D as a percentage of total business expenditures on R&D (BERD)

United States 7.0; Germany 3.3; France 5.7; Canada 12.0; Denmark 23.8; Korea 3.2; Switzerland 8.6; Israel 4.9; Italy 2.8; China (Shanghai); Australia 3.8; Spain 3.1; New Zealand 20.9; Finland 2.4; South Africa 4.2; Iceland 51.4; Norway 2.0; Poland 0.6

StatLink http://dx.doi.org/10.1787/335645331710

Source: OECD (2007), *Science, Technology and Industry: Scoreboard 2007*, OECD Publishing.

Patents

Measuring the output and quantifying scientific and technological processes is important to the design and assessment of related policies. Statistics can help in answering fundamental policy questions, such as: "to what extent are companies inventive?" "What is the importance of international technology transfers?" or "What is the role of company networks in the innovation process?" Patents provide extremely useful information that can help answer such questions. Filing a patent means that the research project has resulted in some invention. In addition, patent documents include valuable information, like the name and address of the inventor and of the owner (usually a business or university), the technological category of the invention, the date of filing (considered to be close to the date of invention), citations to prior art (the sources of the invention), etc. In addition, patent data are available for nearly all countries in the world.

Patent databases are constituted by patent offices for the purpose of administering the patent system. They consist in millions of records, corresponding to patent applications filed each year. Hence the marginal cost for statisticians of using this data is relatively low. In addition, patent information is public, hence raising no legal obstacles to access worldwide. The value of patent data is increased when the data are cleaned and harmonized properly, so they can be readily used by statisticians.

Patent indicators need to be carefully designed and interpreted, since patents are generated by complex legal and administrative processes and are influenced by sophisticated business strategies. Failing to controlling for these factors can result in biased or meaningless statistics. For instance, it is irrelevant to compare the numbers of patents issued in two different countries, since legal criteria for issuing patents are country specific.

Background information on patent data and guidelines for compiling and interpreting indicators are reported in the *OECD Partent Manual* (forthcoming).

▶ **Key definitions**

Patent: a legal title protecting an invention, conferring to its owner the right to exclude others from using in any manner the invention without the owner's consent on a given territory. Patents are issued by national patent offices, which grant them under particular conditions relating notably to the novelty of the invention.

Patent Co-operation Treaty (PCT): a unified procedure for filing patent applications to protect inventions abroad. A PCT application is an international, preliminary application to a patent, which may be followed by national applications at a later stage.

4 AN OVERVIEW OF OECD ECONOMIC STATISTICS

Figure 4.5.4 – **Share of countries in nanotechnology patents filed under PCT** [1]
2004

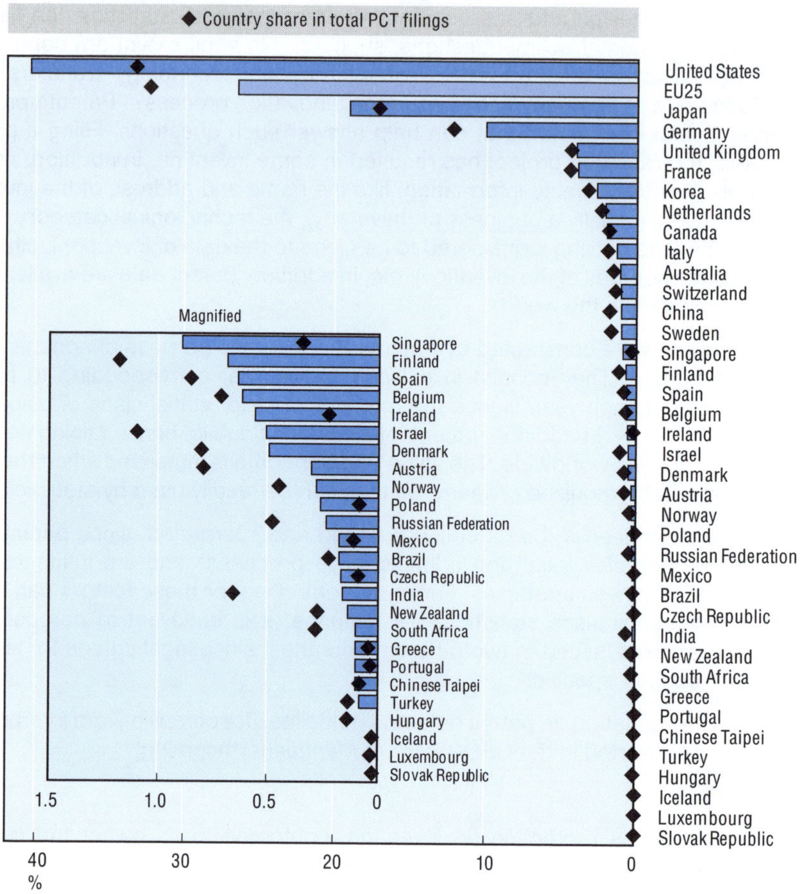

♦ Country share in total PCT filings

United States	
EU25	
Japan	
Germany	
United Kingdom	
France	
Korea	
Netherlands	
Canada	
Italy	
Australia	
Switzerland	
China	
Sweden	
Singapore	
Finland	
Spain	
Belgium	
Ireland	
Israel	
Denmark	
Austria	
Norway	
Poland	
Russian Federation	
Mexico	
Brazil	
Czech Republic	
India	
New Zealand	
South Africa	
Greece	
Portugal	
Chinese Taipei	
Turkey	
Hungary	
Iceland	
Luxembourg	
Slovak Republic	

StatLink http://dx.doi.org/10.1787/335686838251

1. Patent applications filed under the Patent Co-operation Treaty, at international phase, designating the European Patent Office.

Source: OECD (2007), *Science, Technology and Industry: Scoreboard 2007*, OECD Publishing.

AN OVERVIEW OF OECD ECONOMIC STATISTICS 4

Further information

Publications
OECD (2002), *Frascati Manual: Proposed Standard Practice for Surveys on Research and Experimental Development*, OECD Publishing.
OECD/Eurostat (2005), *Oslo Manual – Guidelines for collecting and interpreting innovation data, 3rd edition*, OECD publishing/European Communities.
OECD (2005) *Guide to Measuring the Information Society*, OECD Publishing.
OECD (2006), *Biotechnology Statistics 2006*, OECD Publishing.
OECD (2006), *Information Technology Outlook 2006*, OECD Publishing.
OECD (2007), *Communications Outlook 2007*, OECD Publishing.
OECD (2007), *Main Science & Technology Indicators 2007/1*, OECD Publishing.
OECD (2007), *OECD Science, Technology and Industry: Scoreboard 2007*, OECD Publishing.
OECD (2007), *Compendium of Patent Statistics 2007*, OECD Publishing.
OECD (2008, forthcoming), *Patent Manual*, OECD publishing.

Online databases
OECD Science, Technology and R&D Statistics, available at *www.sourceoecd.org/database/oecdstat*

Websites
www.oecd.org/sti/biotechnology/framework
www.oecd.org/sti/biotechnology/inventory
www.oecd.org/sti/frascatimanual
www.oecd.org/sti/ICTindicators
www.oecd.org/sti/ipr-statistics
www.oecd.org/sti/measuring-scitech
www.oecd.org/sti/oslomanual

4 AN OVERVIEW OF OECD ECONOMIC STATISTICS

4.6 Globalisation

The term "globalisation" has been widely used to describe the increasing internationalisation of financial markets and of markets for goods and services, as well as other production factors (i.e. labour). Globalisation refers above all to a dynamic and multidimensional process of economic integration whereby national resources become more and more internationally mobile while national economies become increasingly interdependent. Traditional statistics no longer suffice to analyse fully the magnitude and consequences of globalisation, and they need to be supplemented by, and combined with, other indicators. Therefore, the OECD developed a wide range of statistics and indicators to provide a more comprehensive portrait of globalisation.

The OECD Handbook on Globalisation

The Handbook on Economic Globalisation Indicators is devoted to measuring the magnitude of the globalisation process and its economic impact, a task which encompasses a potentially large number of areas. Priority was given to all the above driving forces of globalization. The first chapter of the Handbook sets out to **define the concept of economic globalisation**. It also proposes a limited list of reference indicators based on the current availability of the underlying data and policy issues.

The second chapter concerns **foreign direct investment**. It reviews the basic concepts and definitions that apply, including references to the existing manuals, namely the IMF Balance of Payments Manual (5th edition) and the OECD Benchmark Definition of Foreign Direct Investment (3rd edition). It also gives an overview of the data that are currently available and their possible extension, and discusses the main indicators related to international investment.

The third chapter deals with the **economic activity of multinational enterprises**. It develops all the concepts and definitions regarding multinationals, notably the concept of control of an enterprise and the identification of the country of residence of the parent company or the investor which has the ultimate control over its activities. Building on national statistical agencies' best practices, pragmatic and operational recommendations will be made in order to enhance international comparability of indicators and basic data.

The fourth chapter is devoted to the **internationalisation of technology**. Several forms of internationalisation are analysed: the internationalisation of R&D, technological balance of payments and trade in high-technology products.

The fifth chapter deals with certain aspects of the **globalisation of trade**. It focuses on several aspects of the role multinational firms play in international trade, particularly intra-firm trade, as well as other indicators provided on shifts in the structure of international trade, such as intra-industry trade, trade in intermediate goods, intra- and extra- regional trade, methods of evaluating trade balances based on capital ownership and the measurement of international subcontracting.

AN OVERVIEW OF OECD ECONOMIC STATISTICS 4

As far as the economic dimension of globalisation is concerned, three main domains have to be considered: international trade; foreign direct investment; and the activities of multinationals. Moreover, mobility of the labour force is fundamental to understanding how the global economy works nowadays. Therefore, migration statistics are also considered in this section, although they are not usually considered a branch of economic statistics. Finally, the section also considers statistics on aid flows, a fundamental tool for monitoring policies carried out to support the development of poorer countries.

International trade

International trade in goods and services is a major component of the globalisation process. It is a principal channel of economic integration and a driver for economic growth. Overall trade can represent very significant amounts, exceeding sometimes that of GDP. Trade in goods typically represents over two-thirds of total trade, but trade in services is catching up.

According to United Nations guidelines, international merchandise trade statistics are customs-based and record all goods that add to, or subtract, from a country's stock of material resources by entering (imports) or leaving (exports) its economic territory. Goods simply being transported through a country, or goods temporarily admitted or withdrawn (except for goods for inward or outward processing), are not included in the international merchandise trade statistics. The complex nature of customs and statistical needs necessitate a very detailed commodity classification. The Harmonized Commodity Description and Coding System (Harmonized System, or HS) provides such details. While this nomenclature is based on the nature of the commodity, the Standard International Trade Classification, Revision 3 (SITC, Rev.3), which classifies commodities according to their stage of production, is also used and is considered more suitable for economic analysis.

All OECD countries use the United Nations guidelines, so far as their data sources allow. Depending on the trade system in use (general or special), there may be differences across countries in coverage. In the general trade system, the statistical territory coincides with the economic territory; while under the narrower special trade system, only traded goods in free circulation are recorded. The introduction by the European Union of the single market in 1993 resulted in some loss of accuracy for intra-EU trade because customs documents were no longer available to record all imports and exports. VAT declarations are used instead. Note that while the OECD data mostly follow the UN recommendations, trade statistics reported by Eurostat follow the Community definitions. As a result, OECD trade statistics for European Union countries are not strictly comparable with those reported by Eurostat.

International trade in services is growing in importance around the world. Traditional services – transport and insurance on merchandise trade, as well as travel – account for about half of total international trade in services. But trade in newer types of services, particularly those that can be conducted via the Internet, is growing rapidly.

4. AN OVERVIEW OF OECD ECONOMIC STATISTICS

International trade in services is defined according to the 5th edition of the *IMF Balance of Payments Manual* (BPM5) as service transactions between residents and non-residents of an economy. Services include transport (both freight and passengers), travel (mainly expenditure on goods and services by tourists and business travellers), communications services (postal, courier and telecommunications), construction services, insurance and financial services, computer and information services, royalties and licence fees, other business services (merchanting, operational leasing, professional and technical services, etc.), personal, cultural and recreational services and government services not included in the list above.

Trade negotiators take a broader view of international trade in services, including issues of market access, that is not strictly confined to international trade in the economic sense. Thus, in addition to balance of payments trade, they may also wish to know about delivery of services through the commercial presence of foreign-owned affiliates or through the presence of foreign persons. Both the balance of payments view and the broader view are elaborated in the Manual on Statistics of International Trade in Services (MSITS), jointly published by various international organisations.

BPM5 was issued in 1993 and countries began to implement it in the mid-1990s. MSITS was published in 2002 and implementation has been progressing steadily since. The comparability of trade in services data within the balance of payments has been improved by the application of these standards, by use of partner-country data and comparative methodological studies. Data on sales of services by foreign-owned affiliates are increasingly available, but are less well-developed and less well-harmonized than those from the balance of payments.

Growth in merchandise trade 1996 – 2006 was marked by very fast growth in the BRIC economies (Brazil, Russian Federation, India and China) and in smaller, often central-European, OECD countries. The weight of OECD countries in world trade declined during this decade, from 74% to 67%, and that of G7 countries from 49% to 41%. Between 2000 and 2005, the fastest-growing OECD exports in services were computer and information services, financial, insurance services and other business services.

▶ **Key definitions**

Exports are usually valued *free on board* (f.o.b.), and **imports** are valued by most countries at *cost, insurance and freight* (c.i.f.), *i.e.* the cost of the goods plus the costs of insurance and freight to bring the goods to the borders of the importing country.

Trade-to-GDP-ratio: the sum of exports and imports divided by GDP, this ratio measures a country's "openness" or "integration" into the world economy. It represents the combined weight of total trade in a the overall economy, a measure of the degree of dependence of domestic producers on foreign markets and their trade orientation (for exports), and the degree to which domestic demand relies on the foreign supply of goods (for imports). It should be noted that this indicator can also be expressed as the average of exports and imports (not as the sum of both).

AN OVERVIEW OF OECD ECONOMIC STATISTICS 4

Figure 4.6.1 – **Relative growth of exports of goods**
Growth over the period 1996-2006, OECD total = 1

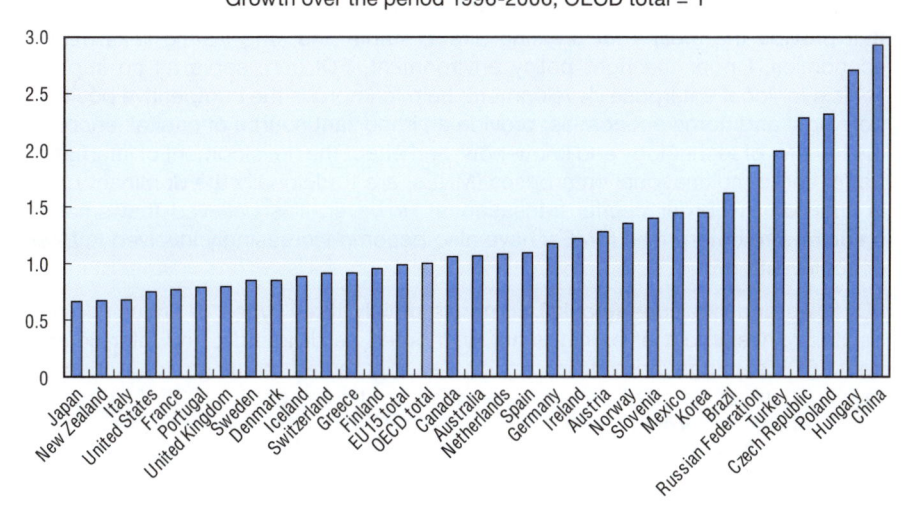

Sources: OECD (2007), *International Trade by Commodity Statistics*, OECD Publishing.
UN, *Commodity Trade Statistics Database*.

Figure 4.6.2 – **Relative annual growth in exports of services**
Growth over the period 1997-2006, OECD total = 1

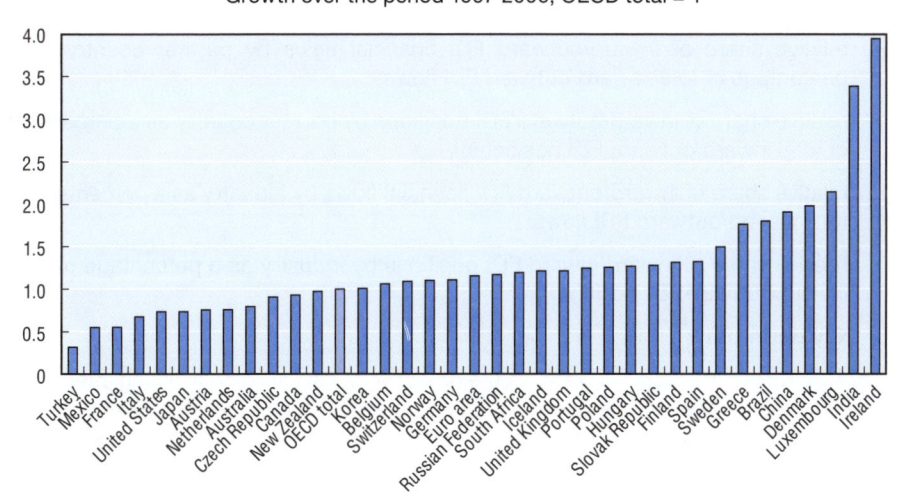

Source: OECD (2007), *Statistics on International Trade in Services*, OECD Publishing.

UNDERSTANDING ECONOMIC STATISTICS – ISBN 978-92-64-03312-2 – © OECD 2008   123

4 AN OVERVIEW OF OECD ECONOMIC STATISTICS

Foreign direct investment

Foreign direct investment (FDI) statistics measure cross-border investments that provide the means for creating direct, stable and long-lasting links between economies. Under the right policy environment, FDI can: serve as an important vehicle for local enterprise development; help to improve the competitive position of both host and home economies; provide an important source of capital; encourage the transfer of technology and know-how; and effect the development of international trade. Large multinational enterprises (MNEs) are traditionally the dominant players in such cross-border capital transactions. However, it is believed that small and medium-size enterprises (SMEs) have also become increasingly involved in foreign direct investment.

FDI flows and positions (stocks) comprise mainly three types of financing: equity capital; reinvestment of earnings not distributed as dividends; and inter-company debt. FDI earnings arise from equity, *i.e.* distributed earnings (dividends) and reinvestment of earnings in that enterprise; and from debt. OECD FDI statistics are compiled according to the *Benchmark Definition of Foreign Direct Investment* (see box) and are based on national statistics broken down by partner country and industrial activity according to ISIC.Rev.3.

FDI-based indicators are among the most widely available and commonly used measures of globalisation. For example, to measure the extent of globalisation through FDI (total FDI or by industry), inward/outward FDI financial flows, income flows and FDI positions are divided by GDP. To measure the contribution of host and investing economies or of industries to globalisation through FDI, the following indicators are calculated:

- relative share of inward/outward FDI financial flows by partner country as a percentage of total inward/outward FDI flows;
- relative share of inward/outward FDI positions by partner country as a percentage of total inward/outward FDI positions;
- relative share of inward/outward FDI financial flows by industry as a percentage of total inward/outward FDI flows;
- relative share of inward/inward FDI positions by industry as a percentage of total inward/outward FDI position.

▶ **Key definitions**

Foreign direct investment: reflects the objective of establishing a lasting interest by a resident enterprise in one economy *(direct investor)* in an enterprise resident in an economy other than that of the investor *(direct investment enterprise)*. For statistical consistency, the ownership of 10% or more of the voting power of a resident enterprise by a non-resident investor is the evidence of a long-term relationship between the direct investor and the direct investment enterprise and a significant degree of influence on the management of the enterprise.

AN OVERVIEW OF OECD ECONOMIC STATISTICS 4

Foreign direct investor: an entity that has a direct investment enterprise resident in an economy other than the economy of residence of the foreign direct investor. A direct investor could be: an individual; a group of related individuals; an incorporated or unincorporated enterprise; a public or private enterprise; a group of related enterprises; a government; estates, trusts and other organisations that own a direct investment enterprise; or any combination of the above.

Direct investment enterprise: an incorporated enterprise (a subsidiary or associate company) or an unincorporated enterprise (including a branch) in which a non-resident investor owns 10% or more of the voting power of the incorporated enterprise, or the equivalent of the unincorporated enterprise.

Direct investment positions (stocks of investment): provide, for a given reference date, information on the total stock of investment made by an investing country abroad, or investment received at a given point in time. These data allow a structural analysis of investments by partner country and by industry.

Direct investment financial transactions: show the net FDI inflows and outflows with assets (acquisitions less disposals/redemptions) and liabilities (incurrence less discharges), presented separately by instrument (equity, debt) in any given reference period.

Direct investment income: provides information on the earnings of direct investors and of the direct investment enterprises. The concept of income is closely related to direct investment positions since it is the size of the overall investment that produces the income, not just the most recent transactions. Income relates to recent performance and allows short-term analysis of investment activity.

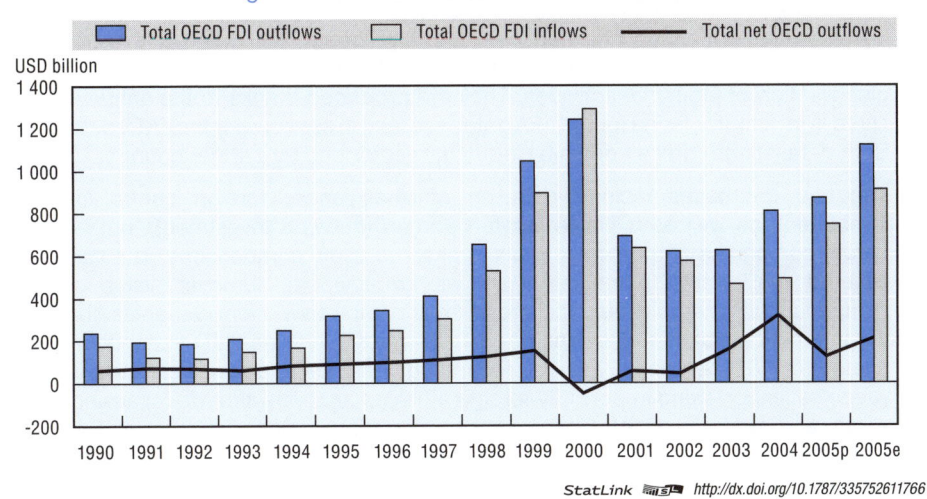

Figure 4.6.3 – **FDI Flows to and from OECD**

p: provisional.
e: estimated value.
Source: OECD (2006), *International Direct Investment Statistics Yearbook*, OECD Publishing.

4. AN OVERVIEW OF OECD ECONOMIC STATISTICS

> **OECD Benchmark Definition of Foreign Direct Investment**
>
> The *Benchmark Definition of Foreign Direct Investment (Benchmark Definition)* sets the world standard for direct investment statistics since it is fully compatible with the underlying concepts and definitions of the *IMF Balance of Payments Manual (BPM)*. The main focus is FDI statistics encompassing direct investment positions and related direct investment financial and income flows.
>
> In terms of detail and breakdowns, the *Benchmark Definition* goes beyond the aggregate statistics of the functional category "direct investment" of the balance of payments financial account and of the international investment position. To support these recommendations, the *Benchmark Definition* provides guidance on how to compile comprehensive breakdowns by partner country. The revised version completed in 2008 provides guidance on new data breakdowns, such as mergers and acquisitions, pass-through funds (via special purpose entities), and direct investment positions by ultimate investing country. By setting the global standard for FDI measurement, the *Benchmark Definition* complements the *OECD Handbook on Economic Globalisation Indicators*.
>
> The *Benchmark Definition* aims to meet a number of objectives, including: a single point of reference for FDI statistics; clear guidance for countries developing or changing their statistical systems for recording direct investment; international standards for FDI taking into account the effects of globalisation; a better basis for economic analysis of direct investment; practical guidance to users of direct investment statistics, including the relations of FDI to other measures of globalisation; and an objective basis for measuring methodological differences that may exist between partner country national statistics.

Activity of multinationals

The Activities of Foreign Affiliates (AFA) and the Foreign Affiliates Trade in Services (FATS) databases have been created in the framework of OECD work on the globalisation of industrial activities. They are produced thanks to the annual OECD surveys in manufacturing for the AFA database, and in services for the FATS database. Both datasets are broken down by industrial sector and by partner country.

The two databases include data on affiliates under foreign control (inward investment) as well as affiliates located abroad (outward investment), but also on parent companies and national totals in order to allow comparisons. The variables covered are: activity variables (such as employment, turnover, value added, compensation of employees and gross fixed capital formation); variables linked to the internationalisation of science and technology (such as R&D expenditure and number of R&D personnel, but also technology balance of payments); trade-related variables (exports and imports by foreign affiliates and intra-firm trade) arranged by sector and not by product. Unlike data on direct investment flows, which cover all transactions representing more than 10% of firms' capital, data on the activity of affiliates are based on the notion of control.

While data on the manufacturing sector have been available since the beginning of the 1980s, the OECD did not start collecting data on the activity of affiliates in services until the second half of the 1990s, and data are not yet available for all OECD countries. There are more variables covered in the AFA than in the FATS database, but the latter includes more partner countries. The number of countries having data on the activities of their affiliates abroad is more limited, as is the number of variables collected.

▶ **Key definitions**

Control of an enterprise: implies the ability to appoint a majority of administrators empowered to direct an enterprise, to guide its activities and determine its strategy. In most cases, this ability can be exercised by a single investor holding a majority (more than 50%) of the shares with voting rights. The notion of control allows all of a company's activities to be attributed to the controlling investor. This means that variables such as a company's turnover, staff or exports are all attributed to the controlling investor and the country from which he comes.

Foreign affiliate: restricted to affiliates under foreign control that are majority-owned. Accordingly, the geographical origin of a foreign affiliate is the country of residence of the ultimate controller. An investor (company or individual) is considered to be the investor of ultimate control if it is at the head of a chain of companies and controls directly or indirectly all the enterprises in the chain without itself being controlled by any other company or individual.

The share of foreign affiliates in employment: the ratio between employment by foreign affiliates and total employment in the compiling country. Employment data can be used to determine the share of affiliates under foreign control in host country employment, or to help determine the extent to which employment by affiliates under foreign control complements or substitutes for domestic (home country) employment by parent companies or other domestic firms.

Share of foreign affiliates in turnover: the ratio between turnover by foreign affiliates and total turnover in the compiling country. Unlike value added, turnover indicates the extent to which affiliates under foreign control are used to deliver outputs originating in the affiliates themselves or in other firms.

Share of R&D expenditure performed by foreign affiliates: it shows the share of industrial R&D under foreign control and that which is controlled by the residents of the compiling countries. It is aimed at measuring the growing internationalisation of R&D activities of multinational firms linked to an increase in the number of R&D laboratories located abroad.

Share of intra-firm trade in the total trade of a country: intra-firm trade refers to trade between enterprises belonging to the same group, located in different countries. For inward investment, the ratio of intra-firm trade to the total trade of countries publishing the relevant data is quite high. Once foreign investments have been made, these transactions reflect centralised decisions made as part of a group's global strategy. This indicator can also be calculated in terms of total trade by affiliates under foreign control.

4. AN OVERVIEW OF OECD ECONOMIC STATISTICS

Figure 4.6.4 – **Employment in manufacturing and services in affiliates under foreign control**
As a percentage of total employment, 2005 or latest available year

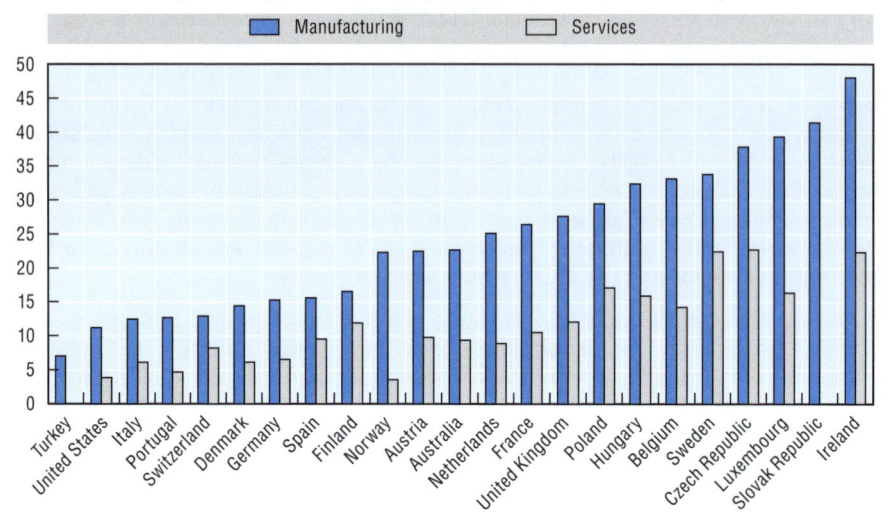

Source: OECD (2007), *OECD Science, Technology and Industry: Scoreboard 2007*, OECD Publishing.

Migration statistics

Since the end of the 1990s, issues related to international migration have received increasing attention from policy makers. This reflects, among other things, the increasing international movements that have taken place following the fall of the Iron Curtain and the growing globalisation of economic activity. In addition, demographic imbalances between developed and developing countries and large differences in real wages have tended to encourage, today as in the past, the movements of workers from economies where they are in surplus to those where they are most in need. Until recently, it has been difficult to provide an accurate and comparative overview of stocks of migrants and of migration flows in OECD countries because commonly used data sources do not all define the migration phenomenon in the same way.

To improve the international comparability of migration statistics, the OECD created in 2005 a new database on the immigrant population by country of residence, country of birth and educational attainment. This database compiles OECD population censuses and register data around the year 2000. For the first time, it provides a picture of brain drain/brain exchange, both within OECD countries and from non-OECD countries to the OECD area (based on estimates of emigration rates), based on demographics and educational attainment. After release of the first version of the database, the follow-up was expanded to include more data on demographic labour force characteristics, such as occupation and sector, field of study and year of arrival.

A preliminary set of standardised statistics on permanent-type migration flows, compiled and published for the first time in 2006, has been recently updated. An extension is currently being created to cover temporary movements.

In addition, the OECD International Migration Database contains annual series on foreign and foreign-born populations, migration flows (inflows into/outflows from selected OECD countries) and naturalisations. It also includes statistics on the employment status of foreigners and foreign-born by gender for selected years. These data are published in the annual report *International Migration Outlook*. This report also include country notes describing recent trends in migration movements and policies, including standardised tables on migration flows and stocks, macroeconomic indicators such as real GDP, components of population growth and labour market outcomes.

Figure 4.6.5 – **Foreign-born persons with tertiary attainment**
As a percentage of all residents with tertiary attainment, circa 2000

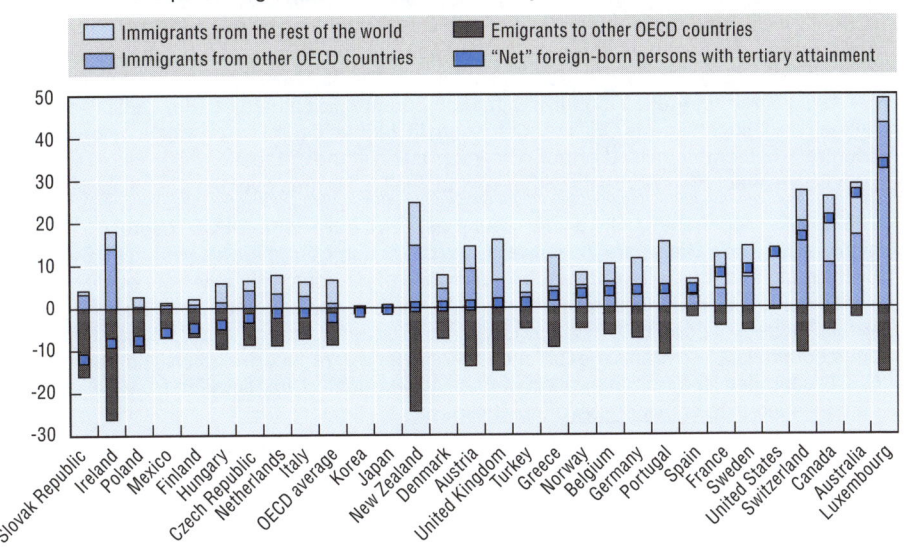

StatLink http://dx.doi.org/10.1787/335841121510

Source: OECD (2007), *International Migration Statistics*, OECD Publishing.

4. AN OVERVIEW OF OECD ECONOMIC STATISTICS

> **International mobility of the highly skilled: the "brain circulation"**
>
> The issue of the extent of gains (or losses) from international migration is one that periodically comes to the forefront of policy agendas. Countries are afraid of losing their "best and brightest" to movements abroad, whether for study or for longer-term expatriation, if not always permanent settlement. On the other hand, countries that recruit significant numbers of highly educated persons from developing countries are accused of contributing to brain drain from these countries and of hampering their economic development.
>
> Concern with "brain drain" is not limited to developing countries. It arose in a number of European countries in the late 1990s, when it was feared that many high technology graduates were leaving their home countries for high-paying jobs elsewhere, especially in the United States. Concern arises periodically when statistics are published on international students abroad or on the emigration of highly educated persons. Rarely evoked are the gains from immigration of the highly educated.
>
> Until recently, there was little information on the actual extent of movement and on the net balance between immigration and emigration of persons with university qualifications. This is why a few years ago the OECD launched a special census data collection, whose data are now included in the International Migration Database. Most censuses in member countries were conducted around 2000, and the results are currently available for almost all of them. Several countries, however, do not have a population census, so data from population registers or from large sample surveys have been used instead. The database currently includes data on the foreign-born in OECD countries by place of birth, nationality and educational attainment (three levels), and new data on employment by occupation have recently become available. These figures concern the number of native and foreign-born persons with tertiary education living in each country. Expatriates in the OECD area are defined as residents in any OECD country born in another OECD country or in a non-OECD country, whether naturalised or not. The information in the database therefore reflects the cumulative effect of movements within, and to, the OECD area over the past decades.
>
> The results show that only a few countries gain from intra-OECD migration of the highly educated. These are Australia, Canada, Luxembourg, Norway, Spain, Sweden, Switzerland and the United States. If immigration of persons with university qualifications from outside the OECD is factored in, however, the balance becomes significantly positive for another set of countries, including Belgium, Germany, Greece and Portugal. For most other countries, the negative net balance is considerably reduced. In short, although many OECD countries lose from migration of the highly educated, immigration from developing countries tends to considerably offset the loss.

AN OVERVIEW OF OECD ECONOMIC STATISTICS 4

Development aid statistics

Statistics on financial flows to developing countries are reported to the OECD by the 23 members of the Development Assistance Committee (DAC), international organisations and some non-DAC donor countries (although reporting may vary from year to year for these donors). Reporting is usually carried out by the country's official aid agency, and is based on common definitions and standard classifications agreed by the DAC and the DAC Working Party on Statistics.

The most important statistical category in the measurement of development aid is official development assistance (ODA). ODA activities are financed through grants and "soft" (or concessional) loans to countries on the DAC List of ODA Recipients and have the promotion of economic development and welfare of recipient countries as their main objective. ODA also includes some expenditures which occur in the donor country such as administrative costs, some support to students from developing countries, aid to refugees in the donor country and the promotion of development awareness.

Most donor countries have committed to reaching the ODA target of 0.7% of donors' GNI, which was adopted by the United Nations in 1970, and has become a benchmark of aid policy. However, as the Figure below shows, in 2006 only five countries met this target. Several other international targets exist in respect to ODA, notably more recent ones set at the G8 Gleneagles summit and UN Millennium +5 summits in 2005, where donors committed to increase their aid. The pledges made at these summits, combined with other commitments, implied lifting aid from USD 80 billion in 2004 to USD 130 billion in 2010 (at 2004 prices and exchange rates).

A series of targets has also been agreed to for aid to the least-developed countries (LDCs), the best known being an undertaking to spend 0.15% of donors' national income on this group.

DAC data also address types and quality of aid provided. Types of aid include investment projects, programme aid, technical cooperation, cash and commodity aid, humanitarian aid and debt relief. An important measure of aid quality is the degree to which procurement is tied to the donor country's goods and services. The DAC Recommendation on untying ODA to the least developed countries has increased the amount of aid that is untied, so as to ensure value for the money spent in aid procurement. DAC members have also gradually improved the terms on which they offer aid: the vast majority of aid is now given as grants.

The data are available on-line through an interactive database which comprises the DAC annual aggregate statistics and the Creditor Reporting System on individual aid activities.

4. AN OVERVIEW OF OECD ECONOMIC STATISTICS

Figure 4.6.6 – **Net ODA in 2006**
As a percentage of gross national income (GNI)

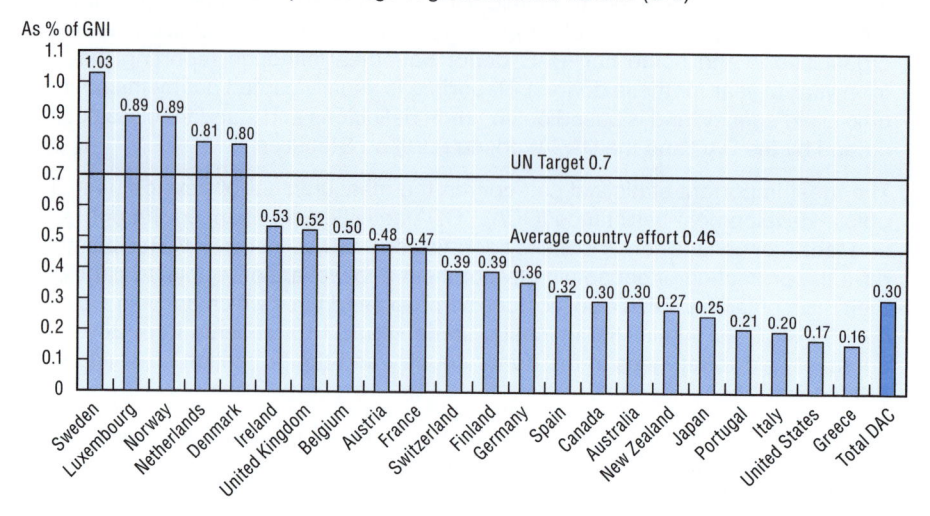

Country	As % of GNI
Sweden	1.03
Luxembourg	0.89
Norway	0.89
Netherlands	0.81
Denmark	0.80
Ireland	0.53
United Kingdom	0.52
Belgium	0.50
Austria	0.48
France	0.47
Switzerland	0.39
Finland	0.39
Germany	0.36
Spain	0.32
Canada	0.30
Australia	0.30
New Zealand	0.27
Japan	0.25
Portugal	0.21
Italy	0.20
United States	0.17
Greece	0.16
Total DAC	0.30

UN Target 0.7
Average country effort 0.46

StatLink http://dx.doi.org/10.1787/335850520144

Sources: OECD (2007), *Geographical Distribution of Financial Flows to Aid Recipients, 2001-2005*, OECD Publishing.
OECD (2008), *OECD Journal on Development: Development Co-operation Report 2007, Statistical Annex*, OECD Publishing.

AN OVERVIEW OF OECD ECONOMIC STATISTICS 4

Further information

Publications
Lindner, A., et al. (2001), "Trade in Goods and Services: Statistical Trends and Measurement Challenges", *OECD Statistics Brief*, No. 1, OECD Publishing, www.oecd.org/std/statisticsbrief.
IMF (1993), *Balance of Payments Manual*, 5th edition, IMF, Washington, DC.
OECD (1999), *Classifying Educational Programmes: Manual for ISCED-97 Implemention in OECD Countries*, 1999 Edition, OECD Publishing.
OECD (2002), *International Mobility of the Highly Skilled*, OECD Publishing.
OECD (2002), *Measuring Globalisation: The Role of Multinationals in OECD Economies, Volume II: Services*, 2001 Edition, OECD Publishing.
OECD (2004), *International Trade by Commodity Statistics – Definitions*, OECD Publishing.
OECD (2004), *Promoting Trade in Services: Experience of the Baltic States*, OECD Publishing.
OECD (2005), *Measuring Globalisation: OECD Economic Globalisation Indicators 2005*, OECD Publishing.
OECD (2005), *Measuring Globalisation: OECD Handbook on Economic Globalisation Indicators*, OECD Publishing.
OECD (2005), *Trade and Structural Adjustment: Embracing Globalisation*, OECD Publishing.
OECD (2005), "Counting Immigrants and Expatriates in OECD Countries – A New Perspective", *Trends in International Migration: SOPEMI – 2004 Edition*, OECD Publishing.
OECD (2006), *Education at a Glance: OECD Indicators 2006*, OECD Publishing.
OECD (2006), *Export Credit Financing Systems in OECD Member Countries and Non-Member Economies: 2005 Update*, OECD Publishing.
OECD (2006), *International Direct Investment Statistics Yearbook*, OECD Publishing.
OECD (2006), *Liberalisation and Universal Access to Basic Services: Telecommunications, Water and Sanitation, Financial Services, and Electricity*, OECD Trade Policy Studies, OECD Publishing.
OECD (2006), *Aid for Trade: Making it Effective*, The Development Dimension, OECD Publishing.
OECD (2006), *Trade Based Money Laundering*, OECD Publishing.
OECD (2007), *Annual Report on the OECD Guidelines for Multinational Enterprises 2007: Corporate Responsibility in the Financial Sector*, OECD Publishing.
OECD (2007), *Infrastructure to 2030 (Vol.2): Preparing the Future*, OECD Publishing.
OECD (2007), *International Investment Perspectives: Freedom of Investment in a Changing World*, OECD Publishing.
OECD (2007), *International Trade by Commodity Statistics*, OECD Publishing.
OECD (2007), *Measuring Globalisation: Activities of Multinationals – Volume I: Manufacturing, 2000-2004*, OECD Publishing.
OECD (2007), *Monthly Statistics of International Trade*, OECD Publishing.
OECD (2007), *Statistics on International Trade in Services*, OECD Publishing.
OECD (2008), *Measuring Globalisation: Activities of Multinationals – Volume II: Services, 2000-2004*, OECD Publishing.
United Nations (1998), *International Merchandise Trade Statistics: Compilers Manual*, United Nations, New York, http://unstats.un.org/unsd/trade/methodology.htm.

Online databases
OECD International Trade by Commodity Statistics
OECD Statistics on Measuring Globalisation
OECD Monthly Statistics of International Trade
OECD International Development Statistics
OECD Statistics on Trade in Services by Service Category.
OECD Statistics on Trade in Services by Partner Country.
Available at www.sourceoecd.org/database/oecdstat.

Websites
www.oecd.org/statistics/globalisation
www.oecd.org/statistics/trade
www.oecd.org/dac/stats
www.oecd.org/sti/measuring-globalisation
www.oecd.org/sti

4. AN OVERVIEW OF OECD ECONOMIC STATISTICS

4.7 Short-term economic indicators

One of the OECD flagship publications is *Main Economic Indicators*, which represents the largest collection of short-term economic indicators for OECD countries. It contains monthly and quarterly data covering a long period of time (for some indicators, 40 years or more). The OECD collects a wide range of intra-annual economic indicators concerning the state of various industrial and services sectors (production, orders, turnover, etc.), as well as costs and prices. Moreover, the OECD has promoted the development of opinion surveys about the current economic situation of enterprises and households, as well as about expectations on future developments: therefore, the OECD has built a unique database containing this type of data, widely used by analysts and policy makers. Finally, the Organisation has developed over time a very successful system of cyclical indicators, able to provide early signals of changes in economic growth, not only for OECD countries, but also for the most important non-member economies.

Economic activity indicators

Short-term economic activity indicators are intended to be useful for understanding short-term movement of various economic activities such as production, sales, orders received, work started, work in progress, or stocks accumulated. At present, such indicators are available for a few selected industries, such as industrial sector, construction sector, wholesale and retail trade sectors, and some services sectors. This information is normally collected in almost all OECD countries at quarterly or monthly frequency using surveys and/or administrative sources, depending upon subjects or countries. Further information is noted in country metadata.

Data for industrial production, orders and stocks for manufacturing goods, as well as data for turnover for retail trade come from sample surveys, while information on orders received, work started or progress in construction are normally collected from administrative sources. Data are expressed in various units, such as indices with averages for a reference year equal to 100, physical units (*e.g.* numbers, square or cubic meters), percentages, etc.

Depending on countries and sectors, production can be measured from deflated turnover or sales, value added, physical output, raw material inputs, hours worked or other employment data. Samples generally include all units whose employment is above or equal to a certain threshold. Some countries apply random sampling under this threshold. Data refer to the whole period (i.e. entire month or quarter).

▶ **Key definitions**

Index of industrial production (IIP): one of the main indicators of short-term economic analysis, the index provides information on the goods produced by establishments engaged in mining (including oil extraction), manufacturing, and the production of electricity, gas and water (*i.e.* sectors C, D and E of ISIC Rev.3). Data are generally presented in indices that measure volume changes in output, as well as in physical volume, or in a ratio. Weights for IIP are estimated from gross value added at factor cost of the base year. Countries make their own estimates if there

AN OVERVIEW OF OECD ECONOMIC STATISTICS 4

are non-replies, and seasonal and working day adjustments are common practices among OECD member countries.

Index of services production (ISP): measures changes over time in the volume of output for the services sector. More precisely, ISP is defined as the ratio of the volume of output produced by the services industries in a given time period to the volume produced by the same industries in a specified base period.

Retail trade index: turnover of retail sales units. Turnover comprises the totals invoiced by the observation unit during the reference period, and this corresponds to gross sales of goods or services supplied to third parties. Retail trade index includes the activities listed in Division 52 of ISIC Rev.3 or NACE Rev. 1. However, there are significant differences among OECD member countries in activity coverage.

Sales of manufactured goods: value or volume of manufactured goods sold or delivered domestically or in foreign markets. Data generally exclude discounts, returns, allowances and taxes. Manufactured goods can be further disaggregated by type, such as intermediate, investment and consumer (durables or non-durables) goods.

Orders of manufactured goods: orders received by manufacturing units from domestic and foreign markets during the reference period for immediate or future delivery. Production-related services as well as consumption taxes, packaging and shipping and transportation costs are included. VAT, rebates, re-sales without further processing and cancellations are excluded.

Permit issued for construction: refers to various measures (*e.g.* floor area, physical volume, monetary value) of approved construction-work permits by type of structure and building use. In addition to new construction, the data cover alterations, extensions, repair and/or renovation of already existing structures, depending on countries.

Work started for dwelling construction: generally refers to the number of dwellings for which construction work commenced in the reference period. In some cases, data may refer to gross surface or physical volume of construction work started for dwellings or buildings. Construction is considered as underway once a foundation has been laid or is in preparation (for example, when digging has begun).

Stocks of manufactured goods: generally refers to products (*i.e.* output and input products) remaining in the reporting unit at the end of the reference period. Output products comprise finished products of own manufacturing (products ready for sale) plus finished products manufactured by others (products for resale without additional manufacturing by the reporting unit). Input products include raw materials, semi-manufacture and materials needed for distribution of the finished products. Thus, stocks generally comprise the sum of raw materials, intermediate and finished goods.

Rate of capacity utilisation: ratio between the actual output and the maximum that could be produced with existing plant and equipment.

4 AN OVERVIEW OF OECD ECONOMIC STATISTICS

Figure 4.7.1 – **Industrial production**
12-month rate of change

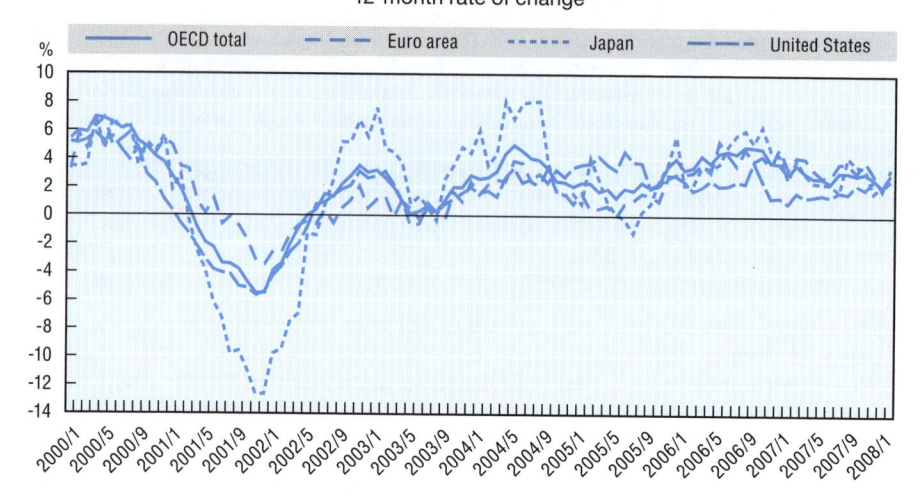

Source: OECD (2008) *Main Economic Indicators*, OECD Publishing.

StatLink ⟶ http://dx.doi.org/10.1787/335857028335

AN OVERVIEW OF OECD ECONOMIC STATISTICS   4

The OECD revision database

First releases of official statistics are often revised in subsequent releases, sometimes substantially. Such revisions can impact policy decisions, since revisions to first-published data may alter the previous assessment of the state of the economy. This may occur through a changed interpretation based on the revised data themselves or the impact the revisions may have on econometric models. While this is a recognised issue of key importance, many producers of official statistics do not quantify expected revisions to their data, and economists do not have the required data to test the sensitivity of their econometric models to revisions in input data. This important gap in knowledge required to effectively use official statistics motivated the OECD to develop a unique product: the *Main Economic Indicators Original Release Data and Revisions Database*, freely available at: http://stats.oecd.org/mei/default.asp?rev=1 .

This product allows both users and producers of official statistics to study the magnitude and direction of subsequent revisions to official statistics and for economists to test the likely effectiveness of econometric models in simulated real-time. The database interface contains full time series, as far back as 1960 in some cases, for 21 key economic variables as originally published in each monthly edition of the OECD Main Economic Indicators CD-Rom, from February 1999 onwards, for OECD countries, the Euro area, China, India, Brazil, South Africa and the Russian Federation. This database is updated on a monthly basis and provides the raw data needed by economists to test the performance of their econometric models in simulated real time.

The revision analysis website also provides access to: comprehensive revisions analysis studies performed by the OECD for GDP (see chart), index of industrial production and retail trade volume; automated programs; a detailed user guide and revision analysis tool allowing users to perform their own revisions analysis based on the OECD methodology; and information on reasons for revisions, together with recommended practices to aid producers of official statistics in establishing a transparent revisions policy for economic statistics.

Figure 4.7.2 – **Mean absolute revision to first published estimates of quarter-on-previous-quarter growth rates for GDP at different intervals**
Period 1995 – 2004

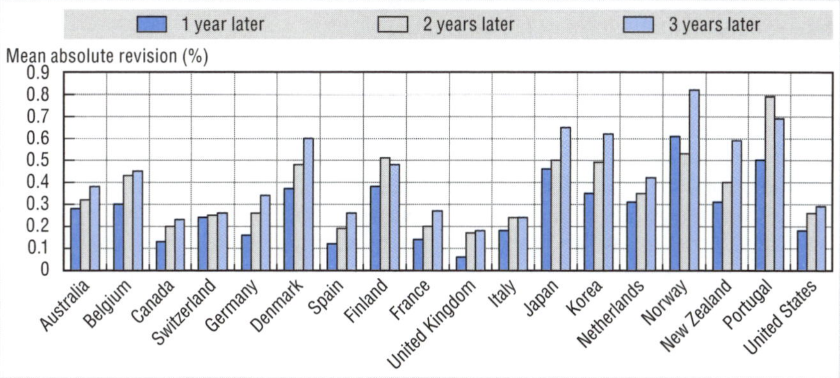

StatLink http://dx.doi.org/10.1787/336004167350

Cost of labour

The cost of labour is an important factor influencing the development of inflation in an economy, as increases in the cost of labour ultimately place pressure on the producers of goods and services to pass on these costs in the form of price increases. Consequently, central banks monitor closely the development of labour costs in their analysis of the economy and in their deliberations concerning monetary policy.

Direct payment for labour services in the form of wages and salaries generally accounts for around 80% of total labour costs. Other labour costs include: bonus payments; payments in kind related to labour services (*e.g.* food, fuel, housing); severance and termination pay; employers' contributions to pension schemes, casualty and life insurance and workers compensation; cost of employee training, welfare amenities and recruitment; taxes on employment (*e.g.* payroll tax); and fringe benefits tax.

Short-term statistics on the evolution of labour costs tend to focus on the wages and salaries component, as this constitutes the bulk of labour costs and data is generally available at a high frequency (*e.g.* from payrolls). In addition, wages and salaries are the component of labour costs most likely to change in the short term, and indeed, changes in other components of labour costs are often linked to changes in the wages and salaries component.

The OECD aims to present short-term statistics (*i.e.* monthly or quarterly) on the growth rate of *hourly earnings* in member countries for manufacturing industries and total private sector, with earnings defined as wages and salaries (including bonuses) plus payments in kind.

A more complete measure of labour costs' potential influence on inflation comes from assessing the evolution of *unit labour costs* (ULCs). Unit labour costs measure the average cost of labour per unit of output. They are calculated as the ratio of total labour costs to real output, or equivalently, as the ratio of mean labour costs per hour to labour productivity (output per hour). As such, ULCs represent a link between productivity and the cost of labour in producing output. Consequently, increases in ULCs often signal pressures faced by producers of goods and services to pass these costs on in the form of higher prices.

The OECD System of ULC Indicators calculates annual and quarterly measures according to a specific methodology to ensure data are comparable across OECD countries. Data are available for all OECD countries and the Euro area for a wide range of sectors (including total economy, manufacturing, industry, market services and the business sector). Annual time series also include a suite of related indicators such as: exchange rate-adjusted unit labour costs; labour income share ratios; labour productivity measures; and labour compensation per unit labour input measures. Quarterly unit labour cost indexes produced through the OECD system therefore represent a key short-term economic statistic for monitoring labour cost evolution in OECD member countries in regards to associated inflationary pressures.

AN OVERVIEW OF OECD ECONOMIC STATISTICS 4

Figure 4.7.3 – **Unit labour cost (industry)**
Quarter-on-previous-quarter rate of change

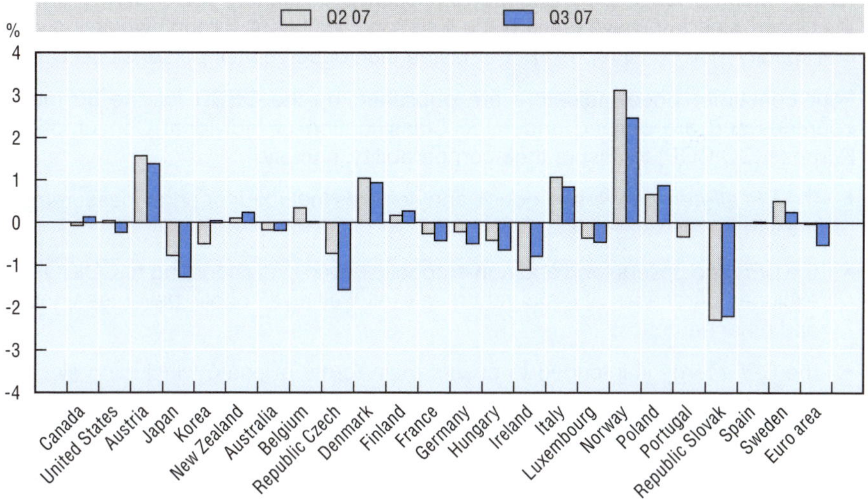

Source: OECD (2008), *Main Economic Indicators*, OECD Publishing.

Consumer prices and other inflation measures

Inflation measures the change in the overall price level of goods and services. It is an averaging concept and has to be distinguished from price changes in individual products, or from price change comparisons between products. For example, if the price of strawberries compared with the price of mushrooms is higher in autumn than it was during the summer, this is not a sign of inflation. Inflation is the average price change in a set of goods and services. Because many different sets of products can be considered, there are also many measures of inflation, with differences in scope and differences in use.

The single most important measure of inflation is the *consumer price index* (CPI). CPIs have a long history dating back to the 18th century (one of the first purposes of CPIs was to compensate wage-earners for a rising price level by adjusting wage rates in proportion to the CPI, a procedure known as indexation). CPIs measure the average change in prices for a basket of goods and services typically purchased by specific groups of households. Averages are formed by observing the price changes for goods and services and by weighting these price changes by the share that each group of goods or services occupies in the total expenditure of households. Thus, even small changes in the price of a product that has a large expenditure weighting can affect the overall index of consumer prices.

Note also that because expenditure shares are average shares across all households, they reflect a consumption pattern that may be more or less appropriate for specific groups of households. For example, low-income households tend to spend a larger

4. AN OVERVIEW OF OECD ECONOMIC STATISTICS

share of their income on food and housing than high-income households. Thus, the same change in food prices will affect inflation for low-income households more than for high-income households. Recently, statistical agencies (*e.g.* in Germany, France and the United Kingdom) have put in place 'inflation calculators' through which individuals can specify their consumption patterns and then observe their personalized CPI.

Four consumer price indicators are published by the OECD for the 30 member countries and are defined under the Classification of Individual Consumption by Purpose (COICOP) to assure their comparability, namely:

- the *CPI all-items* covers all goods and services included for price measurement in the CPI;
- the *CPI food* covers food and non-alcoholic beverages according to COICOP 01. It excludes purchases of restaurant meals, as well as alcoholic beverages, tobacco and other narcotics;
- the *CPI energy* is intended to covers main forms of energy, including electricity, gas and other fuels (COICOP 04.5) and fuels and lubricants for personal-transport equipment (COICOP 07.2.2);
- the *CPI All items less food less energy* provides an indication about "core inflation", *i.e.* the inflation that does not take into account the most volatile price components.

These four indicators are aggregated by the OECD into five zone areas: OECD-Total, OECD-Europe, Major Seven, OECD-Total excluding high-inflation countries, OECD-Europe excluding high-inflation countries. CPI data for zones, based on national indices, are annual chain-linked Laspeyres indices. The weights for individual links are based on the previous year's household private final consumption expenditure based on national accounts data.

The OECD also publishes the most recent prices data for the Euro zone, the European Union and a number of non-member economies (Brazil, China, India, Indonesia, Russian Federation and South Africa). The Euro zone (15 countries) and the European Union area (27 countries) refer to the Harmonised Index of Consumer Prices (HICP) published by Eurostat. HICPs are consumer price indices compiled on the basis of a harmonized coverage and methodology for European countries.

Another central measure of inflation is the *deflator of GDP*. This requires some extra explanation. Gross domestic product (GDP) corresponds to the value of all final expenditure on final goods and services produced in the economy. Final expenditure comprises private consumption, investment, government expenditure and exports minus imports. The deflator of GDP is the price index of this expenditure. A rise in the GDP deflator thus signals that, on average, the prices of final expenditure have gone up. Because GDP is a broader concept than private consumption, the GDP deflator may move differently, for example, from the deflator for private consumption, which is a component of the broader GDP deflator. The deflator for private consumption is closely related but not identical to the CPI described earlier. Along with the deflator for private consumption, there are also deflators for other expenditure categories, such as investment.

AN OVERVIEW OF OECD ECONOMIC STATISTICS 4

The chart below presents some inflation measures for the United States. It is immediately apparent that the price level of investment goods rises at a much lower rate than the overall price level. To a large extent, this reflects technical change and declining prices for information and communication technology goods. It is also apparent that the CPI rises relatively quickly compared to the other price indices and shows more volatility.

Figure 4.7.4 – **Different measures of inflation, United States**
Percentage change from preceding quarter

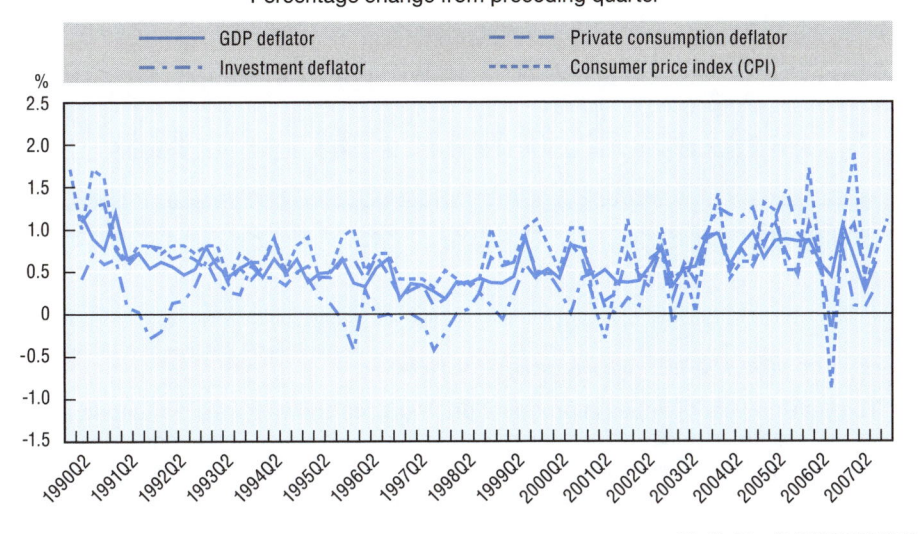

StatLink http://dx.doi.org/10.1787/336063618666

Sources: OECD (2008), *Quarterly National Accounts*, OECD Publishing.
OECD (2008), *Main Economic Indicators*, OECD Publishing.

While consumer prices and investment-good prices measure price changes from the perspective of those who purchase or use goods and services, *producer prices* measure inflation from the perspective of those who produce goods and services. Thus, producer price indices measure the average change in output prices, irrespective of who purchases the goods and services. Producer prices comprise prices of final products (those purchased by consumers, invested or exported) and prices of intermediate products (those used by other producers). Thus, producer price inflation has a different scope from consumer price inflation or from the price developments for total GDP.

Figure 4.7.5 presents the year-on-year changes in producer price indices for the manufacturing sector in selected OECD countries. Producer prices are of interest because they tend to rise or fall with a lead time relative to the price indices for final expenditure, and this can provide useful signals to policy makers. Producer prices are also important tools for statisticians in calculating the output of particular industries at constant prices, so that productivity developments can be monitored, for example.

4 AN OVERVIEW OF OECD ECONOMIC STATISTICS

Figure 4.7.5 – **Producer price indices: manufacturing**
Average annual growth in percentage

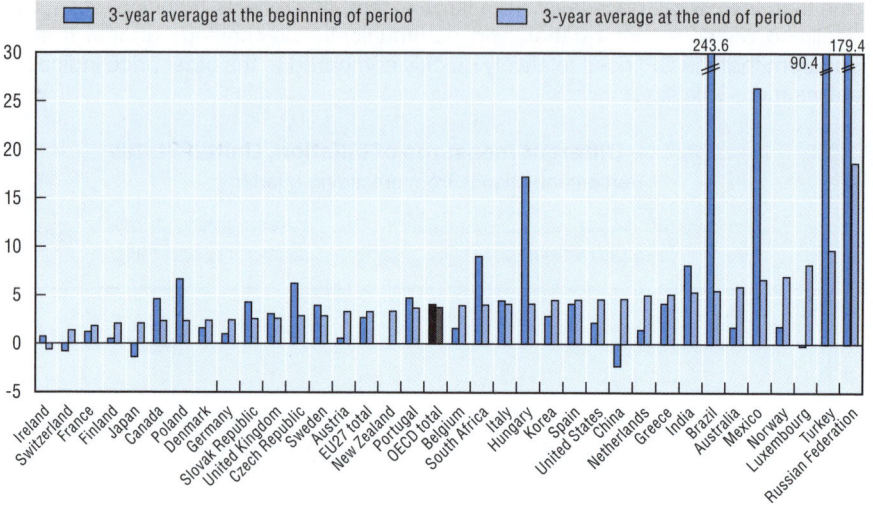

Source: OECD (2007), *Main Economic Indicators*, OECD Publishing.

The year-on-year changes in producer price indices shown here are intended to refer to the producer price indices for manufacturing. However, many countries do not calculate such indices for the manufacturing sector alone, or they calculate wholesale price indices rather than producer prices indices. Wholesale prices include taxes and transport and trade margins in addition to the ex-factory cost of goods. There are also differences between countries in how they adjust prices for quality changes, in the frequency with which the weights are updated, and in the formulae used to derive the price indices.

The OECD Handbook on Hedonic Prices

Deflators for real output, real input and real investment – for producing productivity measures or value added in national accounts – are derived primarily from price indices estimated by statistical agencies. Whether the deflators are consumer price indices or producer price indices, changes in the quality of the products has long been recognised as perhaps the most serious measurement problem in estimating price indices. In national accounts, any error in the deflators creates an exactly equivalent error of opposite sign in the real output, real input, real investment and real consumption measures. For this reason, discussing the problems posed by quality change in price indices is the same thing as discussing the problems of quality change in quantity indices, and therefore in measures of productivity change as well.

The issue of quality changes has become more relevant since the development of information and communication technologies (ICT) accelerated in the last 20 years. Since then, a lot of work has been devoted to understanding the contribution of ICT products to economic growth and to measures of labour productivity. Different quality adjustment methodologies are employed for ICT products across OECD countries, and they seemingly make large differences in the trends of price movements for these products. As pointed out some years ago, changes in computer equipment deflators among OECD countries ranged from plus 80% to minus 72% for the decade of the 1980s; the largest decline occurred in the US hedonic price indices for computer equipment.

International comparisons of productivity growth are clearly affected by these inconsistencies. If different quality adjustment procedures among OECD countries make the data non-comparable, then the measured growth of ICT investment and of ICT capital stocks will not be comparable across OECD countries. Therefore, in 2004 the OECD published the *Handbook on Hedonic* Prices to review the methods employed to adjust for quality change in price indices.

A natural division is between "conventional" methods typically employed by the statistical agencies of many OECD countries, which are discussed in the Handbook, and hedonic methods for adjusting for quality change (alternatively known as hedonic price indices). The latter have a prominent place in price indices for ICT products in several OECD countries. Hedonic methods for producing quality adjusted price indices are thus reviewed in the Handbook, which also goes beyond the economic literature in significant respects, particularly in the comparison of conventional and hedonic methods. In particular, the Handbook compares and contrasts the logic of hedonic methods and conventional methods and the results of employing them in different circumstances. Although most of the examples in the handbook are drawn from ICT products, the principles in it are very general and apply as well to price indices for non-ICT products that experience rapid quality change, and also to price indices for services, which are affected by quality changes fully as much as price indices for goods, though sometimes that has not been sufficiently recognised.

The Handbook sets out principles for "best practice" hedonic indices. These principles are drawn from experience with hedonic studies on a wide variety of products. The Handbook also considers some objections that have been raised to hedonic indices.

4. AN OVERVIEW OF OECD ECONOMIC STATISTICS

> **What inflation measures tell us and what they don't**
>
> The scope of goods and services that should be included in the CPI has been a subject of debate. While inclusion of some items is obvious, consideration of others is not. The single most important item of discussion has been the cost of housing to house owners who occupy their own dwelling. There is no rental transaction because the owner rents the dwelling to himself. It has been argued that the purchase of a house resembles more a financial investment than a purchase of another consumer product, and the implicit rent associated with home ownership should therefore be excluded from the consumer price index, just as other financial assets (such as shares or bonds) are outside the scope of the CPI. Other statisticians would argue that the main purpose of a dwelling is to provide housing services and the price of these housing services should be reflected in the CPI, whether the house is owned by its occupier or whether it is rented.
>
> Note, however, that even when owner-occupied housing is recognized as part of the CPI, it is normally not the purchase price *as such* that enters the CPI but an estimate of the rent that the owner "pays to himself". Over longer periods, the price of rents tends to follow the purchase price of houses, but in the short run this may not be the case. Thus, users are sometimes astonished to find that rapidly rising prices in property markets they experience in their daily lives are only slowly, or not at all, reflected in their country's CPI. The subjective perception of price developments by consumers may also be different from measured inflation because individuals tend to purchase durable consumer goods, such as TV sets or computers, only once in several years. Thus, individuals hardly perceive price changes (for example, price declines for information-technology goods), but of course these price changes are picked up in the measured CPI.

Business tendency surveys and consumer opinion surveys

Business tendency surveys are carried out to obtain qualitative information for use in monitoring the current business situation and forecasting short-term developments. Information from these surveys has proved of particular value in forecasting turning points in the business cycle. The information collected in business tendency surveys is described as qualitative because respondents are asked to assign qualities, rather than quantities, to the variables of interest. Compared to traditional statistical surveys, which usually cover only variables on one aspect of an enterprise's activity, business tendency surveys collect information about a wide range of variables selected for their ability, when analysed together, to give an overall picture of a sector of the economy. For example, most business surveys collect information on production, order books, new orders, stocks of finished goods, exports, employment and prices.

The statistical series derived from business tendency surveys are particularly suitable for monitoring and forecasting business cycles. The cyclical profiles of the series are in many cases easy to detect because they contain no trend. Usually the series are seasonally adjusted (at least to some extent) by the respondents, and this adds to the smoothness of the series. The series usually do not need revisions. This and the fact that they reflect assessments and expectations by businessmen facilitate their use in forecasting and in predicting turning points in the business cycle, in particular.

A harmonised system of business tendency surveys has been developed by the European Union and the OECD. Harmonised business tendency survey data has proved reliable and useful for policy makers. Another advantage of using the harmonised system is that it allows participating countries to compare their business tendency survey results with those of neighbouring or competing countries. It also makes it possible to construct regional totals or totals for economic groupings. And in a world of increasing globalisation, the ability to make comparisons among countries and regions is clearly an advantage. The harmonised system includes surveys of four sectors: industry, which covers manufacturing, as well as mining and quarrying, gas, water and electricity, depending on their importance; construction; retail trade; services.

These sectors have been selected because they cover the kinds of economic activities that are most sensitive to cyclical fluctuations. Agriculture is primarily influenced by climate, and many social and government services – health, education, defense and public administration, for example – respond slowly, if at all, to movements in the business cycle. Business surveys for these activities are therefore less relevant. In addition to their sensitivity to business cycles, industry, construction and trade are interesting activities for economic analysis because they are sectors whose movements are usually correlated with three key macro-economic aggregates – industry with GDP, construction with gross fixed capital formation and retail trade with private consumption.

Consumer opinion surveys also provide qualitative information that has proved useful for monitoring the current economic situation. Typically, they are based on a sample of households, and respondents are asked about their intentions regarding major purchases, their economic situation now compared with the recent past and their expectations for the immediate future.

▶ **Key definitions**

Confidence indicators based on a single survey question: answers to questions on the "general business situation" will usually be based on a combination of factors, such as respondents' appraisal of order books and expected new orders, as well as expectations about interest rates, exchange rates and political developments. These are confidence indicators and may be used as leading indicators for predicting short-term economic developments.

Composite confidence indicators: rather than relying on answers to a single question, a set of survey variables can be combined into a single composite confidence indicator, which summarises economic agents' assessments of, and expectations for, the general economic situation.

4. AN OVERVIEW OF OECD ECONOMIC STATISTICS

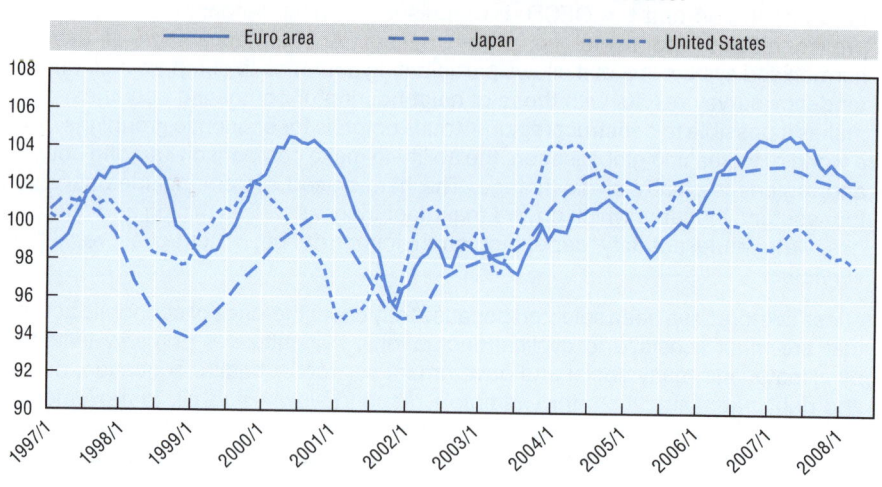

Figure 4.7.6 – **Business confidence indicator**

Composite leading indicators

Economic development in market economies is characterised by a succession of cycles with alternating phases of expansion and contraction in economic activity. The cycle may be defined by reference to the absolute level of economic activity. A downturn occurs when economic activity falls in absolute terms, and an upturn occurs when it begins to increase in absolute terms. This can be described as the classical definition of a cycle. The alternative is to define cycles in terms of growth rates. A downturn occurs when the growth of economic activity falls below the long-term trend, and an upturn occurs when the growth rate rises above it. Growth cycle contractions/expansions include slowdowns/pick-ups, as well as absolute declines/increases in activity, whereas classical cycle contractions/expansions include only absolute declines/increases.

Many survey series provide advance warning of a turning point in aggregate economic activity as measured by GDP or industrial production. The ability of business tendency survey data to predict the cycle's turning point makes them very suitable as leading indicators. Moreover, business tendency survey data can be combined with quantitative statistics to obtain a more structured cyclical indicator system, in particular, the construction of leading indicators.

Cyclical indicator systems are constructed around a reference series, *i.e.* a target series that reflects overall economic activity and whose cyclical development it is intended to predict. The reference series is used to establish the "timing classification" of statistical indicators into leading, coincident or lagging indicators. Statistical series are normally selected for inclusion in a cyclical indicator system if they meet the following criteria: relevance – there must be an economic rationale for expecting a leading relationship; cyclical behaviour – the length and consistency of lead is obviously important as is cyclical conformity (general fit), the absence

AN OVERVIEW OF OECD ECONOMIC STATISTICS 4

of extra or missing cycles and the smoothness of the series over time; practical considerations – these include the frequency of publication (at least quarterly and preferably monthly), no large revisions, timeliness of publication and availability of a long time series with no breaks.

The OECD composite leading indicators (CLIs) are aggregate time series that show a leading relationship with the growth cycles of key macro-economic indicators (the average lead is six months). Typically, they are constructed to predict the cycles of total industrial production or gross domestic product in industry, which are chosen as proxy measures for the aggregate economy. OECD CLIs are calculated by combining component series in order to cover, as far as possible, the key sectors of the economy. These component series cover a wide range of short-term indicators, such as observations or opinions about economic activity, housing permits, financial and monetary data, etc. For each country, the series are selected according to the following criteria: economic significance; cyclical behaviour; data quality. Some transformations are required prior to aggregation, such as "smoothing", in order to reduce the irregularity of the final composite indicator. In general, for each country, component series of the CLI have equal weights. The aggregation of components series into the CLI reduces the risk of "false signals", changes in the indicator due to irregular movements that do not correspond to any later developments in the aggregate economy.

The OECD system of leading indicators is based on the "growth cycle" approach, which measures deviations from the long-term trend. A contractionary phase signals a decline in the rate of growth of the economy, though not necessarily an absolute decline in economic activity. This is distinct from classical cycles that are defined as a succession of periods of absolute growth and decline in economic activity. Peaks and troughs of growth cycles tend to appear earlier in time than those of classical cycles.

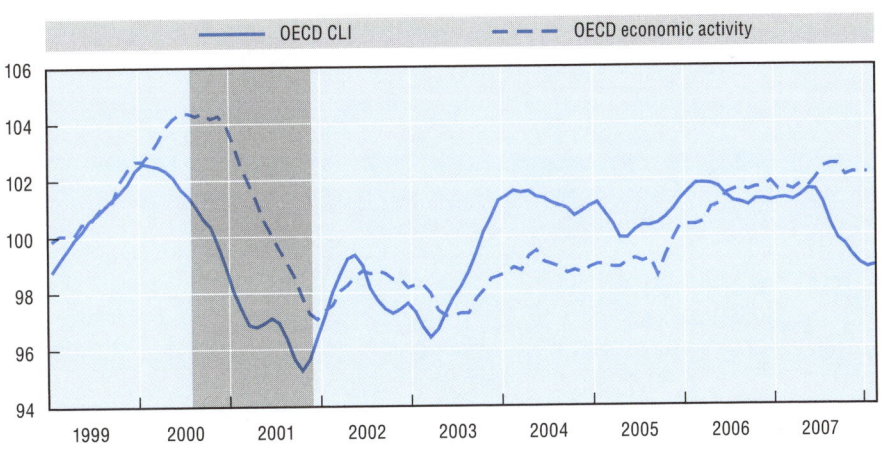

Figure 4.7.8 – **OECD leading indicator**

Note: The grey area represents downswings in economic activity.
Source: OECD (2008), *Main Economic Indicators*, OECD Publishing.

4. AN OVERVIEW OF OECD ECONOMIC STATISTICS

Further information

Publications

Brook, A.M. et al. (2004), "Oil Price Developments: Drivers, Economic Consequences and Policy Responses", *OECD Economics Department Working Papers*, No. 412, OECD Publishing.
OECD (2007), *Cyclical Indicators and Business Tendency Surveys*, www.oecd.org/dataoecd/20/18/1844842.pdf.
OECD (2001), *Composite Leading Indicators: A Tool for Short-Term Analysis*, www.oecd.org/dataoecd/4/33/15994428.pdf.
OECD (2003), *Business Tendency Surveys: A Handbook*, OECD Publishing.
OECD (2007), *OECD Economic Outlook*, Vol. 2007/2, No. 82, OECD Publishing.
OECD (2008), *Main Economic Indicators*, OECD Publishing.

Online databases

Business tendency and consumer opinion indicators
Composite Leading Indicators (MEI)
Industry and services statistics (MEI)
Labour Cost
Prices and Price Indices
Quarterly National Accounts
Available at *www.sourceoecd.org/database/oecdstat*.

Websites

http://stats.oecd.org/mei/
www.oecd.org/std/cli-ts
www.oecd.org/std/mei
www.oecd.org/std/labour
www.oecd.org/std/qna/statistics

AN OVERVIEW OF OECD ECONOMIC STATISTICS 4

4.8 Labour statistics

Labour statistics come from both statistical surveys and administrative sources. Extremely important is the Labour Force Survey (LFS), carried out in almost all OECD countries at quarterly or monthly frequency, using definitions established by the International Labour Office (ILO). In most OECD countries, LFS covers the population aged 15 years and over. The choice of the 15-64 population as the working age population was made according to the accepted retirement age, but the proportion of persons working after 65 years varies from one country to the other. Differences in the lower limit also exist between countries.

On a monthly basis, the OECD publishes "standardised unemployment rates" (SUR). In EU countries, the LFS follows the Eurostat recommendations, which are a detailed version of the ILO guidelines. For other countries, OECD collects directly the data from NSOs. For those countries, the LFS follows ILO guidelines.

The Statistical Annex of the OECD *Employment Outlook* contains a lot of annual labour statistics, such as employment/population ratios; activity and unemployment rates, by gender, selected age groups and educational attainment; part-time employment; annual hours worked; long-term unemployment; and public expenditures and participant stocks in labour market programmes. The *2007 Employment Outlook* includes, for the first time, selected earnings-related indicators. Finally, this database contains a number of statistics on labour market performances and on features of the institutional and regulatory environment affecting the functioning of labour markets. Among these are the following: annual hours of work data for comparisons of trends over time; gross earnings by percentile for deriving measures of earnings dispersion for full-time workers by gender; gross mean and median earnings of full-time workers by age group and gender; statutory minimum wages; public expenditure on labour market programmes and number of participants; trade union density rates in OECD member countries.

▶ **Key definitions**

Total population: all nationals present in, or temporarily absent from the country, and aliens permanently settled in the country. It includes national armed forces stationed abroad; merchant seamen at sea; diplomatic personnel located abroad; civilian aliens resident in the country; displaced persons resident in the country. It excludes foreign armed forces stationed in the country; foreign diplomatic personnel located in the country; civilian aliens temporarily in the country.

Total labour force (or currently active population): comprises all persons who fulfil the requirements for inclusion among the employed or the unemployed as defined below. Civilian labour force corresponds to total labour force excluding armed forces.

Total employment: all persons (including armed forces), above a specified age, who during the reference period (either one week or one day), performed some work (at least one hour) for wage or salary (paid employment) or profit or family gain (self-employment), in cash or in kind, including those who have a job but were not at work (because of illness, vacation, etc.).

Unemployment: the unemployed comprise all persons above a specified age, who during the reference period were at the same time: *a)* without work (*i.e.* were not in paid employment or self-employment); *b)* currently available for work (*i.e.* were available for paid employment or self-employment); *c)* seeking work (*i.e.* had taken specific steps in a recent specified period to seek paid employment or self-employment). As the source is the LFS, this group is referred as "surveyed unemployed".

Registered unemployment: in all OECD countries, governments operate employment agencies at which unemployed persons of working age may register as a job seeker, regardless of whether they are covered by unemployment insurance. These unemployed job seekers are referred to as "registered unemployed". Such administrative statistics are sensitive to changes in regulations and consequently are not comparable through time and among countries. Nevertheless, in some countries they are the only unemployment data available on a monthly basis.

Participation rate: the ratio between the total labour force and the population. Since there is no international definition concerning the age range to take into account, for comparability reasons the OECD publishes participation rates: total labour force as a percentage of the total population; total labour force as a percentage of the 15-64 population. Participation rates calculated according to national definitions may take into account the age group represented in the labour force survey.

Employment rate: the ratio between the employed and the working age population (the OECD includes in this category persons aged 15-64). In addition to the employment rate as defined above, the OECD also publishes the ratio of employment as a percentage of the total population.

Unemployment rate: the ratio between the number of unemployed and the total labour force. Since members of the armed forces should, by definition, be included among persons in employment, total labour force should be used to calculate the unemployment rate in accordance with ILO recommendations. Nevertheless, to increase the comparability between OECD member countries, the OECD publishes the unemployment rate taking into account the civilian labour force.

AN OVERVIEW OF OECD ECONOMIC STATISTICS 4

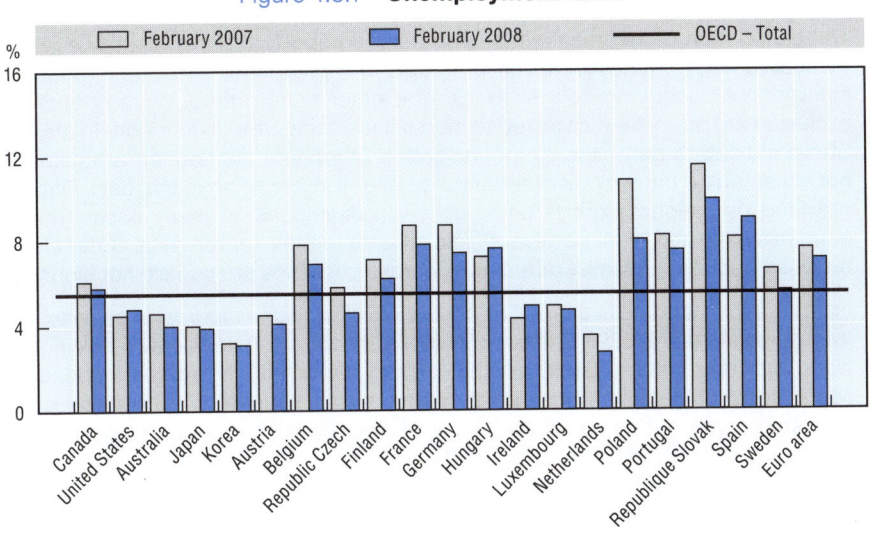

Figure 4.8.1 – **Unemployment rates**

Further information

Publications
OECD (2007), *OECD Economic Outlook*, OECD Publishing.
OECD (2007), *OECD Employment Outlook*, OECD Publishing.
OECD (2007), *Labour Force Statistics*, OECD Publishing.
OECD (2008), *Main Economic Indicators*, OECD Publishing.

Online databases
OECD Employment and Labour Markets
Available at *www.sourceoecd.org/database/oecdstat*

Websites
www.oecd.org/statistics/labour
www.oecd.org/std/labour
www.oecd.org/els/employment

4 AN OVERVIEW OF OECD ECONOMIC STATISTICS

4.9 Income distribution and households' conditions

The distribution of incomes within a country is important for at least two reasons. Inequalities may create incentives for people to improve their situation through work, innovation or acquiring new skills. On the other hand, crime, poverty and social exclusion are often seen as linked to inequalities of income distribution. In the OECD Social Indicators database, some indicators of income distribution are computed, notwithstanding the serious comparability issues still existing in this field. Data were provided by national experts using common definitions. In many cases, however, countries have had to make several adjustments to their source data. Small changes between periods and small differences across countries are usually not significant.

In this context, income is defined as *household disposable income*, broadly following the definitions of the 1993 *System of National Accounts*. It consists of earnings from work, property income (such as interest and dividends), and pensions and other social security benefits; income taxes and social security contributions paid by households are deducted. The equality of disposable incomes among individuals is normally measured by the *Gini Coefficient*. This is a common measure of equality and ranges from 0 in the case of "perfect equality" (each share of the population gets the same share of income) to 100 in the case of "perfect inequality" (all income goes to the share of the population with the highest income). Household income is adjusted to take account of household size.

Figure 4.9.1 – **Distribution of household disposable income among individual**
Measured by Gini Coefficients

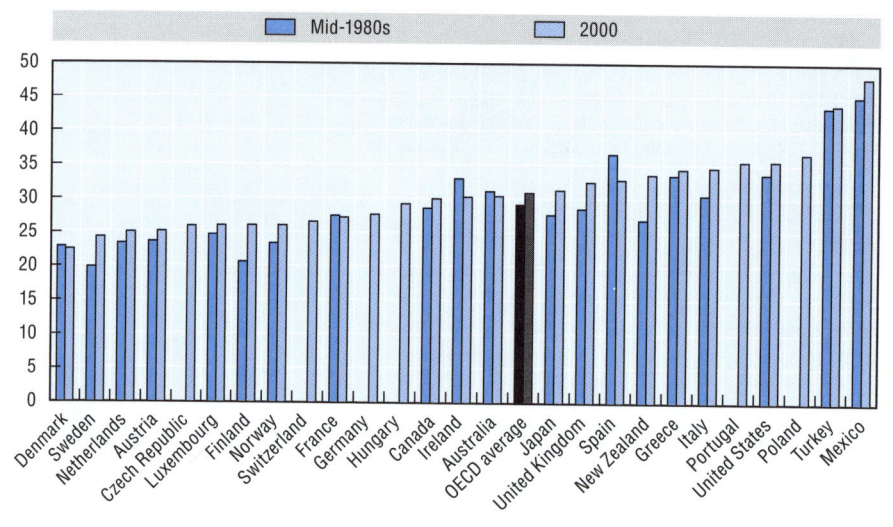

StatLink http://dx.doi.org/10.1787/336141325048

Source: Förster, M. and M. Mira d'Ercole (2005), "Income Distribution and Poverty in OECD Countries in the Second Half of the 1990s", *OECD Social Employment and Migration Working Papers*, No. 22, OECD Publishing.

AN OVERVIEW OF OECD ECONOMIC STATISTICS 4

There is considerable variation in levels of income inequality across OECD countries. For years around 2000, the Gini coefficient of income inequality is lowest in Denmark and Sweden, and highest in Mexico and Turkey – the two OECD countries with lowest per capita income. On average, across the 20 countries for which data are available since the mid-1980s, the Gini coefficient of income inequality increased from 29 to 31, but this increase may be within the margin of error for statistics on income distribution. The safest conclusion is that, for these 20 countries as a whole, there was little or no change.

There were, however, some striking changes for several countries when years around 2000 are compared with the mid-1980s. Household income distribution became markedly more equal in Spain and Ireland, and there were smaller reductions in inequality in Australia, Denmark and France.

At the other end of the scale, the Gini coefficients increased (greater inequality) by 10-20% in Norway, Japan, Italy and the United Kingdom and by over 20% in Sweden, New Zealand and Finland. Note, however, that despite the large increase in Sweden, the Gini coefficient is still one of the lowest in the OECD area.

In view of the strong demand for cross-national indicators on the situation of families, the OECD has recently developed a new *database on family outcomes and family policies* with indicators for all OECD countries. The database builds on indicators from different databases maintained by the OECD (for example, the OECD Social Expenditure database and the OECD Education database) and other international organisations. For some other indicators, for example about the use of parental leave or the use of out-of-school-hours care, information is derived from questionnaires sent by the OECD to member countries.

The OECD Family database aims to contain data on: the structure of families (size and composition, fertility patterns and marital and partnership status); the labour market position of families (employment status of family members, gender differences in employment conditions, workplace hours and time for caring); public policies for families and children (*i.e.* general tax/benefit support for families with children, public provisions for child-related leave, public spending on childcare and early education); child outcomes (child health, child poverty, education and literacy, social participation). By the end of 2008, some 30 to 35 indicators should be released, including: typology of childcare benefits; net parental fees by family type and income level; and trends in the income position of different household types. The first batch of indicators was released by the end of 2006, but work is ongoing on the preparation of new indicators for release throughout 2008.

4 AN OVERVIEW OF OECD ECONOMIC STATISTICS

Further information

Publications

Jomo, K.S. (2001), "Globalisation, Liberalisation, Poverty and Income Inequality in Southeast Asia", *OECD Development Centre Working Papers*, No. 185, OECD Publishing.
Kayizzi-Mugerwa, S. (2001), "Globalisation, Growth and Income Inequality: The African Experience", *OECD Development Centre Working Papers*, No. 186, OECD Publishing.
OECD (2004), *Income Disparities in China: An OECD Perspective*, OECD Publishing.
OECD (2005), *Extending Opportunities: How Active Social Policy Can Benefit Us All*, OECD Publishing.
OECD (2007), *Society at a Glance: OECD Social Indicators – 2006 Edition*, OECD Publishing.
Uchimura, H. (2005), "Impact of Changes in Social Institutions on Income Inequality in China", *OECD Development Centre Working Papers*, No. 243, OECD Publishing.
OECD (2008, forthcoming), *Growing Unequal*.

Websites

www.oecd.org/statistics/social
www.oecd.org/els/social/family/database

4.10 Monetary and financial statistics

This section highlights financial data collected by the OECD to support macroeconomic and financial markets analysis, as well as the preparation of policy advices. In particular, the following areas are covered: monetary aggregates, balance of payments and interest rates. All data are collected and disseminated in the context of *Main Economic Indicators*.

Monetary aggregates

Monetary aggregates measure the amount of money circulating in an economy. They are expressed in current prices ("nominal" terms) because the amount of money required by an economy reflects current levels of economic activity and price.

There are many monetary aggregates. Statistically, they are items on the balance sheet of the banking system. Although they may be taken from either side of the balance sheet (since credit series, which are banking assets, are sometimes labelled monetary aggregates), they are normally taken from the liabilities side. On the balance sheet, the liabilities items are ordered, starting with very narrow definitions of money (such as notes and coins) and gradually widening through various types of bank accounts (*e.g.* sight deposits, term deposits) to very broad items, which include sophisticated products like financial derivatives.

There were no internationally recognised standards for compiling monetary aggregates until the IMF published its Monetary and Financial Statistics Manual in 2000. Cross-country comparability suffered as a result. Now, notably, the European Central Bank's framework for constructing Euro area monetary aggregates is consistent with IMF principles and non-euro EU countries are also required to report data to ECB according to the framework, as are EU candidate countries as part of their application process.

▶ **Key definitions**

Narrow money: covers highly liquid forms of money (money as a means of exchange). A general definition of narrow money (M1) is: currency, *i.e.* banknotes and coins, plus overnight deposits.

Broad money: includes the less liquid forms (money as a store of value). A general definition of broad money (M3) is: M1 *plus* deposits with an agreed maturity of up to two years and deposits redeemable at notice of up to three months, repurchase agreements, money market fund shares/units and debt securities up to two years.

4 AN OVERVIEW OF OECD ECONOMIC STATISTICS

Figure 4.10.1 – **Broad Money**
Year-on-year growth rates

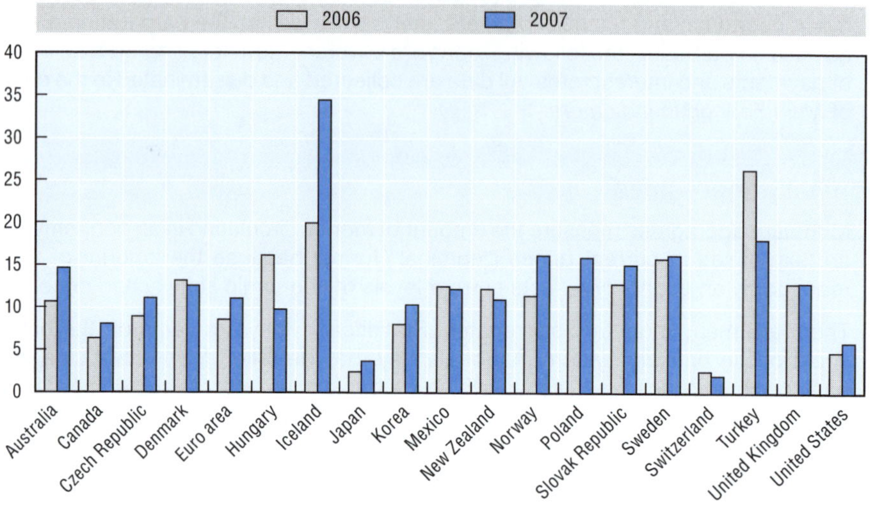

Source: OECD (2008), *Main Economic Indicators*, OECD Publishing.

Balance of payments statistics

The balance of payments is a statistical statement that provides a summary of economic transactions of an economy with the rest of the world, for a specific time period. The transactions are for the most part between residents and non-residents of the economy. The transactions include: goods, services and income; those involving financial claims on, and liabilities to, the rest of the world; and transfers. A transaction is defined as an economic flow that reflects the creation, transformation, exchange, transfer or extinction of economic value and involves changes in ownership, of goods or assets, the provision of services, labour or capital. Transactions are recorded using a double-entry method.

Balance of payments data are important for economic and monetary policy formation and analysis, both for short-term and structural information, as well as an indicator of monetary stability. Payment imbalances and trends in trade in goods and services, the current account, and in financial flows in inward and outward foreign investment attract particular attention. The balance of payments data also provide much detailed information and links to specialised statistical frameworks, such as those on international trade in services, and foreign direct investment.

Balance of payments data are compiled in accordance with the 5th edition of the Balance of Payments Manual published by the IMF (BPM5), and presented according to the Standard Presentation. There is virtually complete concordance in concepts between the balance of payments and the rest of the world account of SNA93. Closely related to the flows in the balance of payments framework is the international investment position (IIP), which provides at a specific date, such as the end of a quarter, a statement of an economy's financial assets and liabilities, with their composition, vis-à-vis the rest of the world.

The OECD balance of payments dataset collects a limited set of the main flow variables, with a primary purpose of providing a timely OECD wide set of variables for short-term economic analysis. Data are collected from all member countries and important non-member economies. These main variables include:

- Current account (trade in goods, trade in services, income, current transfers)
- Capital account
- Financial account (direct investment, portfolio investment, financial derivatives, other investment, change in reserve assets)
- Net errors and omissions

Figure 4.10.2 – **Current account balance of payments**
As a percentage of GDP, average 2004-2006

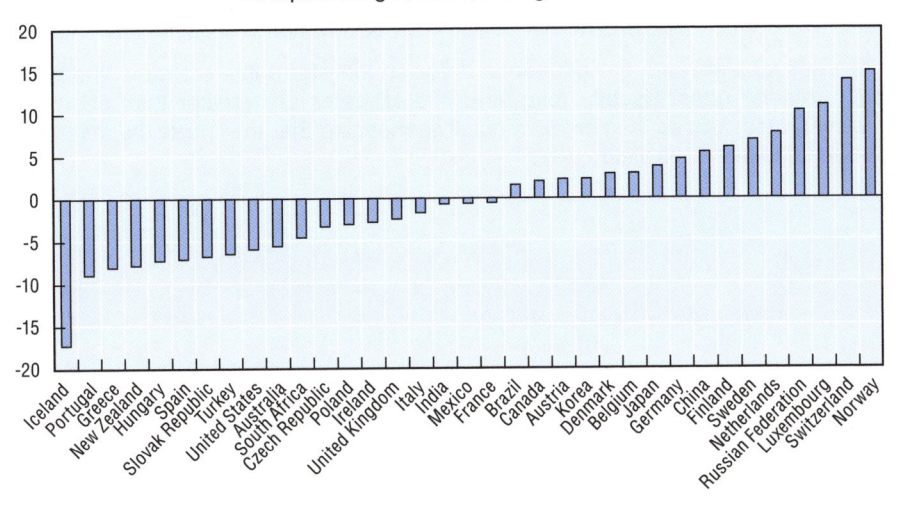

Sources: For member countries and South Africa: OECD (2007), *Main Economic Indicators*, OECD Publishing. For Brazil, China, India and Russian Federation: National sources.

Interest rates

Interest rates are defined as the price paid for borrowing money and compensating the lenders for deferring their expenditures; simply stated, the interest rate is the cost of money and is expressed as an annual percentage. Many factors can affect interest rates, such as the supply and demand for money, the inflation rate, the amount, purpose and period of the transaction, the strength of the national currency, the pace of economic growth and government policy. As a consequence, there will be numerous rates applying to the large number of transactions in effect at any one time in any one country. While efforts have been made by the OECD to select rates that ensure as much international comparability as possible, the fact remains that the institutional features of each country's financial markets are distinct and often markedly different from those of other countries.

▶ **Key definitions**

Immediate interest rate (or < 24hrs): used as a term to describe official discount rates and call-money rates. The official discount rate is the rate at which Central Banks make advances to, or discount eligible bills of exchange for, selected banks and other financial intermediaries. Day-to-day loans usually refer to operations on the money market between banks to balance temporary surpluses and shortages of liquidity. Call money generally refers to secured or unsecured "at-call" loans made by banks to money market dealers.

Short-term interest rate: usually either the three-month interbank offer rate or the rate associated with Treasury bills, Certificates of Deposit or comparable instruments, each with three-month maturity.

Long-term interest rate: the yield on 10-year government bonds, in most cases.

Interest rate spread: the difference between long-term interest rates and short-term interest rates. Usually, long-term interest rates are greater than short-term interest rates, and so the spread is positive, meaning that the longer the maturity of a bond, the higher its yield.

AN OVERVIEW OF OECD ECONOMIC STATISTICS 4

Table 4.10.1 – Interest rates
February 2008

Country	Short-term interest rates	Long-term interest rates
Australia	7.69	6.29
Austria *	..	4.08
Belgium *	..	4.15
Canada	3.88	3.85
Czech Republic	3.94	4.48
Denmark	4.37	4.08
Finland *	..	4.06
France *	..	4.08
Germany *	..	3.95
Greece *	..	4.33
Hungary	7.73	..
Iceland	19.00	9.80
Ireland *	..	4.22
Italy *	..	4.35
Japan	0.76	1.43
Korea	5.28	5.28
Mexico	7.51	..
Netherlands *	..	4.05
New Zealand	8.82	6.40
Norway	5.91	4.39
Poland	5.94	..
Portugal *	..	4.27
Slovak Republic	..	4.36
Spain *	..	4.14
Sweden	4.21	4.02
Switzerland	2.80	3.06
United Kingdom	5.61	4.62
United States	3.06	3.74
Euro area	4.36	4.14

StatLink http://dx.doi.org/10.1787/336536361073

Note: Member of the Euro area are indicated with an asterisk.

Source: OECD (2008), *Main Economic Indicators*, OECD Publishing.

4. AN OVERVIEW OF OECD ECONOMIC STATISTICS

Further information

Publications
IMF (1993), *Balance of Payments Manual*, 5th edition, IMF, Washington, DC.
OECD (2006), *Export Credit Financing Systems in OECD Member Countries and Non-Member Economies*, OECD Publishing.
OECD (2008), *Main Economic Indicators*, OECD Publishing.
UN, EC, IMF, OECD, UNCTAD and the WTO (2002), *Manual on Statistics of International Trade in Services*, United Nations, New York.

Online databases
Main Economic Indicators.
OECD Economic Outlook Statistics.
Financial Indicators (MEI).
Available at *www.sourceoecd.org/database/oecdstat*.

Websites
www.oecd.org/eco/sources-and-methods
www.oecd.org/std/mei
http://stats.oecd.org/mei/

AN OVERVIEW OF OECD ECONOMIC STATISTICS 4

4.11 National accounts

Since its foundation, the OECD has played a fundamental role in the development of national accounts, contributing to the preparation of guidelines and handbooks on specific issues, as well as to the various editions of the System of National Accounts (SNA). This section presents the wide range of data currently collected and disseminated by the OECD, as well as those compiled by the Secretariat. In particular, the following areas are covered: economic accounts (including the database on productivity and the STAN database developed for industrial analysis), input-output, financial accounts, quarterly national accounts and purchasing power parities. All together, the OECD databases concerning national accounts represent a unique source of comparable statistics for international and national analyses. Since 2005, a large part of national accounts databases are updated on a rolling basis, as soon as the data become available from national sources.

Economic accounts

There are three principal types of economic accounts published by national statistical offices: national accounts; balance of payments; and government finance statistics. The second two are essentially components of the first, but provide much more detail than is generally found in the national accounts, and they are dealt with elsewhere in this chapter.

The standards governing national accounts are enshrined in two international reference manuals: the *System of National Accounts 1993* (SNA 93), which is recognised globally, and the European version, the *European System of Accounts 1995* (ESA 95). The ESA 95 is consistent with the SNA 93 but is more prescriptive. The SNA 93 is published jointly by the United Nations, the Commission of the European Communities, the International Monetary Fund, the Organisation for Economic Co-operation and Development and the World Bank. An updated version of the SNA 93 is being developed and is scheduled for release in two parts in 2008 and 2009. An updated version of ESA 95 will follow.

The national accounts consist of an integrated set of macroeconomic accounts, balance sheets and tables based on internationally agreed concepts, definitions, classifications and accounting rules. Together, these principles provide a comprehensive accounting framework within which economic data can be compiled and presented in a format that is designed for purposes of economic analysis, decision-taking and policy making.

The national accounts record production, consumption and the accumulation of wealth. They also record the income generated by production, the distribution of income among the factors of production and uses of the income, either by consumption or the acquisition of assets. When fully implemented, the national accounts record the value of an economy's stock of assets and liabilities at the beginning and end of a period (usually a year) and changes arising from production and transfers of income, as well as recording events that bring about changes in the value of the wealth stock. Such events can include revaluations, write-offs, growth and depletion of natural assets, catastrophes and transfers of natural assets to economic activity.

4. AN OVERVIEW OF OECD ECONOMIC STATISTICS

Accounts for the economy as a whole are supported by accounts for the various sectors of the economy, such as those relating to the government, households and corporate entities. The framework also embraces other, more detailed accounts, such as financial accounts and input-output tables. And it provides for additional analyses through social accounting matrices and satellite accounts designed to reflect specific aspects of economic activity, such as tourism, health and the environment. National accounting information can serve many different purposes. In general terms, the main purpose of national accounts is to provide information that is useful for economic analysis and the formulation of macroeconomic policy.

Of all the variables in the national accounts, the most prominent is gross domestic product (GDP). GDP is the standard measure of the value of goods and services produced by a country in its economic territory during a period of time (see Chapter 2 for a complete definition). Although it is a measure of production and not welfare, GDP has commonly been used as a proxy measure of the welfare of a country, but attention is increasingly being given to other factors. By removing price changes, a temporal volume measure of GDP shows how quickly production is growing over time. By taking account of price differences between countries, a spatial volume measure shows how production in one country compares with other countries. If either of these measures is divided by the number of persons in the population, GDP per capita is obtained, which is useful in making comparisons over time or between countries.

Figures 4.11.1 presents annual growth rates in the volumes of GDP for main geo-economic zones, while Figure 4.11.2 compares the level of GDP per capita for member countries in 2006.

Figure 4.11.1 – **Real GDP growth**
Annual growth in percentage

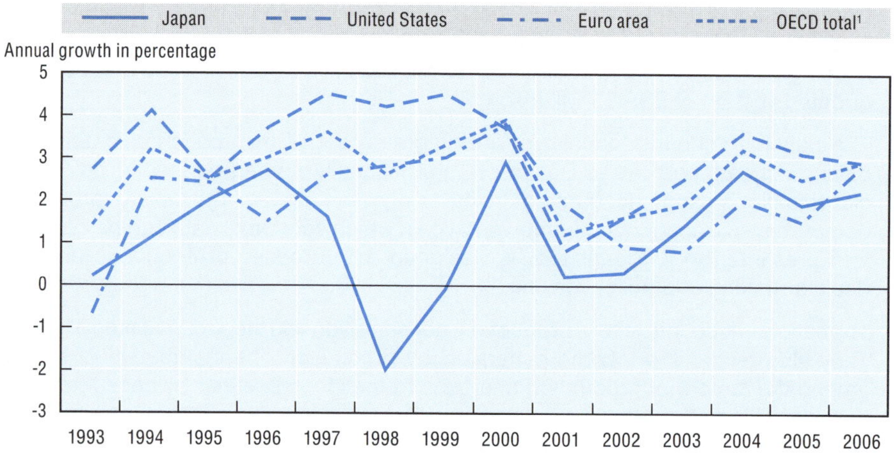

1. Excluding Czech Republic, Hungary, Poland and Slovak Republic.

Source: OECD (2007), *National Accounts of OECD Countries*, OECD Publishing.

AN OVERVIEW OF OECD ECONOMIC STATISTICS 4

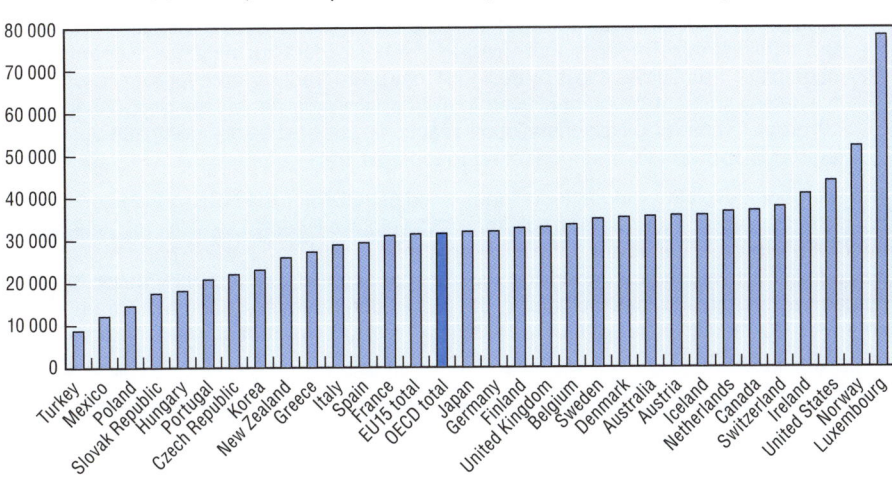

Figure 4.11.2 – **GDP per capita**
US dollars, current prices and PPPs, 2006 or latest available year

Source: OECD (2007), *National Accounts of OECD Countries*, OECD Publishing.

Handbook on the non-observed economy

To improve the exhaustiveness of GDP, the OECD, IMF, ILO and CIS STAT have published *Measuring the Non-Observed Economy: A Handbook*. The term "non-observed economy" (NOE) refers to those economic activities that should be included in GDP but are often not because they are not covered in the statistical surveys or administrative records from which the national accounts are constructed, namely:

- **Underground activities:** legal activities deliberately concealed from government to avoid paying taxes or social charges or to avoid the costs associated with legislation on safe working conditions or protection of consumers' rights. Sometimes, the activities are only partly concealed and may be reported to the tax authorities at lower-than-actual values, so as to reduce taxes rather than eliminate them entirely.

- **Illegal activities:** underground activities that involve the production or exchange of illegal goods and services, such as narcotics, prostitution, trade in stolen goods, smuggling and audio-video counterfeiting. Illegal activities should be included in the GDP providing they involve transactions between willing buyers and sellers. Theft, extortion and most kinds of fraud, for example, do not meet this definition and fall outside the production boundary.

- **Production of goods for own use:** these activities are usually legal but they may be omitted from the national accounts because there are no observable transactions between buyers and sellers since they are one and the same. In OECD countries, construction and maintenance of dwellings is probably the most important example of production for own use. In transition and developing countries growing ones own food is often an important activity.

4. AN OVERVIEW OF OECD ECONOMIC STATISTICS

> **Handbook on the non-observed economy** *(cont.)*
>
> - **Statistical deficiencies:** activities omitted simply because the statistical surveys and administrative records that provide the basic data for national accounts are incomplete. Sometimes this is by design: it may be impractical to cover every producer in a survey so a cut-off point is used to exclude the smallest enterprises. Otherwise, the problem arises from poor statistical practices: out-of-date or incomplete business register, inappropriate treatment of non-response, etc.
>
> The *Handbook* explains various techniques to adjust GDP for the NOE in the short term, but the emphasis is on longer-term solutions. It develops a five-part strategy for measuring the NOE, with practical advice for each step. The ultimate aim is to upgrade the survey and administrative sources underlying the national accounts so that they cover the full range of economic activities included in the production boundary. Such a programme to improve the exhaustiveness of GDP will usually need to be part of an overall programme of statistical reform.

Productivity

Productivity is commonly defined as a ratio of a volume measure of output to a volume measure of inputs and measures how efficiently production inputs are being used in the economy to produce outputs. While there is no disagreement on this general notion, a look at the productivity literature and its various applications reveals very quickly that there is neither a unique purpose for, nor a single measure of, productivity. The two most commonly used measures of productivity are labour productivity and multi-factor productivity. Labour productivity is a single factor measure that relates output to the number of hours worked. Multi-factor productivity aims at capturing several factors of production. Typically, labour and capital input measures are combined into an indicator of combined inputs. Then, multi-factor productivity is measured as the ratio between output and combined inputs. More detailed explanations of productivity measures can be found in the OECD manual *Measuring Productivity* (2001).

There is a general understanding that productivity matters for the standard of living and economic growth, but to answer more specific analytical questions, different measures of productivity are required. In one way or another, the various productivity measures relate to the broader objectives of tracing technology, technical change and efficiency in the economy, in an industry or in a sector. More specific analytical reasons why the OECD is interested in the measurement of productivity include:

- productivity growth is considered a key source of economic growth and competitiveness, and as such it forms a basic statistic for many international comparisons and country assessments;

- productivity data are also used in the analysis of labour and product markets of OECD countries. For example, the OECD has analysed the links between productivity and product market regulation;

- productivity change constitutes an important element in modelling the productive capacity of OECD economies. This permits computation of capacity utilisation measures, themselves important in gauging the position of economies within the business cycle and for forecasting economic growth. In addition, the degree to which an economy's capacity is used informs analysts about the pressures from economic demand and thereby about the risk of inflationary developments.

Figure 4.11.3 – **Growth in GDP per hour worked**
Average annual growth in percentage, 1995-2000 and 2001-2006

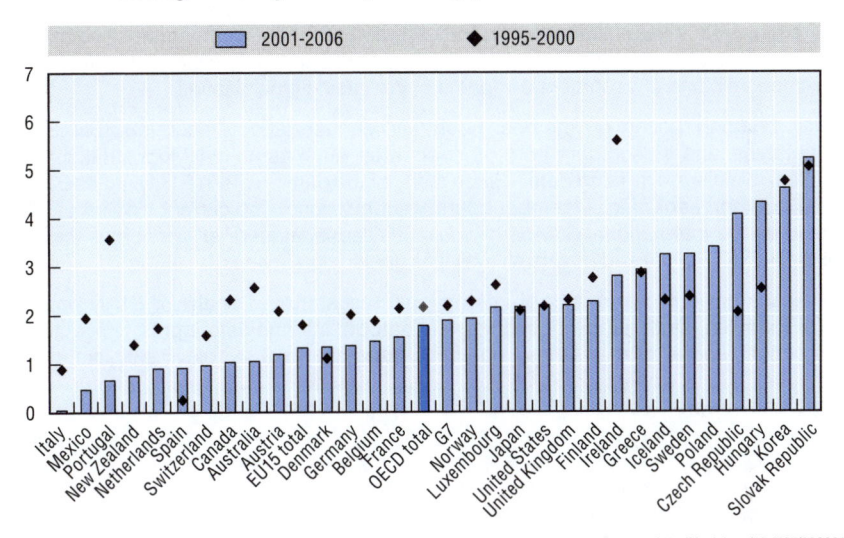

Source: OECD Productivity Database.

4. AN OVERVIEW OF OECD ECONOMIC STATISTICS

> **The STAN database for industrial analysis**
>
> The STAN industry database provides analysts and researchers with a comprehensive tool for analysing industrial performance at a relatively detailed level of activity across OECD countries. It includes annual estimates of output, labour input, investment and international trade, from 1970 onwards, which allow users to construct a wide range of indicators to focus on areas such as productivity growth, competitiveness and general structural change. Through the use of a standard industry list, comparisons can be made across countries. The industry list provides sufficient detail to enable users to highlight high-technology sectors and is compatible with those used in other datasets in the STAN family, such as business expenditure on R&D, harmonised input-output tables and bilateral trade by industrial activity. Combining these datasets can help provide insights into the socio-economic and environmental impacts of increasing globalization.
>
> STAN is primarily based on member countries' annual national accounts (SNA93) by activity tables, and it uses data from other sources, such as national industrial surveys/censuses, to estimate missing detail. Since many of the data points in STAN are estimated, they do not represent official member country submissions. The current version of STAN is based on the *International Standard Industrial Classification of all economic activities, Revision 3* (ISIC Rev. 3) and covers all activities (including services).
>
> To meet the basic requirements of international research and analysis, STAN provides several variables, such as: production (gross output), intermediate inputs, value added, labour cost, wages and salaries, operating surplus, total employment, number of employees, hours worked, gross fixed capital formation (investment), capital stock, imports and exports. Variable coverage for each country depends on: whether national statistical offices compile the measures by industrial activity in the context of annual national accounts; the extent of *back estimates* made by national statistical offices after revisions of national accounts; and the availability of business survey/census data (for detailed sectors). Where possible and appropriate, STAN provides time series in both nominal terms (current prices) and real terms (volumes). More information is available at *www.oecd.org/sti/stan*.

Input-output tables

Input-output (I/O) tables describe the sale and purchase relationships between producers and consumers within an economy. I/O tables are estimated in the context of national accounts: some countries estimate annual I/O tables, while others do it every three or five years. I/O tables represent a fundamental tool for analytical purposes and they can be produced by illustrating flows between the sales and purchases (final and intermediate) of *industry outputs* or by illustrating the sales and purchases (final and intermediate) of *product outputs*.

The OECD I/O database is presented on the former basis, reflecting in part the collection mechanisms for many other data sources, such as research and development data, employment statistics, pollution data and energy consumption, which are in the main collected by establishments, and so industry. The 2006 edition of OECD I/O tables consists of matrices of inter-industrial transaction flows of goods and services (domestically produced and imported) in current prices, for 27 OECD countries (*i.e.* all

AN OVERVIEW OF OECD ECONOMIC STATISTICS — 4

OECD member countries except Iceland, Mexico and Luxembourg) and eight non-member countries (Argentina, Brazil, China, Chinese Taipei, India, Indonesia, Israel and Russia), covering the years from the mid-1990s to the early 2000s. Through the use of a standard industry list (based on 48 industrial sectors classified following the ISIC Rev. 3) comparisons can be made across countries. Moreover, the industry breakdown allows high-technology manufacturing activities, such as pharmaceuticals, computers, communication equipment and aircraft to be studied, although for some countries some of these sectors are not separately identified.

Many of the *industry-by-industry* input-output tables have been derived from member countries' supply-use tables, using the fixed-product sales structure assumption. Furthermore, some additional adjustments have been made to the supply-use tables, usually to deal with disclosure problems. As such, the input-output tables should not be regarded as official country estimates. If the supply-use tables are consistent with equivalent estimates in the National Accounts and the STAN Database, the I/O tables maintain this consistency. Not all countries, however, integrate their supply-use tables into the national accounts' production process, and therefore differences may exist on occasion.

The database is a very useful empirical tool for economic research and structural analysis at the international level. It highlights inter-industrial relationships and covers not only manufacturing but also services. When used in conjunction with other OECD databases on industrial structures (such as the STAN Database, the Business Research & Development Expenditures by Industry – ANBERD and the Bilateral Trade Database – BTD), it provides a tool for consistent economic analysis of growth, structural change, productivity, competitiveness and employment at both the sectoral and macroeconomic levels. Increasingly, I/O tables are also being used in environmental analysis, for example, to measure direct and indirect pollutants produced by industrial sectors within an economy, and importantly, "linkages" between economies.

Financial accounts and balance sheets

The financial accounts (flows) together with the financial balance sheets (stocks) form the full Financial Accounts, which belong to the System of National Accounts (SNA). In particular, the financial accounts are part of the accumulation accounts; they record, by type of instrument, the financial transactions between institutional sectors. The financial balance sheets, corresponding to the final sets of information of the accounts, record the stocks of financial assets and liabilities held by the institutional sectors, and give their net worth at the end of the accounting period.

The financial accounts permit analysts and policy makers to have a better understanding of the interactions between the "real" economy and the financial activities of OECD member countries. While, as a general rule, the financial accounts are to be recorded on a non-consolidated basis, consolidated accounts are also useful for certain types of analyses, such as deriving a better account of the financial position of the various economic players, in particular for financial corporations and for general government.

4. AN OVERVIEW OF OECD ECONOMIC STATISTICS

▶ **Key definitions**

Institutional sectors: composed of those institutional units capable of engaging in transactions with other units and grouped together into five main categories, some of which are divided into sub-sectors: *non-financial corporations*; *financial corporations*; *general government*; *households*; *non-profit institutions serving households* – NPISH. To these five sectors, which together comprise the *total economy* sector, is added the *rest of the world* sector, which reflects transactions and assets/liabilities vis-à-vis non-residents.

Transactions: describe the net acquisition of financial assets and the net incurrence of liabilities during the reporting year. The transactions accounts include a balancing item (net acquisition of assets less net incurrence of liabilities) and the final net lending(+) / net borrowing(-).

Stocks: correspond to the amount of financial assets and liabilities at a point in time. The stocks accounts also present a balancing item that corresponds to the net value (assets less liabilities).

Assets and liabilities: grouped into seven categories of instruments, most of them divided into sub-instruments, which are ordered according to their liquidity: *monetary gold and SDRs*; *currency and deposits*; *securities other than shares*; *loans*; *shares and other equities*; *insurance technical reserves*; and *other accounts receivable/payable*. All *assets* have a counterpart *liability*, except for monetary gold and SDRs.

Consolidated accounts: in these accounts, all transactions and stock positions between sub-sectors of the same sector, as well as between institutional units of the same sub-sector, are eliminated.

Quarterly national accounts

Quarterly national accounts are a central instrument for short-term analysis and have a very important role in economic policy making. This is because they provide timely indicators of economic developments and enable detailed analysis of the behaviour of economies around turning points in the business cycle. Annual accounts are very useful for structural analysis but tend to hide the pattern of growth around turning points because peaks or troughs in economic activity generally cut across years.

Business and government economists are the major users of quarterly national accounts data. Both analyse current trends and make short-term forecasts of economic developments, and contribute to the discussion and co-ordination of economic policies. Quarterly national accounts are much used by government economists in order to provide the macroeconomic framework for the government budget. Timely and reliable data are of the essence, although these two requirements are often in conflict with each other.

OECD Quarterly national accounts (QNA) comprise comparable macroeconomic data for all 30 member countries on a quarterly basis. They feed directly into the OECD Secretariat's modelling, forecasting and analytical work and are used by outside researchers for the same purpose. They are, however, less detailed than

AN OVERVIEW OF OECD ECONOMIC STATISTICS 4

annual accounts, although countries have developed their quarterly accounts in a quite impressive way over the last six years.

Data are collected from countries on the basis of a standard questionnaire for European member countries and by various means for non-European member countries. All countries' quarterly accounts are now consistent with the 1993 System of National Accounts (1993 SNA).

Most countries produce "chain" volume estimates, which are generally derived by first calculating values at previous year prices then chaining them together in order to produce continuous volume time series. These estimates provide better indicators of growth than estimates derived using a fixed-price structure, that is only revised every five or 10 years, as was commonly done by many member countries until quite recently.

Most countries produce seasonally adjusted quarterly series and some of them produce series that are also adjusted for variations in the number of working days. Unless they are forced to do so, the sum of the four quarters of seasonally adjusted/working-day adjusted data will not be equal to the corresponding annual series. Some countries do this, but others do not.

OECD QNA provide a selection of time series from countries' quarterly national accounts for the following accounts: gross domestic product components by expenditure, by cost structure and by industry; gross fixed capital formation by product and gross fixed capital formation by institutional sector; components of disposable income; saving and net lending/borrowing. They also comprise some area totals and a consistent set of volume and price indices.

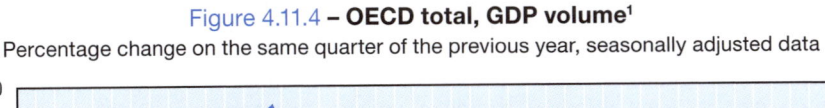

Figure 4.11.4 – **OECD total, GDP volume**[1]
Percentage change on the same quarter of the previous year, seasonally adjusted data

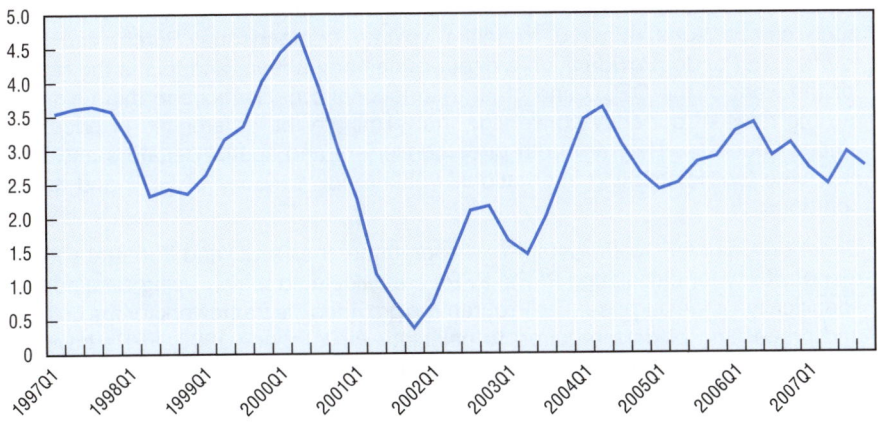

StatLink http://dx.doi.org/10.1787/336285670358

1. Derived from volume data converted into US dollars using fixed 2000 PPPs of GDP.

Source: OECD (2008), *Quarterly National Accounts*, OECD Publishing.

4 AN OVERVIEW OF OECD ECONOMIC STATISTICS

Figure 4.11.5 – **Quarterly GDP volume growth**
Fourth quarter 2007 or latest available quarter
Percentage change on the previous quarter, seasonally adjusted data

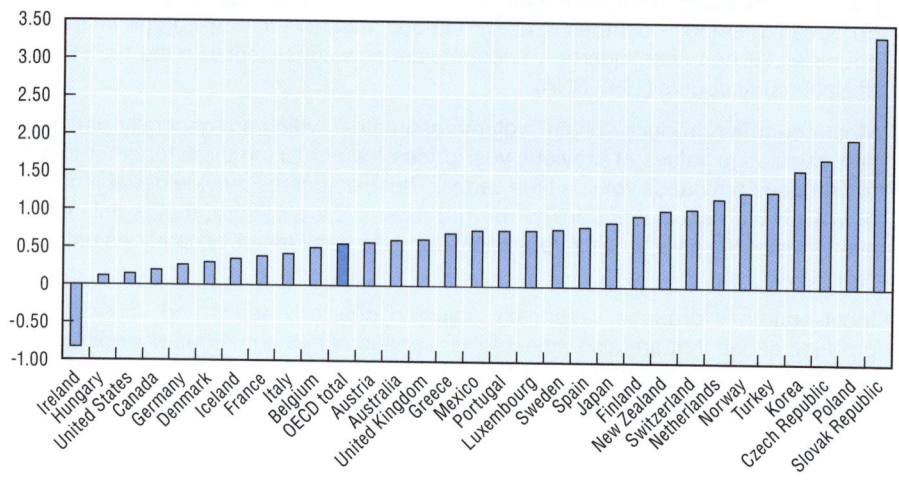

Source: OECD (2008), *Quarterly National Accounts*, OECD Publishing.

StatLink http://dx.doi.org/10.1787/336287662250

Purchasing power parities

How does one compare economic data between countries that is expressed in units of national currency? And in particular, how should measures of production and gross domestic product (GDP) be converted? The use of market exchange rates, while straightforward, turns out to be an unsatisfactory solution for many reasons – primarily because exchange rates reflect so many more influences than the direct-price comparisons required to make volume comparisons. Purchasing Power Parities (PPPs) do provide such a direct-price comparison, and this is the rationale for the work of the OECD and other international organisations in this field. PPPs are the rates of currency conversion that eliminate the differences in price levels among countries. They are both price converters and spatial deflators and are an adequate tool for making international volume comparisons of GDP and its main components.

Under the Joint OECD-Eurostat PPP Programme, the OECD and Eurostat share the responsibility for calculating PPPs. PPPs are calculated mainly using data collected specifically for the purpose. The Programme provides the framework for the collection and processing of data required to calculate PPPs. Since 1990, PPPs have been calculated every three years for member countries of the OECD and annually for EU countries.

PPPs are key statistical tools for international volume comparisons. However, there is a lack of understanding of the methodology and also of how, and when, PPPs should be used. The following box summarises how PPPs should be used.

AN OVERVIEW OF OECD ECONOMIC STATISTICS 4

Recommended uses	• To make spatial volume comparisons of GDP (size of economies), GDP per head (economic welfare), GDP per hour worked (labour productivity) • To make spatial comparisons of comparative price levels • To group countries by their volume index of GDP per head and/or their comparative price levels of GDP
Uses with limitations	• To analyse changes over time in relative GDP per capita and relative prices • To analyse price convergence • To make spatial comparisons of cost of living • To use PPPs calculated for GDP and its component expenditures as deflators for other values, such as household income
Not recommended uses	• As precise measures to establish strict rankings of countries • As a means of constructing national growth rates • As measures to generate output and productivity comparisons by industry • As measures to undertake price level comparisons at low levels of aggregation • As indicators of the undervaluation or overvaluation of currencies • As equilibrium exchange rates

▶ **Key definitions**

Indices of real final expenditure: volume measures that reflect the relative magnitudes of the product groups or aggregates being compared. At the level of GDP, they are used to compare the economic size of countries.

Indices of real final expenditure per head: standardised measures of volume that reflect the relative levels of the product groups or aggregates being compared after adjusting for differences in the size of populations among countries. At the level of GDP, they are used to compare the economic well being of populations.

Comparative price levels: ratio of PPPs to exchange rate. They provide a measure of the differences in price levels among countries by indicating for a given product group or aggregate the number of units of common currency needed to buy the same volume of the product group or aggregate in each country. At the level of GDP, they provide a measure of the differences in the general price levels of countries.

4. AN OVERVIEW OF OECD ECONOMIC STATISTICS

Figure 4.11.6 – **Comparative price levels and indices of real GDP per head**
OECD = 100, 2006

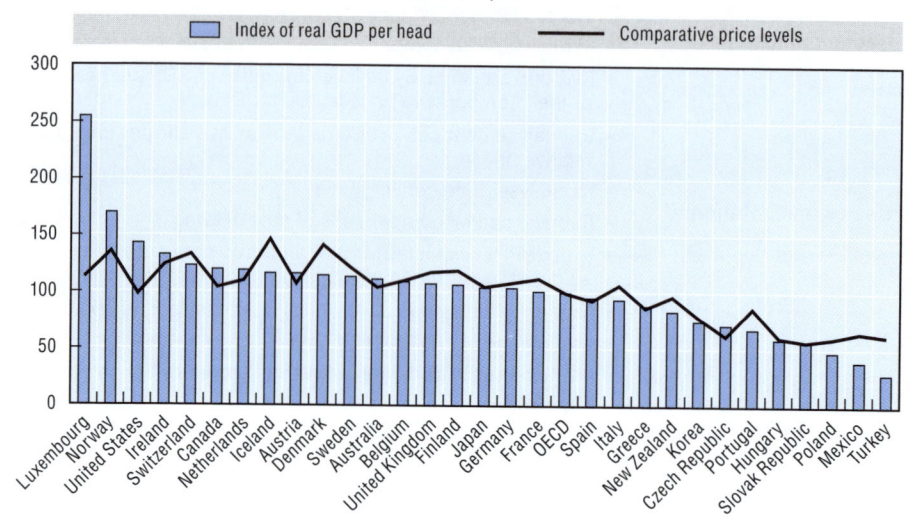

StatLink http://dx.doi.org/10.1787/336358623634

AN OVERVIEW OF OECD ECONOMIC STATISTICS 4

Further information

Publications

Ahmad, N., *et al.* (2003), "Comparing Labour Productivity Growth in the OECD Area: The Role of Measurement", *OECD Science, Technology and Industry Working Papers*, No. 2003/14, OECD Publishing.

Maddison, Angus (2003), *The World Economy: Historical Perspectives*, OECD Publishing.

OECD and African Development Bank (2007), *African Economic Outlook 2006/2007*, OECD Publishing.

OECD (2000), *System of National Accounts 1993: Glossary*, OECD Glossaries, OECD Publishing.

OECD (2001), "The Measurement of Productivity: What Do the Numbers Mean?", *Measuring Productivity – OECD Manual Measurement of Aggregate and Industry-level Productivity Growth*, OECD Publishing, pp. 29-61.

OECD (2003), *The Sources of Economic Growth in OECD Countries*, OECD Publishing.

OECD (2004), "Clocking In (and Out): Several Facets of Working Time", *OECD Employment Outlook*, 2004 Edition, OECD Publishing.

OECD (2007), *Latin American Economic Outlook 2008*, OECD Publishing.

OECD (2007), *OECD Economic Outlook*, Vol. 2007/2, No. 82, OECD Publishing.

OECD (2007), *Purchasing Power Parities and Real Expenditures: 2005 Benchmark Year*, OECD Publishing.

OECD (2008), *Main Economic Indicators*, OECD Publishing.

OECD (2008), *National Accounts of OECD Countries*, OECD Publishing.

Pilat, D. and P. Schreyer (2004), "The OECD Productivity Database – An Overview", *International Productivity Monitor*, No. 8, Spring, CSLS, Ottawa, pp. 59-65.

Schreyer, P. and D. Pilat (2001), "Measuring Productivity", *OECD Economic Studies*, OECD Publishing.

UN, OECD, IMF, Eurostat (eds.) (1993), *System of National Accounts 1993*, United Nations, Geneva, *http://unstats.un.org/unsd/sna1993*.

Van Ark, B. (2004), "The Measurement of Productivity: What Do the Numbers Mean?", in G. Gelauff, L. Klomp, S. Raes and T. Roelandt (eds.), *Fostering Productivity – Patterns, Determinants and Policy Implications*, Elsevier, Amsterdam; Boston, pp. 29-61.

Yamano N. and Ahmad N., "The OECD Input-Output Database: 2006 Edition", *OECD Science, Technology and Industry Working Papers*, 2006.

Online databases

National Accounts of OECD Countries
OECD Economic Outlook Statistics
Quarterly National Accounts
Available at *www.sourceoecd.org/database/oecdstat*

Websites

www.oecd.org/eco/sources-and-methods
www.oecd.org/statistics/productivity
www.oecd.org/statistics/productivity/compendium
www.oecd.org/std/ppp
www.oecd.org/std/qna/statistics
www.theworldeconomy.org

4 AN OVERVIEW OF OECD ECONOMIC STATISTICS

4.12 OECD Economic forecasts

In common with member government administrations and other public and private sector analysts, the OECD's Economics Department routinely monitors the world economy and in this context produces macroeconomic forecasts covering prospective world developments over a coming two-year period. The OECD forecasts include projections for key macroeconomic variables in each of it 30 member countries, as well as international trade and payments, and broad developments in key non-OECD economies and regions. An important feature of the exercise is the treatment of the world economy as a coherent and integrated whole, with individual country and regional assessments made under a consistent set of assumptions, giving particular attention to international consistency in trade and financial developments. Importantly, the OECD projections and the accompanying analysis have a clear focus on framing the policy debate in Member countries. The resulting forecasts are published twice a year in the *OECD Economic Outlook* and the associated OECD Economic Outlook database.

The OECD's macroeconomic projections are best characterised as being "conditional" rather than "pure" forecasts, since they depend on specific sets of assumptions including those about prevailing macroeconomic and structural policies, exchange rates and world commodity prices. Fiscal policy assumptions are based on current legislation, as well as announced measures and stated policy intentions when they are embodied in well-defined programmes with legislative support. Monetary policies are assumed to be set so as to achieve stated objectives, notably in relation to maintaining low inflation, and take into account monetary and financial market conditions and policy announcements. Nominal exchange rates against the US dollar are generally assumed to remain constant at the level prevailing on a pre-specified cut-off. Crude oil prices are typically assumed to remain constant in nominal terms based on average prices during the period leading up to the cut-of date; other commodity prices are typically assumed to remain constant in real terms.

Projections for individual OECD Member countries are, in general, made on a quarterly frequency and typically include:

- Main domestic demand components (consumption, investment and stock-building) as well as exports and imports, determining output (GDP) in "real" terms, as well as corresponding deflators and other important price measures;

- Labour market developments as summarised by employment, unemployment and participation rates and corresponding wage cost and earnings developments;

- Appropriation accounts for main institutional sectors;

- International trade and payments, including sub-balances of the current account, such as the balances on goods and services, foreign investment income and transfers.

A large number of other important macroeconomic variables are also included in the projections, including supply potential and output gaps, short- and long-term interest rates and indicators of world trade and competitiveness.

AN OVERVIEW OF OECD ECONOMIC STATISTICS 4

Table 4.12.1 – Economic Outlook N.82, Summary of projections

	2007	2008	2009	2007 Q4	2008 Q1	2008 Q2	2008 Q3	2008 Q4	2009 Q1	2009 Q2	2009 Q3	2009 Q4	Fourth quarter 2007	Fourth quarter 2008	Fourth quarter 2009
							Per cent								
Real GDP growth															
United States	2.2	2.0	2.2	1.3	1.1	1.5	1.8	1.9	2.2	2.5	2.7	2.8	2.6	1.6	2.5
Japan	1.9	1.6	1.8	1.7	1.5	1.6	1.7	1.8	1.8	1.9	1.9	1.9	1.3	1.7	1.9
Euro area	2.6	1.9	2.0	1.7	1.8	1.9	2.0	2.0	2.0	2.0	2.0	2.0	2.2	1.9	2.0
Total OECD	2.7	2.3	2.4	2.0	1.9	2.0	2.2	2.3	2.5	2.6	2.7	2.7	2.6	2.1	2.6
Inflation															
United States	2.6	2.1	2.0	2.4	2.5	2.0	1.9	1.9	2.1	1.9	1.9	2.0	2.5	2.1	2.0
Japan	-0.5	-0.3	0.3	-1.0	-0.2	0.1	0.1	0.3	0.3	0.4	0.5	0.5	-0.8	0.1	0.4
Euro area	2.2	2.2	2.3	2.3	2.3	2.2	2.2	2.2	2.3	2.3	2.3	2.3	2.4	2.2	2.3
Total OECD	2.3	2.1	2.1	2.3	2.3	2.1	2.1	2.0	2.1	2.0	2.0	2.1	2.4	2.1	2.1
Unemployment rate[1]															
United States	4.6	5.0	5.0	4.8	4.8	4.9	5.0	5.1	5.1	5.0	5.0	4.9	4.8	5.1	4.9
Japan	3.8	3.7	3.6	3.8	3.8	3.8	3.7	3.7	3.7	3.6	3.5	3.5	3.8	3.7	3.5
Euro area	6.8	6.4	6.4	6.5	6.5	6.5	6.4	6.4	6.4	6.4	6.4	6.4	6.5	6.4	6.4
Total OECD	5.4	5.4	5.3	5.4	5.4	5.4	5.3	5.3	5.3	5.3	5.3	5.2	5.4	5.3	5.2
World trade growth	7.0	8.1	8.1	8.2	8.0	8.0	8.0	8.0	8.1	8.2	8.2	8.2	7.7	8.0	8.2
Current account balance[2]															
United States	-5.6	-5.4	-5.3												
Japan	4.7	4.8	5.2												
Euro area	0.2	-0.1	-0.2												
Total OECD	-1.4	-1.4	-1.4												
Cyclically-adjusted fiscal balance[3]															
United States	-3.0	-3.4	-3.4												
Japan	-3.4	-3.9	-3.6												
Euro area	-0.6	-0.6	-0.4												
Total OECD	-2.0	-2.2	-2.1												
Short-term interest rate															
United States	5.3	4.6	4.7	5.0	4.8	4.6	4.6	4.6	4.6	4.6	4.7	4.8			
Japan	0.7	0.6	0.9	0.8	0.7	0.6	0.6	0.6	0.7	0.8	0.9	1.2			
Euro area	4.3	4.2	4.1	4.7	4.4	4.2	4.1	4.1	4.1	4.1	4.1	4.1			

StatLink http://dx.doi.org/10.1787/336536447544

1. Per cent of the labour force.
2. Per cent of GDP.
3. Per cent of potential GDP.

UNDERSTANDING ECONOMIC STATISTICS – ISBN 978-92-64-03312-2 – © OECD 2008

4. AN OVERVIEW OF OECD ECONOMIC STATISTICS

The assessment process uses a combination of analytical methods and expert judgment, involving a broad exchange of views among OECD country experts and topic specialists, also taking into account a variety of statistics and information based on econometric models of key macroeconomic relationships. International consistency is ensured through the use of the OECD's world trade model (Pain *et al*, 2005), and discussions between country and trade specialists.

In assessing the current near-term situation, particular weight is also given to separate models that make use of high-frequency indicators to provide estimates of GDP growth in the major OECD economies in the two quarters following the last quarter for which data has been published (Sédillot and Pain, 2005). These models incorporate high-frequency information released before the official national accounts data, including "soft" indicators, such as business and consumer surveys, and "hard" indicators, such as industrial production and retail sales, with use made of monthly and quarterly data and a variety of estimation techniques.

A further "reality check" on the OECD projections is provided by discussions with member country government experts and economic forecasters. While giving due consideration to the comments and suggestions from member countries, the projections and analysis published in the *Economic Outlook* reflect the independent assessment of world economic conditions by the OECD staff economists.

Further information

Publications
OECD (2007), *OECD Economic Outlook*, Vol. 2007/2 No. 82, OECD Publishing.
F. Sédillot and N. Pain (2005), "Indicator models for real GDP growth in the major economies", *OECD Economic Studies*, No. 40, 2005/1.
N. Pain, *et al.* (2005), "The New International Trade Model", *OECD Economic Department Working Papers,* No. 440, August.

Online databases
OECD Economic Outlook database, available at *www.sourceoecd.org/database/oecdstat*

Websites
www.oecd.org/oecdeconomicoutlook
www.oecd.org/eco/sources-and-methods

4.13 Territorial statistics

Territorial statistics are an important tool in assessing the economic performance of regions and in evaluating regional development policies. While national averages can hide wide regional differences in economic conditions, regional statistics enable the identification of those regions that outperform their country as a whole and those that lag behind. The patterns of development may differ widely in urban and rural areas, and some areas may lag behind even when the national economy is performing well.

The word "region" can mean very different things both within and among countries. To address this issue, the OECD has classified regions within each member country into two Territorial Levels (TLs). The higher level (Territorial Level 2) consists of 335 macro-regions (*i.e.* for the US, it consists of 51 states) while the lower level (Territorial Level 3) is composed of 1 679 micro-regions (*i.e.* for the US it consists of 179 groups of counties). This classification – which for European countries is largely consistent with the Eurostat classification – facilitates greater comparability of regions at the same territorial level. Indeed, these two levels, which are officially established and relatively stable in all member countries, are used by many as a framework for implementing regional policies.

A second important issue for the analysis of regional economies concerns the different "geography" of each region. For instance, in the United Kingdom one could question the relevance of comparing the highly urbanised area of London to the rural region of the Shetland Islands, despite the fact that both regions belong to the same territorial level (TL3). To take account of these differences, the OECD has established a regional typology according to which TL3 regions have been classified as Predominantly Urban, Predominantly Rural and Intermediate. This typology, based on the percentage of regional population living in rural or urban communities, enables meaningful comparisons between regions belonging to the same type and level.

OECD regional statistics cover a wide range of topics, from demographic variables to economic accounts and from labour data to social and innovation indicators. Time series are available for 7 to 10 years periods according to the variable.

Regional statistics allow for the calculation of measures of concentration and disparity within countries. In 2003, Portugal. Sweden and the United Kingdom displayed the highest concentration of GDP, followed closely by Korea, Australia and Finland. GDP was more evenly distributed in the Slovak Republic, the Czech Republic and the Netherlands. During the period 1998-2003, concentration increased most in Hungary and Poland and decreased in the Czech Republic and Portugal. The largest regional disparities in labour productivity in 2003 were found in Mexico and Turkey, followed by the United States. According to this index, the countries with the smallest disparities were Sweden and Denmark. During the period 1998-2003, the Gini index increased the most in Australia, Ireland and Canada and decreased in Poland, the Slovak Republic and Spain.

4 AN OVERVIEW OF OECD ECONOMIC STATISTICS

▶ Key definitions

Index of geographic concentration: the geographic concentration index compares the geographic distribution of GDP, for example, to the area of all regions. The index lies between 0 (no concentration) and 100 (maximum concentration). The value of the index is affected by the size of the regions; therefore, differences in geographic concentration between two countries may be partially due to differences in the average size of regions in each country.

Gini index of inequality: the Gini index measures the extent to which the distribution of employment among regions within an economy, for example, deviates from a perfectly equal distribution. The Gini index measures the area between the Lorenz curve and the hypothetical line of absolute equality, expressed as a percentage of the maximum area under the line. A Gini index of zero represents perfect equality, and 100 indicates perfect inequality.

The quest for an OECD definition of metropolitan regions

In assessing regional competitiveness policies governments are increasingly called to compare the economic and social performance of metropolitan regions across countries. The scope of what we can learn from this international comparison however is limited by the lack of a comparable definition of metropolitan region. Although almost each country has its own definition, these definitions vary significantly.

A first non-definitive methodology has been developed by the OECD for a comparable definition of metropolitan regions. This methodology is based on four criteria:

- The first criterion concerns the size of the population. A threshold of 1.5 million people is set to consider the region as metropolitan.

- Second, the density of population should exceed a critical value set at 150 people per km^2.

- Third, it is also fundamental that these regions with large and dense populations constituting urban areas represent a self-contained labour market. In order to define labour markets, commuting flows are used to calculate net migration rates. A region is considered metropolitan if the net commuting rate does not exceed 10% of the resident population.

- The fourth criterion has been set to include a small number of important cities in their national context. Therefore, cities with less than 1.5 million people, but that account for more than 20% of their national population, are included.

AN OVERVIEW OF OECD ECONOMIC STATISTICS 4

Figure 4.13.1 – **Index of geographic concentration of GDP**

2003 | 1998

Country	Value
Portugal	56
Sweden	55
United Kingdom	54
Korea	51
Australia	50
Finland	50
Canada	49
Norway	49
Spain	48
Austria	48
Japan	47
Mexico	46
United States	46
Turkey	44
France	41
Hungary	39
OECD26 average	38
Ireland	38
Greece	38
Poland	37
Germany	36
Italy	36
Denmark	35
Belgium	33
Netherlands	29
Czech Republic	27
Slovak Republic	24

StatLink http://dx.doi.org/10.1787/336418331644

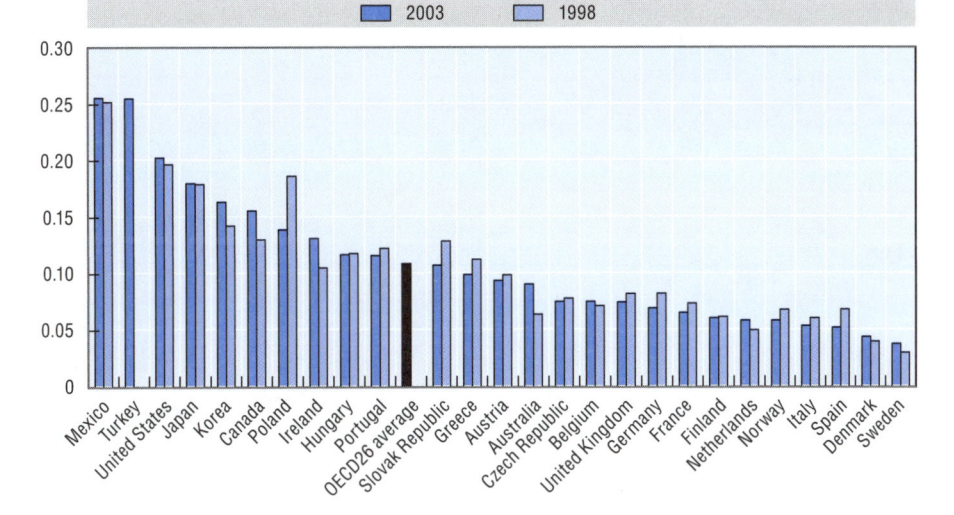

Figure 4.13.2 – **Gini index of inequality of GDP per worker**

2003 | 1998

Source: OECD (2007), *OECD Regions at a Glance*, OECD Publishing.

StatLink http://dx.doi.org/10.1787/336453644613

4. AN OVERVIEW OF OECD ECONOMIC STATISTICS

Further information

Publications
OECD (2007), *OECD Regions at a Glance*, OECD Publishing.

Online database
OECD Regional Statistics, available at *www.sourceoecd.org/database/oecdstat*.

Websites
www.oecd.org/regional/regionsataglance

4. AN OVERVIEW OF OECD ECONOMIC STATISTICS

4.14 Economic history: long-term statistics of the world economy

The OECD has been collecting economic data for several decades now, and many key time series go back as far as the 1960s. However, for those studying the underlying causes and patterns of growth in the world economy, even half a century is too brief a period to be able to make meaningful analyses. In this respect, the OECD Development Centre has made some important contributions to the field of economic history. In particular the work of the respected economist, Angus Maddison, has been especially influential. Maddison's work presents and analyses quantitative data for key economic variables from as far back as 960AD, and covering all regions of the world. By bringing together this information Maddison aims to quantify long-term changes in world income and population in a comparable way, and as such, to begin to offer explanations. Obviously, the further into the past such investigations delve, the weaker the evidence and the greater the reliance on clues and conjecture. However, such exercises are useful and necessary as the differences in the pace and pattern of change in major parts of the world economy have deep roots in the past. The two Maddison's most influential statistical publications are:

The world economy

In this seminal work, Maddison brings together statistics on such variables as GDP, population, agricultural production, and merchandise exports, covering the past millennium. On the basis of comprehensive and detailed data, he argues that advances in population and income over the past millennium have been sustained by three interactive processes:

a) conquest or settlement of relatively empty areas which had fertile land, new biological resources, or a potential to accommodate transfers of population, crops and livestock;

b) international trade and capital movements;

c) technological and institutional innovation.

He shows that over the past millennium, world population rose 22–fold. Per capita income increased 13–fold, world GDP nearly 300–fold. This contrasts sharply with the preceding millennium, when world population grew by only a sixth, and there was no advance in per capita income.

From the year 1000 to 1820 the advance in per capita income was a slow crawl – the world average rose about 50 per cent. Most of the growth went to accommodate a fourfold increase in population. Since 1820, world development has been much more dynamic. Per capita income rose more than eightfold, population more than fivefold.

Chinese economic performance in the long-run

In this book Maddison provides a detailed analysis of the development of the Chinese economy over the past millennium and the prospects for the next quarter century. He demonstrates that Chinese per capita income was higher than that of Europe from the tenth to the early fifteenth century and it was the world's biggest economy for several centuries thereafter, before falling into decline. Its extraordinary progress in the reform period since 1978 has been a resurrection,

4. AN OVERVIEW OF OECD ECONOMIC STATISTICS

not a miracle and it is likely to resume its normal position as the world's number one economy by 2015. He applies standard OECD measurement techniques to estimate the pace of Chinese progress and finds somewhat slower growth, nearly 8 per cent a year rather than the 9.6 per cent of Chinese Bureau of Statistics. Instead of using the exchange rate to measure the level of Chinese performance, which greatly understates China's role in the world economy, Maddison uses purchasing power parity to convert yuan into US dollars and finds that China accounted for 5 per cent of world GDP in 1978, 15 per cent in 2003 and that this is likely to rise to 23 per cent in 2030.

Table 4.14.1 – **Comparative Levels of Economic Performance, China and Other Major Parts of the World Economy**
1700-2003

	China	Japan	Europe	United States	USSR	India	World
GDP (billion 1990 "international" dollars)							
1700	82.8	15.4	92.6	0.5	16.2	90.8	371.4
1820	228.6	20.7	184.8	12.5	37.7	111.4	694.5
1952	305.9	202	1 730.7	1 625.2	545.8	234.1	5 912.8
1978	935.1	1 446.2	5 268.2	4 089.5	1 715.2	625.7	18 969.0
2003	6 188.0	2 699.3	8 643.8	8 430.8	1 552.2	2 267.1	40 913.4
Population (million)							
1700	138	27	100.3	1	26.6	165	603.2
1820	381	31	169.5	10	54.8	209	1 041.7
1952	569	86.5	398.6	157.6	185.9	372	2 616.0
1978	956	114.9	480.1	222.6	261.5	648	4 279.7
2003	1 288.4	127.2	516	290.3	287.6	1 050	6 278.6
GDP per capita (1990 "international" dollars)							
1700	600	570	923	527	610	550	615
1820	600	669	1 090	1 257	688	533	667
1952	538	2 336	4 342	10 316	2 937	629	2 260
1978	978	12 585	10 972	18 373	6 559	966	4 432
2003	4 803	21 218	16 750	29 037	5 397	2 160	6 516

StatLink http://dx.doi.org/10.1787/336547300101

Table 4.14.2 – **Shares of World GDP**
1700-2003

	1700	1820	1952	1978	2003
China	22.3	32.9	5.2	4.9	15.1
India	24.4	16.0	4.0	3.3	5.5
Japan	4.1	3.0	3.4	7.6	6.6
Europe	24.9	26.6	29.3	27.8	21.1
United States	0.1	1.8	27.5	21.6	20.6
USSR	4.4	5.4	9.2	9.0	3.8

StatLink http://dx.doi.org/10.1787/336551023063

Source: OECD (2007), Development Centre Studies *Chinese Economic Performance in the Long Run – Second Edition, Revised and Updated: 960-2030 AD,* OECD Publishing.

Further information

Publication
Maddison, Angus (2006), *The World Economy: Volume 1: A Millennial Perspective and Volume 2: Historical Statistics*, Development Centre Studies, OECD Publishing.

OECD (2007), Development Centre Studies, *Chinese Economic Performance in the Long Run – Second Edition, revised and updated: 960-2030 AD*, OECD Publishing.

Websites
www.ggdc.net/Maddison/

Chapter 5

Assessing the Quality of Economic Statistics

How can we distinguish between high-quality statistics and data whose quality is poor? And what exactly do we mean by the "quality" of statistical data? Do quality standards exist for statistics? If so, who established them? At present, when users have practically unlimited access to statistical information but often feel bombarded by the media with sometimes conflicting data, the ability to identify high-quality statistics is of paramount importance. This chapter illustrates the basic concepts developed to ascertain the quality of statistical data, and the initiatives launched at the international level to assess the quality of statistics produced by national statistical offices and other producers of official statistics. Given that the international comparability of statistics plays a key role in the decision-making process of major international organisations, the IMF, the OECD and European authorities have worked particularly hard to develop models for assessing statistical quality.

5. ASSESSING THE QUALITY OF ECONOMIC STATISTICS

5.1. The dimensions of quality

From the 1980s onwards, driven by the reorganisation of industrial production in which many developed countries were at that time engaged, the concept of "total quality" passed into the public domain; extensive literature analysed the various aspects of this term, including the application of so-called *Total Quality Management (TQM)* to various fields of activity. Statistics, too, were involved in the revolution triggered by the TQM approach, indeed to such an extent that various national statistical offices and international organisations developed systematic approaches to the quality management of statistics, as well as evaluation frameworks for data quality, particularly that of economic statistics. Furthermore, in the age of the "information society", in which many suppliers of statistical data co-exist and the scarcity of data has given way to an apparent over-abundance, the end users' ability to assess the quality of the statistics has become a prerequisite for selecting the most relevant data for their needs.

According to the definition published by the International Standards Office (ISO) in 1986, quality is the totality of features and characteristics of a product or service that bear on its ability to satisfy stated or implied needs (ISO 8402). Therefore, a product's ability to satisfy user needs determines its quality, and therefore makes the user the sole judge of overall product quality. This contrasts with other approaches that consider the producer best-qualified to assess the quality of the product, on the grounds that the producer alone has knowledge of the production processes.

In a statistical context, for a large part of the last century the term "quality" was primarily seen as a synonym for "accuracy". This view derived from statistical sample surveys in which sampling "errors" (attributable to the incorrect use of benchmarking and to the characteristics of the sample used) could be compounded by more significant non-sampling errors relating to the various stages in the statistical production cycle (activities of interviewers, programming errors in computer procedures, etc.). Typically, in this context, there was conflict between the quality and the timeliness of data, *i.e.* between the accuracy of data and the time needed to produce and disseminate those data.

As a result of work carried out over the past 20 years, the concept of quality in statistics now has much broader significance and is based on a series of "dimensions". For example, according to a survey conducted in 2001, the dimensions most frequently used by European statistical offices to define quality were: relevance, accuracy, timeliness, availability, comparability, coherence, completeness. Similar concepts are used by statistical offices in Canada, the United States and Australia and also by the European Statistical System.

The box on the next page provides short definitions of the various dimensions of quality used by the OECD. In accordance with the central role played by users in the evaluation of quality, these definitions tend to underline the importance of subjective dimensions that go well beyond those of accuracy alone. For example, the same information can be deemed extremely relevant by one user but completely useless by another. The accessibility of a database may be judged positively by a user with good computer skills, but negatively by somebody not used to navigating through databanks.

ASSESSING THE QUALITY OF ECONOMIC STATISTICS 5

Main dimensions of quality for OECD statistics

Relevance

The relevance of a statistic reflects its ability to satisfy the needs of users. This depends on its utility in helping to add to the users' knowledge with regard to the topics of greatest importance to them. The evaluation of relevance is subjective and varies according to the user's needs.

Accuracy

Accuracy represents the level at which the statistical information correctly describes the phenomenon it has been developed to measure. It is normally expressed in terms of the "error" in the statistical data, which can in turn be broken down into different components.

Timeliness and Punctuality

The timeliness of a statistic is the time it takes to disseminate it with regard to the reference period. The timeliness of a statistic has a significant impact on its relevance. In addition, there is a clear trade-off between the timeliness and the accuracy of a statistic. Punctuality implies the existence of a timetable for releasing statistical information and measures the degree to which that timetable is adhered to by the data producer.

Accessibility

The accessibility of a statistic reflects the ease with which it can be identified and utilised by a user. Accessibility therefore depends on the means with which the statistic is made available to the user (paper, electronic medium, etc.), the search procedures required, the user's ability to make use of the statistic, the existence of barriers to access (cost, for example), the provision of user-support services, etc.

Interpretability

Interpretability reflects the ease with which the users can understand the basic characteristics of the statistic and thereby evaluate its utility for their own needs. The adequacy of the information (metadata) provided regarding the coverage of the statistic with regard to the reference universe, its comparability over time and in space, the methods used to collect and generate data, the accuracy of data, etc., are all fundamental factors of interpretability.

Coherence

Coherence relates to the degree to which a particular statistic can be analysed from a temporal and spatial standpoint, or related to other information within analytical and interpretation models. The use of standard concepts, definitions and classifications increases the coherence of the information supplied by various sources, while the existence of changes in methodology can impede the comparability over time of historical series relating to the same parameter.

Credibility

The credibility of a statistic refers to the confidence that users have in the person or entity producing that statistic. It is normally based on the reputation of the producer as demonstrated over time, which in turn relates to factors such as the objectivity, scientific independence, professionalism and transparency shown by the producer in the course of his or her activities.

5. ASSESSING THE QUALITY OF ECONOMIC STATISTICS

The assessment of interpretability can vary substantially between an expert in statistical terms, who has no difficulty reading the methodological notes accompanying statistical tables, and someone without such knowledge. It should also be noted that the credibility dimension of a given statistic does not depend so much on its technical qualities as on the characteristics of the data producer and its reputation, which in turn depend on how the user population perceives the overall quality of the statistics produced.

It is clear how such a multi-faceted definition of quality poses a much greater challenge to producers of statistics than a simple demand to merely produce "accurate" data. This challenge addresses the entire statistical production cycle, from the initial design of statistics to their collection, compilation, dissemination and communication. To meet such an ambitious objective, some statistical offices have developed systematic approaches to quality, such as quality frameworks, which tend to combine technical aspects with those relating to management. These pay constant attention to introducing improvements at every stage of the statistical production process, through methodological, technological and organisational innovations, or by investment in staff training at all levels of the management hierarchy, combined with the adoption of innovative public communication, marketing and data dissemination strategies.

Moreover, some international organisations such as the OECD and Eurostat, have developed and adopted *quality frameworks*. These are designed to enhance the quality of their statistics, through the revision and improvement of internal procedures used to collect, transform and disseminate statistical data sent to them by their member countries, and through the adoption of technologically more advanced instruments to improve data accessibility and interpretability.

5.2. International initiatives for the evaluation of quality

Given the importance of the end user's perspective in quality evaluation, the data dissemination phase becomes crucial in the statistical production cycle: accurate data that are not timely, hard to access and can only be interpreted in parts would indeed be considered of poor quality by most users and would probably be disregarded in favour of data that are more timely and easier to access and read, even if they were only partly accurate. This is where the main risk lies for the producers and the users of official statistical products in the modern "information society": the former risk seeing their efforts to produce accurate statistics facing competition from other producers with less well endowed methodology but better able to deploy aggressive marketing techniques to impose their own products on the media and the general public. The public (because of its limited knowledge of statistical techniques) finds it increasingly difficult to distinguish between information of high technical quality and information based on less rigorous scientific criteria, but with apparently greater relevance and timeliness. The result: users run the risk of making decisions based on approximate or even incorrect data.

ASSESSING THE QUALITY OF ECONOMIC STATISTICS 5

Over the past 10 years, national producers of official statistics and international organisations have given greater attention to the formulation of quality evaluation procedures based on: *a)* critical analyses of national statistical systems (or of specific subject areas) conducted by commissions composed of internationally recognised experts; *b)* multilateral systems for monitoring the quality of the principal economic statistics, as well as the practical application of the UN *Fundamental Principles of Official Statistics*. These procedures have been added to the quality checks regularly carried out by international organisations on the statistics they receive from national producers, as well as to user-satisfaction surveys for statistical information.

International organisations are frequently requested to review and analyse the institutional, methodological and organisational aspects of the production of national statistics. This analysis often entails a series of visits to national statistical offices and other producers of official statistics and the preparation of reports on their various activities and processes, which are then critically assessed by the international organisation and by user groups. The exercise concludes with the drafting of a final report that is normally made public. The statistical systems of Switzerland, Hungary and Portugal have been the subject, within the past decade, of such reviews requested by the country concerned, while all the statistical systems of the European Union were analysed in depth by Eurostat, with regard to both institutional and technical issues. Similar analyses have been made by the OECD of the systems of countries wishing to join that Organisation.

A second type of statistical-quality analysis by international organisations was the initiative launched in 1995 by the IMF following the Mexican financial crisis. Since one of the causes of that crisis was the highly unreliable statistical data on key elements of the economic and financial situation in that country, the IMF launched a project to oblige national producers of economic statistics to improve the information provided on the availability and quality of macroeconomic statistics, and to comply with the UN *Fundamental Principles of Official Statistics*. Under this initiative, known as the *Special Data Dissemination Standard* (SDDS), individual countries update at pre-determined intervals a publicly accessible Internet site (*http://dsbb.imf.org*) displaying statistics relating to 18 parameters (Gross Domestic Product, prices, public deficit, etc.), which are accompanied by appropriate information (metadata) on the methods used to produce those statistics, the organisational procedures governing their release and the institutional status of the producers of official statistics. Given this information, users can more accurately assess the quality of the data provided.

5. ASSESSING THE QUALITY OF ECONOMIC STATISTICS

> **The role of metadata**
>
> The provision of methodological information, or metadata, that define the concepts and methods used in the collection, compilation, transformation, revision and dissemination of statistics, is an essential function of all agencies disseminating statistics at both the national and international levels. A distinction can be made between "structural" metadata – that act as data identifiers and descriptors (needed to identify, use and process data matrixes and cubes) – and "reference" metadata, which describe statistical concepts and methodologies for the collection and generation of data and provide information on data quality.
>
> The need for such methodological information arises from a desire to lend transparency to economic, social and population statistics so that the typical end user can make an informed assessment of their usefulness and relevance to his or her purpose. In recognition of this, methodological transparency is embodied as one of the UN *Fundamental Principles of Official Statistics*. The provision of metadata is therefore an inescapable responsibility of all statistical agencies, in both developed and developing countries, and one that requires adequate planning and resources. In recognition of this, many statistical agencies have embodied their policy on the provision of metadata in their dissemination standards and author guides.
>
> Users of metadata are generally depicted as falling into two broad groups: producers of statistics responsible for designing statistical collections, collecting, processing and evaluating statistics, and disseminating data; and end-users of statistics comprising policy analysts, media, academics, students, etc. The statistical functions of international organisations often fall somewhere in the middle of these broad groups, in that they also perform the role of disseminators of statistics to internal or external end-users. International organisations also use metadata in evaluations and assessments of the comparability of statistics among countries.
>
> The need for the provision of more extensive methodological information is now receiving greater recognition. But actual practices in this area vary considerably in the statistical systems of both developed and developing countries; there are significant differences, for instance, in the amount of methodological detail provided on their websites and in other disseminating media (even in the national language), the frequency of updating, the proximity to the statistics described and ease of access by users.
>
> The four key elements of recommended practice in the compilation and dissemination of metadata relate to the need for the compilation of up-to-date metadata by international organisations and national agencies; providing access to metadata; the methodological items (or metadata elements) that should be incorporated in metadata disseminated; and the use of a common terminology.
>
> The role of metadata and recommended practices in the compilation and dissemination of metadata are outlined in more detail in the recent OECD publication *Data and Metadata Reporting and Presentation Handbook* (available at *http://www.oecd.org/findDocument/0,2350,en_2649_34257_1_119669_1_1_1,00.html*).

ASSESSING THE QUALITY OF ECONOMIC STATISTICS 5

Going into greater detail, the IMF dissemination standards cover four aspects: the content, periodicity and timeliness of economic and financial data; public access; procedures for communicating data to the public; and the intrinsic quality of the data disseminated. For each of these aspects, the standards define from two to four quantitative aspects that can be verified by users (for example, the timeliness of a statistic expressed as the number of days since the reference period). In addition, the standards provide that producers: issue a timetable for the release of statistical data at least three months in advance (to avoid political pressure being applied to delay dissemination); disseminate data simultaneously to all users, or state publicly whether, and under what conditions, politicians or civil servants can have access to the data before other citizens; provide an adequate explanation of the sources and any revisions to data; disseminate comprehensive methodological notes allowing users to understand the methods used to produce data, etc. According to the degree to which these standards are respected, the IMF then carries out an independent assessment of the overall quality of the national statistical system and the statistical data.

The IMF also carries out quality analyses for a number of key economic statistics (national accounts, prices, government accounts, etc.) as part of its Review of Observation of Standards and Codes (ROSC) programme, although in this instance publication of the final report is subject to the approval of the government of the country being examined.

Initially greeted with some scepticism, the IMF's SDDS initiative proved to be highly effective in creating a culture of greater transparency and rigour in the production of statistical data. For example, the requirement to issue a timetable beforehand for the various statistical data or to describe the procedures for releasing data has posed serious problems to some statistical offices, central banks and Finance Ministries, which used to release survey statistics without following a predetermined timetable or to disseminate them first to the government, thereby raising suspicions about the use of statistical information to influence the financial markets or to exert political control over the statistics themselves. Despite the difficulties encountered during the launching stage, the IMF Standards can now be considered part of the common legacy of the producers of statistical information, or at least as goals to work towards. SDDS has undoubtedly helped to increase the transparency of the statistical process, and have facilitated access to data.

In addition, Eurostat has launched initiatives in various statistical domains aimed at assessing the quality of data produced by national statistical offices and by Eurostat itself. This included the development of composite indicators to monitor changes in the various dimensions of quality over time.

However, the careful attention paid by Eurostat to the quality control of national accounts failed to avoid a very real scandal erupting in 2004 regarding the accuracy of data supplied by Greece in support of its accession to the euro area. The decision regarding European Monetary Union and the number of countries who would have taken part in it from 1 January 1999 was taken in May 1998 on the basis of a detailed analysis of the economic and financial position of European member states.

5. ASSESSING THE QUALITY OF ECONOMIC STATISTICS

According to the provisions of the Maastricht Treaty, five basic indicators had to be taken into consideration when assessing the eligibility of the candidacy of an EU member state: the rate of inflation, rate of interest, exchange rate, public deficit/GDP in current prices and public debt/GDP in current prices.

Eleven countries were initially chosen to enter the Monetary Union on 1 January 1999 (Austria, Belgium, Finland, France, Germany, Ireland, Italy, Luxembourg, the Netherlands, Portugal, and Spain while the assessment for Greece was postponed until 2001 with a view to accession from 2002 onwards. In 2001, however, Greece too was allowed to take part in the Monetary Union, although in 2004 it became clear that the statistics relating to Greece's deficit and public debt supplied by the Greek statistical authorities, validated by Eurostat and used as the basis for the decision by the European Council, were not accurate. In particular, based on the revised data, the public deficit/GDP ratio turned out to be well above the maximum 3% threshold established for accession to the Monetary Union.

This discovery cast doubt on both Eurostat's ability to properly assess the quality of the data provided by national statistical offices and the independence of the latter vis-à-vis their governments. The European Council therefore asked the statistical authorities to draw up a Code of Conduct, which was officially approved by the Statistical Programme Committee in February 2005 and promulgated by the European Commission as the "Recommendation on the independence, integrity and accountability of the national and European Community statistical authorities". The Code sets out principles for the functioning of national statistical institutes and of Eurostat itself, underlining the importance of their scientific and organisational independence, the need for them to have adequate resources, etc., and refers to a number of indicators with which to monitor the practical implementation of these principles. Furthermore, the Commission and the European Council gave a mandate to Eurostat to increase the stringency of their qualitative controls on the statistics produced by national statistical authorities, particularly those relating to economic and financial aggregates. New surveillance and verification procedures for statistical processes have been drawn up with the aim of increasing the overall quality and credibility of European statistics.

It is therefore clear that the drive to improve the quality of statistical data is a continuous process, aimed at both national statistical authorities and international and supranational organisations. However, users also need to be vigilant with regard to statistical quality, and the processes used in compilation, by paying close attention to the metadata provided alongside statistical data. Metadata can be used to assess not only the technical characteristics of the statistics, but also the overall credibility of the producer.

ASSESSING THE QUALITY OF ECONOMIC STATISTICS 5

The IMF's Data Quality Assurance Framework (DQAF)

In addition to the SDDS initiative, the IMF has also developed a useful conceptual approach for assessing the quality of statistics produced by national statistical offices, central banks and other producers of official statistics. The DQAF approach provides for three levels of detail: definition of the dimensions of quality; more precise elements that help to define each dimension of quality; indicators to be calculated to assess the degree to which the actual situation matches that which could ideally be predicted on the basis of quality objectives. The first two levels of the DQAF are described below.

Dimensions of quality	Elements
1. Prerequisites of quality	1.1. Legal and institutional environment
	1.2. Resources available
	1.3. Relevance of the information produced
	1.4. Other aspects of *quality management*
2. Assurance of integrity	2.1. Professionalism of statistical work
	2.2. Transparency
	2.3. Ethical standards
3. Methodological soundness	3.1. Use of international standards
	3.2. Scope
	3.3. Use of international classifications
	3.4. Use of international accounting principles
4. Accuracy and reliability	4.1. Source data
	4.2. Critical assessment of source data
	4.3. Statistical techniques used
	4.4. Assessment and validation of intermediate data and statistical outputs
	4.5. Revision studies
5. Serviceability	5.1. Periodicity and timeliness
	5.2. Coherence
	5.3. Revision policy and practice
6. Accessibility	6.1. Data accessibility
	6.2. Metadata accessibility
	6.3. Assistance to users

Source: IMF.

5. ASSESSING THE QUALITY OF ECONOMIC STATISTICS

The Quality Framework and Guidelines for OECD Statistics

The quality of statistics disseminated by an international organization depends on two aspects: the quality of national statistics received; and the quality of internal processes for the collection, processing, analysis and dissemination of data and metadata. The *Quality Framework and Guidelines for OECD Statistics* (QFOS) focuses on improving the quality of data collected, compiled and disseminated by the OECD through an improvement in the Organisation's internal statistical processes and management, though there is a positive spillover effect on the quality of data compiled at the national level.

In the context of the OECD's decentralised statistical environment, the QFOS provides a common framework which can be used to systematically assess, compare and further improve OECD statistics. The QFOS has four elements: a definition of quality and its dimensions; a set of broad principles or core values on which OECD statistical activities are to be conducted and quality guidelines covering all phases of the statistical production process; procedure for assuring the quality of proposed new statistical activities; procedure for evaluating the quality of existing statistical activities on a regular basis.

The OECD views quality in terms of seven dimensions: relevance; accuracy; credibility; timeliness; accessibility; interpretability; and coherence. Another factor is that of cost-efficiency, which is not strictly a quality dimension, but it is still an important consideration in the possible application of one or more of the seven dimensions cited previously for OECD statistical output. In addition to quality dimensions, some "core values" for OECD statisticians have been identified, using the UN *Fundamental Principles of Official Statistics* as the key reference.

To develop specific guidelines, statistical activities have been articulated in seven main phases: definition of the data requirements in general terms; evaluation of other data currently available; planning and design of the statistical activity; extraction of data and metadata from databases within and external to OECD; implementation of specific data and metadata collection mechanisms; data and metadata verification, analysis and evaluation; data and metadata dissemination. For each step the quality concerns and the instruments available to help in addressing them are identified in the QFOS. In particular, a set of guidelines and concrete procedures have been prepared for each step, taking into account good existing practices within the OECD and in other statistical agencies.

All new activities have to be designed and carried out following the quality guidelines. Moreover, existing statistical activities are subject to periodic quality reviews, on a rotation basis over a number of years. The stages envisaged for quality reviews are as follows:

1. identification of the statistical activities for review during the course of the following year;
2. self-assessment by the statistical activity manager and staff, resulting in a brief report that includes a summary of quality problems and a prioritised list of possible improvements;
3. review of, and comments on, the self-assessment report by major users, as well as by the statistical, information technology, and dissemination staff of the OECD;
4. preparation of the final quality report, combining all comments;
5. assignment of resources for selected quality improvement initiatives;
6. feedback by the Chief Statistician to stakeholders on the implementation of quality improvement initiatives proposed.

ASSESSING THE QUALITY OF ECONOMIC STATISTICS 5

As was the case with the authorities responsible for monetary policy, establishing the credibility of national statistical institutes and other producers of economic statistics is a long and complex process that requires an appropriate level of funding. In contrast, as in cases such as that of Greece, the loss of credibility can prove to be an extremely rapid and destructive process, which takes considerable time to recover.

In April 2007, in preparation for the second OECD World Forum on "Statistics, Knowledge and Policy", upon request of the OECD, the European Commission (Eurobarometer) carried out a survey on what citizens know about key economic indicators (GDP, unemployment rate and inflation) in 27 countries. In this context, one of the questions investigated the extent to which citizens trust official statistics. The results show significant differences between countries and a higher level of trust in Nordic countries, while the new EU countries (Romania, Bulgaria, etc.) are at the other end of the scale. On average, 45% of European citizens do not tend to trust official statistics. The results also show a clear positive relation between the level of trust and citizens' belief that policy makers use statistics to make decisions, as well as between the trust in official statistics and thye trust in national governments. These results clearly show how challenging it is for official statisticians to find an institutional set up that can ensure a true independence from government, to communicate the quality of their work and to be perceived as a credible source by citizens.

Figure 5.1 – **Trust in official statistics and belief that policy decisions are based on statistics**
European countries – April 2007

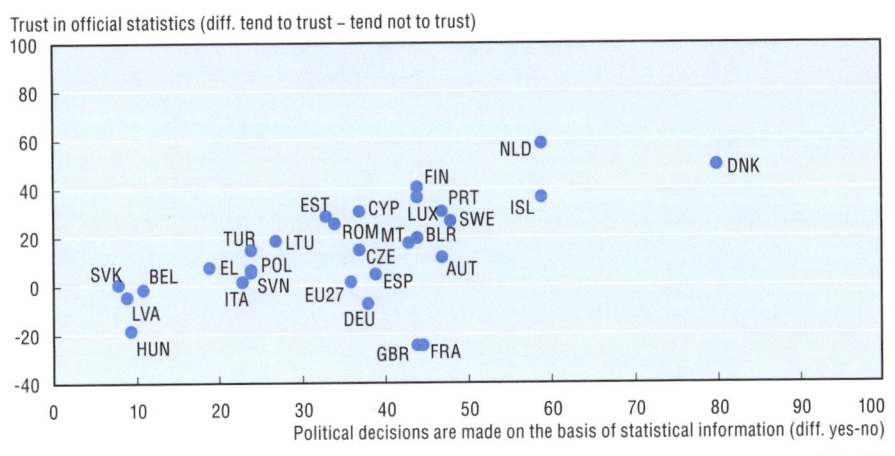

OECD PUBLICATIONS, 2, rue André-Pascal, 75775 PARIS CEDEX 16
PRINTED IN FRANCE
(30 2008 27 1 P) ISBN 978-92-64-03312-2 – No. 56209 2008